W9-BYL-660

Interior Designer's
Portable Handbook

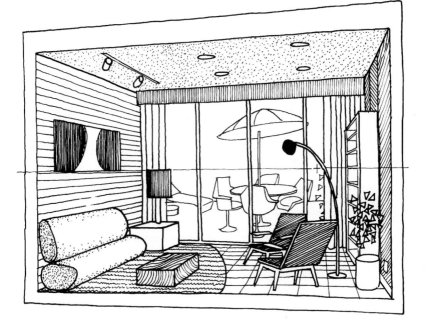

INTERIOR DESIGNER'S
PORTABLE HANDBOOK
FIRST-STEP RULES OF THUMB FOR INTERIOR DESIGN

PAT GUTHRIE
ARCHITECT

McGraw-Hill

New York   San Francisco   Washington, D.C.   Auckland   Bogotá
Caracas   Lisbon   London   Madrid   Mexico City   Milan
Montreal   New Delhi   San Juan   Singapore
Sydney   Tokyo   Toronto

Library of Congress Cataloging-in-Publication Data

Guthrie, Pat.
    The interior designer's portable handbook / Pat Guthrie.
       p.   cm.
    Adaptation of: The architect's portable handbook.
    Includes bibliographical references and index.
    ISBN 0-07-134617-1
    1. Interior decoration Handbooks, manuals, etc.   2. Architectural
design Handbooks, manuals, etc.   I. Guthrie, Pat. Architect's portable
handbook. II. Title.
NK2115.G86 1999
729—dc21
                                          99-31234
                                              CIP

McGraw-Hill

*A Division of The **McGraw·Hill** Companies*

Copyright © 2000 by McGraw-Hill, Inc. All rights reserved. Printed in
the United States of America. Except as permitted under the United
States Copyright Act of 1976, no part of this publication may be reproduced or distributed in any form or by any means, or stored in a data
base or retrieval system, without the prior written permission of the
publisher.

   10 11 12 13 14 15 16   DOC/DOC   0 9 8 7 6 5 4 3

ISBN 0-07-134617-1

*The sponsoring editor for this book was Wendy Lochner, and the
production supervisor was Pamela A. Pelton. It was set in Times Ten
by North Market Street Graphics.*

Printed and bound by R. R. Donnelley & Sons Company.

This book is printed on recycled, acid-free paper containing
a minimum of 50% recycled, de-inked fiber.

Information contained in this work has been obtained by McGraw-
Hill, Inc., from sources believed to be reliable. However, neither
McGraw-Hill nor its authors guarantees the accuracy or complete-
ness of any information published herein, and neither McGraw-
Hill nor its authors shall be responsible for any errors, omissions, or
damages arising out of use of this information. This work is published with the understanding that McGraw-Hill and its authors
are supplying information, but are not attempting to render engineering or other professional services. If such services are required,
the assistance of an appropriate professional should be sought.

Dedicated to:

- *My family (Jan, Eric, and Erin)*
- *Wendy Lochner—who invited me to do this book*

Contents

___ PART 6. WOOD

___ PART 7. THERMAL AND MOISTURE PROTECTION

___ PART 8. DOORS, WINDOWS, AND GLASS

___ PART 9. FINISHES

___ PART 10. SPECIALTIES

Preface

This book is largely adapted from the author's *The Architect's Portable Handbook* (McGraw-Hill, 1998). Many things overlap between the fields of architecture and interior design. In fact, interior design could be considered a specialty in the architectural field. From *The Architect's Portable Handbook* those things dealing with engineering, with the exterior "skin," and the "bones" (structural elements) have largely been deleted. What has been added is a greater emphasis on space planning, interior finishes, equipment, and furniture.

This book is particularly oriented toward those working in the field of interior design at two levels:

1. The interior decorator who selects furnishings and room finishes.
2. The interior designer who does what the decorator does, but who also does space planning and may approach what an architect does for "tenant improvement" or remodel-type projects where whole new spaces are created within an existing building.

In either case, and everything in between, this book should be a help to anyone doing "interiors."

As with *The Architect's Portable Handbook,* this book is laid out in the C.S.I. (Construction Specifications Institute) format. The user would do well to become familiar with this, as it has become a standard in the construction industry.

This book does not deal with aesthetics. There are many books on that subject. Rather, the idea of this book is to provide the designer with fast preliminary facts to save the designer time—so more time can be devoted to the creative side of interior design.

Interior Designer's
Portable Handbook

NOTES

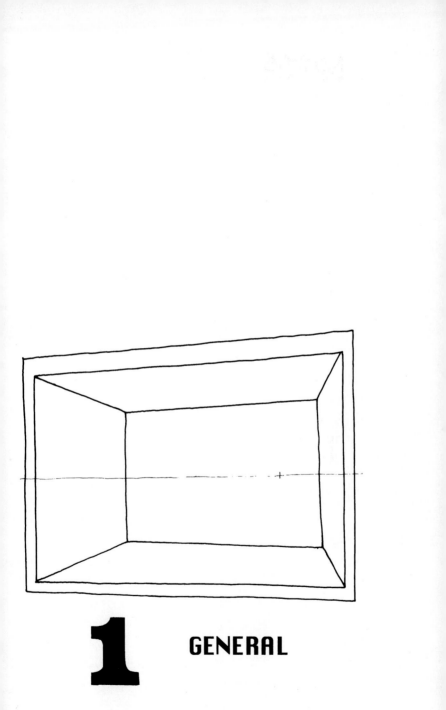

1 GENERAL

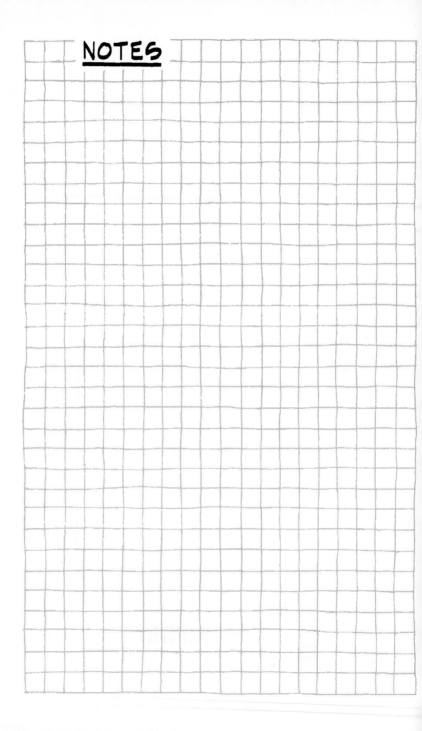

NOTES

___ A. PRACTICE (5) (21) (37) (39) (42)

___ 1. Compensation (fees)

___ *a.* See Appendix A for designer fees as a percentage of installation cost by building type.

___ *b.* Use the American Institute of Architects breakdown of fees as a guide:

___ Schematic design phase	15%	or	
___ Design development	20%	25%	Preliminary design
___ Construction documents	40%	50%	Construction documents
___ Bid/negotiation	5%		
___ Construction administration	20%	25%	Construction administration
	100%	100%	

___ 2. Rules of Thumb for Business Practice

___ *a.* *Watch cash flow:* For a small firm, balance checkbook. For a medium or large firm, use cash statements and balance and income statements. Estimate future cash flow based on past, with 15% "fudge factor," plus desired profit.

___ *b.* *Have financial reserves:* (six months' worth).

___ *c.* *Monitor time by these ratios:*

___ (1) $\text{Chargeable ratio} = \dfrac{\text{direct job labor cost}}{\text{total labor cost}}$

This tells what percent of total labor cost is being spent on paying work. The higher the percent the better. Typical range is 55 to 85%, but lower than *65%* is poor. However, principals often have a 50% ratio.

___ (2) $\text{Multiplier ratio} = \dfrac{\text{dollars of revenue}}{\text{dollars of direct labor}}$

This ratio is multiplied times wages for billing rates. Usually *2.5 to 3.0.* Will vary with firm and time.

___ (3) Overhead rate: looks at total indirect expenses as they relate to total direct labor. An overhead rate of 180 means $1.80 spent for each $1.00 working on revenue-producing projects.

___ (4) Profit: measured as total revenue minus expenses. Expressed as percent of total revenue.

    ___ d. *Monitor accounting reports:* A financial statement consists of:
- ___ (1) Balance Sheet: Tells where you are on a given date by Assets and Liabilities.
- ___ (2) Earnings Statement (Profit and Loss): Tells you how you got there by Income less Direct (job) costs, and Indirect (overhead) costs = Profit, or Loss.

    ___ e. *Mark up for reimbursable expenses* (travel, printing, etc.): Usually 10%.

    ___ f. *Negotiating contracts*
- ___ (1) Estimate scope of services.
- ___ (2) Estimate time, costs, and profit.
- ___ (3) Determine method of compensation: See 4.

    ___ g. *Contract checklist*
- ___ (1) Detailed scope of work, no interpretation necessary.
- ___ (2) Responsibilities of both parties.
- ___ (3) Monthly progress payments.
- ___ (4) Interest penalty on overdue payments.
- ___ (5) Limit length of construction administration phase.
- ___ (6) Cost estimating responsibilities.
- ___ (7) For cost-reimbursable contracts, specify a provisional overhead rate (changes year to year).
- ___ (8) Retainer, applied to fee but not costs.
- ___ (9) Date of agreement, and time limit on contract.
- ___ (10) Approval of work—who, when, where.
- ___ (11) Ways to terminate contract, by both parties.
- ___ (12) For changes in scope, bilateral agreement, and an equitable adjustment in fee.
- ___ (13) Court or arbitration remedies and who pays legal fees.
- ___ (14) Signature and date by both parties.

___ 3. Fees and Purchasing

The interior designer's compensation is more complicated than that for other design professionals. The designer may charge a professional fee. The designer may also be a contractor of sorts by being the purchaser and installer of furnishings, with profit from the difference between wholesale and resold price to the client. The interior designer may use either of these methods or both.

    ___ a. *Professional fees* can be determined by:

___ (1)   Percentage of installed cost (furnishing or interior construction cost, or both).

___ (2)   Lump sum.

___ (3)   Hourly rates. **(Typical rates are \$65 to \$120/hr.)**

___ (4)   Hourly rates with maximum "upset."

___ b.   <u>*Resale compensation*</u> can be determined by:

Designer purchasing furniture from supplier at a discounted amount less than the list price. This usually ranges from 10% to 50% discount. The designer then resells furniture to client at a higher price. The difference is compensation to the designer. Other issues in the resale of furniture are:

___ (1)   Who pays for *freight* (shipping) and insurance? "F.O.B. Factory" means buyer assumes ownership and responsibility when goods are loaded on truck at factory. "F.O.B. Destination" means the manufacturer retains ownership and responsibility of goods until they reach delivery destination. Costs of freight and insurance are borne by the manufacturer in this case.

___ (2)   Cost of *warehousing,* if required, and who is responsible for it needs to be established. As a rule of thumb, shipping is 8% to 12% of discounted price, with 10% as a good average.

___ (3)   Sales tax for resale of furniture.

EXAMPLE

THE INTERIOR DESIGNER SELECTS A PIECE OF FURNITURE WITH MANUFACTURER'S LIST PRICE OF $1000. THE MANUFACTURER OFFERS A 50% DISCOUNT 'TO THE TRADE' AND F.O.B. DESTINATION. THE DESIGNER PURCHASES THE FURNITURE FOR 50% OF $1000, OR $500.

THE DESIGNER MAY THEN RESELL THE FURNITURE TO THE CLIENT AT:

LIST $1000   ($1000 - $500 = $500 COMPENSATION)
+ TAX

DISCOUNT, SAY 25%. ($1000 X .25 = $250 + TAX)

$500 DIFF. BETW'N MANUF. &
DESIGNER

LESS $250   RESALE (+TAX)
$250   COMPENSATION TO
DESIGNER

NOTES

NOTES

__ B. "SYSTEMS" THINKING

In the planning and design of buildings, a helpful, all-inclusive tool is to think in terms of overall "systems" or "flows." For each of the checklist items on the next 2 pages, follow from the beginning or "upper end" through to the "lower end" or "outfall":

__ 1. <u>People Functions</u>

    __ *a.* Follow flow of occupants from one space to another. This includes sources of vertical transportation (stairs, elevators, etc.) including pathways to service equipment.

    __ *b.* Follow flow of occupants to enter building from off-site.

    __ *c.* Follow flow of occupants to exit building as required by code.

    __ *d.* Follow flow of accessible route as required by law.

    __ *e.* Follow flow of materials to supply building (including furniture and off-site).

    __ *f.* Follow flow of trash to leave building (including to off-site).

    __ *g.* Way finding: Do graphics or other visual clues aid flow of the above six items?

__ 2. <u>Heat</u>

    __ *a.* Follow sun paths to and into building to plan for access or blocking.

    __ *b.* Follow excessive external (or internal) heat through building skin and block if necessary.

    __ *c.* Follow source of internal heat loads (lights, people, equipment, etc.) to their "outfall" (natural ventilation or AC, etc.).

    __ *d.* Follow heat flow into materials over a year, a day, etc. and allow for expansion and contraction.

__ 3. <u>Air</u>

    __ *a.* Follow wind patterns through site to encourage or block natural ventilation through building, as required.

    __ *b.* Follow air patterns through building. When natural ventilation is used, follow flow from inlets to outlets. When air is still, hot air rises and cold air descends.

    __ *c.* Follow forced-air ventilation patterns through building to address heat (add or dissipate) and odors.

__ 4. <u>Light</u>

    __ *a.* Follow paths of natural light (direct or indirect sun) to and into building. Encourage or block as needed.

    __ *b.* Follow paths of circulation and at spaces to provide artificial illumination where necessary. This includes both site and building.

___ 5. <u>Energy and Communications</u>

   ___ *a.* Follow electric or gas supply from off-site to transformer, to breakers or panels, and to each outlet or point of connection.

   ___ *b.* Follow telephone lines from off-site to telephone mounting board, to each phone location.

___ 6. <u>Sound</u>

   ___ *a.* Identify potential sound sources, potential receiver locations, and the potential sound paths between the two.

   ___ *b.* Follow sound through air from source to receiver. Mitigate with distance or barrier.

   ___ *c.* Follow sound through structure from source to receiver. Mitigate by isolation of source or receiver.

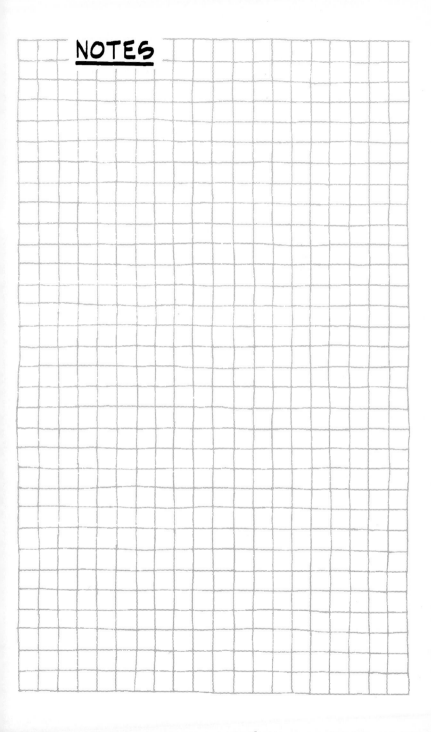

NOTES

NOTES

___ C. SPECIFICATIONS (CSI FORMAT) ⑮

Use this section as a checklist of everything that makes or goes into buildings, to be all-inclusive in the planning and designing of buildings, their contents, and their surroundings:

Bidding Requirements, Contract Forms, and Conditions of the Contract
___ 00010 Prebid information
___ 00100 Instructions to bidders
___ 00200 Information available to bidders
___ 00300 Bid forms
___ 00400 Supplements to bid forms
___ 00500 Agreement forms
___ 00600 Bonds and certificates
___ 00700 General conditions
___ 00800 Supplementary conditions
___ 00900 Addenda

Specifications—By Division

Division 1—General Requirements
___ 01010 Summary of work
___ 01020 Allowances
___ 01025 Measurement and payment
___ 01030 Alternates/alternatives
___ 01035 Modification procedures
___ 01040 Coordination
___ 01050 Field engineering
___ 01060 Regulatory requirements
___ 01070 Identification systems
___ 01090 References
___ 01100 Special project procedures
___ 01200 Project meetings
___ 01300 Submittals
___ 01400 Quality controls
___ 01500 Construction facilities and temporary controls
___ 01600 Material and equipment
___ 01650 Starting of systems/commissioning
___ 01700 Contract closeout
___ 01800 Maintenance

Division 2—Sitework
___ 02010 Subsurface investigation
___ 02050 Demolition
___ 02100 Site preparation
___ 02140 Dewatering
___ 02150 Shoring and underpinning

___ 02160 Excavation support systems
___ 02170 Cofferdams
___ 02200 Earthwork
___ 02300 Tunneling
___ 02350 Piles and caissons
___ 02450 Railroad work
___ 02480 Marine work
___ 02500 Paving and surfacing
___ 02600 Utility piping materials
___ 02660 Water distribution
___ 02680 Fuel and steam distribution
___ 02700 Sewerage and drainage
___ 02760 Restoration of underground pipelines
___ 02770 Ponds and reservoirs
___ 02780 Power and communications
___ 02800 Site improvements
___ 02900 Landscaping

Division 3—Concrete
___ 03100 Concrete formwork
___ 03200 Concrete reinforcement
___ 03250 Concrete accessories
___ 03300 Cast-in-place concrete
___ 03370 Concrete curing
___ 03400 Precast concrete
___ 03500 Cementitious decks and toppings
___ 03600 Grout
___ 03700 Concrete restoration and cleaning
___ 03800 Mass concrete

Division 4—Masonry
___ 04100 Mortar and masonry grout
___ 04150 Masonry accessories
___ 04200 Unit masonry
___ 04400 Stone
___ 04500 Masonry restoration and cleaning
___ 04550 Refactories
___ 04600 Corrosion-resistant masonry
___ 04700 Simulated masonry

Division 5—Metals
___ 05010 Metal materials
___ 05030 Metal finishes
___ 05050 Metal fastenings
___ 05100 Structural metal framing
___ 05200 Metal joists
___ 05300 Metal decking

___ 05400 Cold-formed metal framing
___ 05500 Metal fabrications
___ 05580 Sheet metal fabrications
___ 05700 Ornamental metal
___ 05800 Expansion control
___ 05900 Hydraulic structures

Division 6—Wood and Plastic
___ 06050 Fasteners and adhesives
___ 06100 Rough carpentry
___ 06130 Heavy timber construction
___ 06150 Wood-metal systems
___ 06170 Prefabricated structural wood
___ 06200 Finish carpentry
___ 06300 Wood treatment
___ 06400 Architectural woodwork
___ 06500 Structural plastics
___ 06600 Plastic fabrications
___ 06650 Solid polymer fabrications

Division 7—Thermal and Moisture Protection
___ 07100 Waterproofing
___ 07150 Dampproofing
___ 07180 Water repellents
___ 07190 Vapor retarders
___ 07195 Air barriers
___ 07200 Insulation
___ 07240 Exterior and finish systems
___ 07250 Fireproofing
___ 07270 Fire-stopping
___ 07300 Shingles and roofing tiles
___ 07400 Manufactured roofing and siding
___ 07480 Exterior wall assemblies
___ 07500 Membrane roofing
___ 07570 Traffic coatings
___ 07600 Flashing and sheet metal
___ 07700 Roof specialties and accessories
___ 07800 Skylights
___ 07900 Joint sealers

Division 8—Doors and Windows
___ 08100 Metal doors and frames
___ 08200 Wood and plastic doors
___ 08250 Door-opening assemblies
___ 08300 Special doors
___ 08400 Entrances and storefronts
___ 08500 Metal windows

___ 08600 Wood and plastic windows
___ 08650 Special windows
___ 08700 Hardware
___ 08800 Glazing
___ 08900 Glazed curtain walls

Division 9—Finishes
___ 09100 Metal support systems
___ 09200 Lath and plaster
___ 09250 Gypsum board
___ 09300 Tile
___ 09400 Terrazzo
___ 09450 Stone facing
___ 09500 Acoustical treatment
___ 09540 Special wall surfaces
___ 09545 Special ceiling surfaces
___ 09550 Wood flooring
___ 09600 Stone flooring
___ 09630 Unit masonry flooring
___ 09650 Resilient flooring
___ 09680 Carpet
___ 09700 Special flooring
___ 09780 Floor treatment
___ 09800 Special coatings
___ 09900 Painting
___ 09950 Wall covering

Division 10—Specialties
___ 10100 Visual display boards
___ 10150 Compartments and cubicles
___ 10200 Louvers and vents
___ 10240 Grilles and screens
___ 10250 Service wall systems
___ 10260 Wall and corner guards
___ 10270 Access flooring
___ 10290 Pest control
___ 10300 Fireplaces and stoves
___ 10340 Manufactured exterior specialties
___ 10350 Flagpoles
___ 10400 Identifying devices
___ 10450 Pedestrian control devices
___ 10500 Lockers
___ 10520 Fire protection specialties
___ 10530 Protective covers
___ 10550 Postal specialties
___ 10600 Partitions
___ 10650 Operable partitions

___ 10670 Storage shelving
___ 10700 Exterior protection devices for openings
___ 10750 Telephone specialties
___ 10800 Toilet and bath accessories
___ 10880 Scales
___ 10900 Wardrobe and closet specialties

Division 11—Equipment
___ 11010 Maintenance equipment
___ 11020 Security and vault equipment
___ 11030 Teller and service equipment
___ 11040 Ecclesiastical equipment
___ 11050 Library equipment
___ 11060 Theater and stage equipment
___ 11070 Instrumental equipment
___ 11080 Registration equipment
___ 11090 Checkroom equipment
___ 11100 Mercantile equipment
___ 11110 Commercial laundry and dry-cleaning equipment
___ 11120 Vending equipment
___ 11130 Audiovisual equipment
___ 11140 Vehicle service equipment
___ 11150 Parking control equipment
___ 11160 Loading dock equipment
___ 11170 Solid-waste-handling equipment
___ 11190 Detention equipment
___ 11200 Water supply and treatment equipment
___ 11280 Hydraulic gates and valves
___ 11300 Fluid waste treatment and disposal equipment
___ 11400 Food service equipment
___ 11450 Residential equipment
___ 11460 Unit kitchens
___ 11470 Darkroom equipment
___ 11480 Athletic, recreational, and therapeutic equipment
___ 11500 Industrial and process equipment
___ 11600 Laboratory equipment
___ 11650 Planetarium equipment
___ 11660 Observatory equipment
___ 11680 Office equipment
___ 11700 Medical equipment
___ 11780 Mortuary equipment
___ 11850 Navigational equipment
___ 11870 Agricultural equipment

Division 12—Furnishings
___ 12050 Fabrics
___ 12100 Artwork

___ 12300 Manufactured casework
___ 12500 Window treatment
___ 12600 Furniture and accessories
___ 12670 Rugs and mats
___ 12700 Multiple seating
___ 12800 Interior plants and planters

Division 13—Special Construction
___ 13010 Air-supported structures
___ 13020 Integrated assemblies
___ 13030 Special purpose rooms
___ 13080 Sound, vibration, and seismic control
___ 13090 Radiation protection
___ 13100 Nuclear reactors
___ 13120 Preengineered structures
___ 13150 Aquatic facilities
___ 13175 Ice rinks
___ 13180 Site-constructed incinerators
___ 13185 Kennels and animal shelters
___ 13200 Liquid and gas storage tanks
___ 13220 Filter underdrains and media
___ 13230 Digester covers and appurtenances
___ 13240 Oxygenation systems
___ 13260 Sludge-conditioning systems
___ 13300 Utility control systems
___ 13400 Industrial and process control systems
___ 13500 Recording instrumentation
___ 13550 Transportation control instrumentation
___ 13600 Solar energy systems
___ 13700 Wind energy systems
___ 13750 Cogeneration systems
___ 13800 Building automation systems
___ 13900 Fire suppression and supervisory systems
___ 13950 Special security construction

Division 14—Conveying Systems
___ 14100 Dumbwaiters
___ 14200 Elevators
___ 14300 Escalators and moving walks
___ 14400 Lifts
___ 14500 Material-handling systems
___ 14600 Hoists and cranes
___ 14700 Turntables
___ 14800 Scaffolding
___ 14900 Transportation systems

Division 15—Mechanical
___ 15050 Basic mechanical materials and methods
___ 15250 Mechanical insulation
___ 15300 Fire protection
___ 15400 Plumbing
___ 15500 Heating, ventilation, and air-conditioning
           (HVAC)
___ 15550 Heat generation
___ 15650 Refrigeration
___ 15750 Heat transfer
___ 15850 Air handling
___ 15880 Air distribution
___ 15950 Controls
___ 15990 Testing, adjusting, and balancing

Division 16—Electrical
___ 16050 Basic electrical materials and methods
___ 16200 Power generation—built-up systems
___ 16300 Medium voltage distribution
___ 16400 Service and distribution
___ 16500 Lighting
___ 16600 Special systems
___ 16700 Communications
___ 16850 Electrical resistance heating
___ 16900 Controls
___ 16950 Testing

NOTES

___ D. PROGRAMMING (38)

___ 1. <u>Programming</u> is a process leading to the statement of an architectural problem and the requirements to be met in offering a solution. It is the search for sufficient information to clarify, to understand, to state the problem. Programming is problem seeking and design is problem solving.

___ 2. <u>Use the Information Index</u> on pp. 24–25 as a guide for creating a program for more complex projects.

___ 3. <u>Efficiency Ratios</u>: Use the following numbers to aid in planning the size of buildings and their spaces in regard to the ratio of net area to gross area:

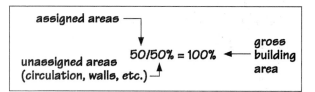

Note: The gross area of a building is the total floor area based on outside dimensions. The net area is based on the interior dimensions. For office or retail space, net leasable area means the area of the primary function of the building, excluding such things as stairwells, corridors, mechanical rooms, etc.

Common Range		
Automobile analogy	For buildings	Ratios
Super Luxury	Superb	50/50
Luxury	Grand	55/45
Full	Excellent	60/40
Intermediate	Moderate	65/35
Compact	Economical	67/33
Subcompact	Austere	70/30
Uncommon Range		·
	Meager	75/25
	Spare	80/20
	Minimal	85/15
	Skeletal	90/10

The following table gives common breakdowns of unassigned areas:

Circulation	16.0	20.0	22.0	24.0	25.0
Mechanical	5.0	5.5	7.5	8.0	10.0
Structure and walls	7.0	7.0	8.0	9.5	10.0
Public toilets	1.5	1.5	1.5	2.0	2.5
Janitor closets	0.2	0.5	0.5	0.5	1.0
Unassigned storage	0.3	0.5	0.5	1.0	1.5
	30.0%	35.0%	40.0%	45.0%	50.0%

NOTES

INFORMATION INDEX

	GOALS What does the client want to achieve & why?	FACTS What is it all about?
FUNCTION What's going to happen in the building? People Activities Relationships	Mission Maximum number Individual identity Interaction/privacy Hierarchy of values Security Progression Segregation Encounters Efficiency	Statistical data Area parameters Manpower/workloads User characteristics Community characteristics Value of loss Time-motion study Traffic analysis Behavioral patterns Space adequacy

FORM What is there now & what is to be there?
Site
Environment
Quality
	Site elements
	(Trees, water, open space,
	    existing facilities,
	    utilities)
	Efficient land use
	Neighbors
	Individuality
	Direction
	Entry
	Projected image
	Level of quality
		Site analysis
		Climate analysis
		Cope survey
		Soils analysis
		F.A.R. and G.A.C.
		Surroundings
		Psychological implications
		Cost/SF
		Building efficiency
		Functional support

ECONOMY Concerns the initial budget & quality of construction. Initial budget Operating costs Lifecycle costs	Extent of funds Cost effectiveness Maximum return Return on investment Minimize oper. costs Maint. & oper. costs Reduce life cycle costs	Cost parameters Maximum budget Time-use factors Market analysis Energy source-costs Activities & climate factors Economic data
TIME Deals with the influences of history, the inevitability of change from the present, & projections into the future. Past Present Future	Historic preservation Static/dynamic Change Growth Occupancy date	Significance Space parameters Activities Projections Linear schedule

CONCEPTS How does the client want to achieve the goals?	**NEEDS** How much money, space, & quality (as opposed to wants)?	**PROBLEM** What are the significant conditions & the general directions the design of the building should take?
Service grouping People grouping Activity grouping Priority Security controls Sequential flow Separated flow Mixed flow Relationships	Space requirements Parking requirements Outdoor space req'mts. Building efficiency Functional alternatives	Unique and important performance requirements which will shape building design.

Enhancement
Climate control
Safety
Special
  foundations
Density
Interdependence
Home base
Orientation
Accessibility
Character
Quality control
	Quality (cost/SF)
	Environmental & site
	  influences on costs
		Major form considerations which will affect building design.

Cost control Efficient allocation Multifunction Merchandising Energy conservation Cost control	Cost estimate analysis Entry budget (FRAS) Operating costs Life cycle costs	Attitude toward the initial budget and its influence on the fabric and geometry of the building.
Adaptability Tailored/loose fit Convertibility Expansibility Concurrent scheduling	Phasing Escalation	Implications of change/growth on long-range performance.

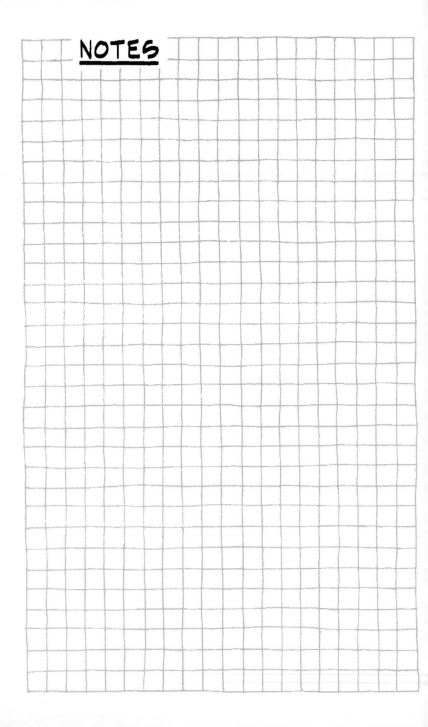

NOTES

___ E. INSTALLATION COSTS

Note: Most costs throughout this book (and this chapter) are from the following sources:

___ 1. This book has rough cost data throughout. Rough costs are **boldface.** See App. A for rough estimates of installed costs by building type.

___ 2. Furniture, Fixtures, and Equipment (FF&E) Costs

    ___ *a.* The interior designer is most often specifying and sometimes installing *furniture.* See Part 12, p. 329 for typical furnishing costs. Also see p. 5 for furniture cost markups and discounts.

    ___ *b.* Fixtures are *built-ins* that may be priced and installed by the interior designer or maybe by a general contractor.

    ___ *c.* Equipment costs often relate to items designed and installed by another specialist designer. Examples would be kitchen equipment by a food service company or medical equipment by a medical equipment supplier. In short, these costs do not involve a general contractor and are not construction costs.

___ 3. General Interior Construction Costs

If the interior designer is doing more than just space planning and specifying furnishings, then tenant improvements or remodel of existing building interiors will probably involve a general contractor and possibly an architect and maybe engineers.

    ___ *a.* If anything structural is involved, retain a structural engineer.

    ___ *b.* If plumbing is modified or added, or heating, ventilation, and air-conditioning (HVAC) is modified or added, retain a mechanical engineer.

    ___ *c.* If lighting or power is modified or added, retain an electrical engineer.

    ___ *d.* Check with the local code enforcing agencies to see if an architect is required.

For general interior construction costs given, subcontractor's overhead and profit, plus tax, are included. Both material (M) and labor (L) are included, usually with a general idea of percentage of each to the total (100%). Because there is room for only one cost per "element," often an idea of possible variation (higher or lower) of cost is given. One must use judgment in this regard to come up with a reasonable but rough cost estimate. As costs change, the user will have to revise costs in this book. The easiest way to do this will be to add historical modifiers, published each year, by various sources. The costs in this book are approx. costs for 1997 and 1998. Over the last few years costs have increased about 2 to 3% per year. Be sure to compound when using this rule of thumb.

<u>EXAMPLE:</u>

A CONSTRUCTION ITEM IN THE BOOK GIVES THE FOLLOWING:
$5.00/SF (40% M & 60% L) (VARIATION OF +100% &
-20%.)
THIS MEANS THAT AS A GOOD AVERAGE THE COST OF THE
ITEM INSTALLED (WITH THE SUBCONTRACTOR'S O.H. & P.) IS
$5/SF, THE MATERIAL COST IS APPROX. $5 X .40 = $2/
SF. THE LABOR COST IS APPROX. $5 X 0.60 = $3/SF.
HOWEVER, A VERY EXPENSIVE VERSION CAN BE ROUGHLY
100% HIGHER ($5 X 2 = $10/SF) OR A CHEAPER VER-
SION CAN BE ROUGHLY 20% LOWER ($5 X 0.80 = $4/
SF, BUT THE APPROX. AVERAGE COST IS $5.00/SF.
NOTE: GENERAL CONTRACTOR'S O.H. & P. NOT INCLUDED.

___ 4. <u>Cost Control and Estimating</u>
   Cost estimating can be time-consuming. It can also be dangerous in that wrong estimates may require time-consuming and expensive redesign. From the beginning of a project, responsibility for cost control (if any) should be clearly established. If the designer is responsible for doing estimates, the designer should consider the following points:
   ___ *a.* Apples to Apples: In discussing costs and budgets with clients and builders, the parties must be sure they are comparing "apples to apples" (i.e., what is included and excluded). Examples of misunderstandings:
      ___ (1) Financing costs (are usually excluded).
      ___ (2) Designers' and consultants' fees.
      ___ (3) City or government fees (are usually excluded).
      ___ (4) Are furniture, fixture, and equipment (FF&E) costs included?

EXAMPLE:

A DESIGNER IS WORKING FOR A "SPEC" BUILDER. THE DESIGNER HAS IN MIND A $60/SF BUDGET. THE SPEC. BUILDER HAS IN MIND A $50/SF BUDGET. THE DESIGNER'S NUMBER HAS A GENERAL CONTRACTOR'S O.H. & P. OF SAY, 20% AS IF THE PROJECT WERE BID OR NEGOTIATED WITH AN INDEPENDENT CONTRACTOR. THE SPEC. BUILDER IS THINKING ABOUT HIS DIRECT COSTS, ONLY. THEY ARE COMPARING "APPLES TO ORANGES", BUT IF THE BUILDER'S NUMBER IS ADJUSTED:

$50/SF × 1.20 = $60/SF

OR IF THE DESIGNER'S NUMBER IS ADJUSTED:

$60/SF × 0.80 = $50/SF

THEN, THEY ARE TALKING "APPLES TO APPLES".

___ *b.* Variables:
   ___ (1) *Location.* Modify costs for actual location. Use modifiers often published.
   ___ (2) *Historical index.* If cost data is old, modify to current or future time by often-published modifiers.
   ___ (3) *Building size.* The $/SF costs may need to be modified due to size of the project.
   ___ (4) *Shape.* More complicated shapes will cause costs to go up. Where single elements are articulated (e.g., rounded corners or different types of coursing and materials in a masonry wall), add 30% to the costs involved.
   ___ (5) *Quality of materials, construction, and design.* Use the following rough guidelines to increase or decrease as needed:

Automobile analogy	For buildings	%
Super Luxury	Superb	+120
Luxury	Grand	+60
Full	Excellent	+20

Intermediate	Moderate	$\underline{100}$
Compact	Economical	−10
Subcompact	Austere	−20

Note: Increasing the quality from lowest to highest can double the cost.

___ *c.* Costs (and construction scheduling) can be affected by weather, season, materials shortages, and/or labor practices.

___ *d.* Beyond a 20-mile radius of cities, extra transportation charges increase material costs slightly. This may be offset by lower wage rates. In dense urban areas, costs for locally supplied material may actually increase.

___ *e.* In doing a total estimate, an allowance for general conditions should be added. This usually ranges from 5 to 15%, with *10%* a typical average.

___ *f.* At the end of a total estimate, an allowance for the general contractor's overhead and profit should be added. This usually ranges from *10 to 20%*. Market conditions at the time of bidding will often affect this percentage as well as all items. The market can swing 10 to 20% from inactive to active times.

___ *g.* Contingencies should always be included in estimates as listed below. On alterations or repair projects, *20%* is not an unreasonable allowance to make.

___ *h.* Use rounding of numbers in all estimating items.

___ *i.* Consider using "add alternates" to projects where the demand is high but the budget tight. These alternates should be things the client would like but does not have to have and should be clearly denoted in the drawings.

___ *j.* It is often wise for the designer to give estimates in a range.

___ *k.* Because clients often change their minds or things go wrong that cannot be foreseen in the beginning, it may pay to advise the client to withhold from his budget a confidential *5 to 10% contingency*. On the other hand, clients often do this anyway, without telling the designer.

___ *l.* Costs can further be affected by other things:
Government overhead ≈+100%
Award-winning designs are often ≈+200 to 300%

___ 5. Cost Control Procedure
___ *a.* At the *predesign phase* or beginning of a project, determine the client's *budget* and what it includes, as

well as anticipated size of the project. Back out all nonconstruction costs such as cost of furniture and fixtures, design fees, etc. Verify, in a simple format (such as $/SF, $/room, etc.) that this is reasonable. See App. A for average $/SF costs as a comparison and guideline.

___ *b.* At the *schematic design phase,* establish a reasonable $/SF target. Include a *15% to 20% contingency.*

___ *c.* At the *design development phase,* as the design becomes more specific, do a "systems" estimate. See Part 13 as an aid. For small projects a "unit" estimate might be appropriate, especially if basic plans not normally done at this time can be quickly sketched up for a "take off." Include a *10% to 15% contingency.*

___ *d.* At the *construction documents phase,* do a full unit "take off." For smaller projects, the estimate in the last phase may be enough, provided nothing has changed or been added to the project. Add a *5% to 10% contingency.*

___ 6. <u>Typical Commercial Building Cost Percentages</u>

Division	New const.	Remodeling
1. General requirements	6 to 8%	about 30%
2. Sitework	4 to 6%	for general
3. Concrete	15 to 20%	
4. Masonry	8 to 12%	
5. Metals	5 to 7%	
6. Wood	1 to 5%	
7. Thermal and moisture protection	4 to 6%	
8. Doors, windows, and glass	5 to 7%	
9. Finishes	8 to 12%	about 30%
10. Specialties*		for divisions
11. Equipment*		8–12
12. Furnishings*	6 to 10%*	
13. Special construction*		
14. Conveying systems*		about 40%
15. Mechanical	15 to 25%	for mech.
16. Electrical	8 to 12%	and elect.
Total	100%	

Note: FF&E (furniture, fixtures, and equipment) are often excluded from building cost budget.

___ 7. <u>Guidelines for Tenant Improvements (TI) in Office Buildings:</u>
  ___ *a.* **Costs for office building frames and envelopes: <u>$25 to $35/SF</u>.**
  ___ *b.* **TI costs range from <u>$20 to $50/SF (in extreme cases $100/SF)</u>.**

___ 8. <u>Guidelines for Demolition</u>
  ___ *a.* Total buildings: ***$3 to $5/SF***
  ___ *b.* Separate elements: ***10% to 50%*** of in-place construction cost of element.

EXAMPLE

PROBLEM: DEVELOP A LIKELY BUDGET FOR A NEW OFFICE TENANT IMPROVEMENT IN A NEW OPEN SPACE "SHELL" BUILDING. THE T.I. SPACE IS TO BE 5000 S.F.

SOLUTION:

		LOW	AVE	HIGH
1. FROM APP A, P. ESTABLISH AVERAGE IN PLACE COSTS ($ $/SF)		10	20	30
2. ASSUME FURNISHINGS ARE 50% & CONST. COSTS ARE 50% OF TOTAL ($/SF)	FURN.	5	10	15
	CONST.	5	10	15
	TOTAL	10	20	30
3. TYPICAL INTERIOR DESIGN FEES ARE (%)		3	4	6
4. CONVERT COSTS TO LUMP SUMS BY MULTIPLYING × 5000 SF. ($)	FURN.	25000	50000	75000
	CONST.	25000	50000	75000
	TOTAL INSTALLED	$50000	$100000	$150000
5. ESTIMATE DESIGNER'S FEE OF % IN LINE 3 × LUMP SUMS IN 4 ($)		$1500	$4000	$9000
6. TOTAL ESTIMATE OF COSTS TO CLIENT		$51500	$104000	$159000

NOTES

NOTES

___ F. HUMAN DIMENSIONS

Note: All dimensions are ranges from several sources in inches and rounded to the nearest inch. Where a range is given, lower numbers tend to be for women and the higher numbers for men. The average of the two tends to be the standard average.

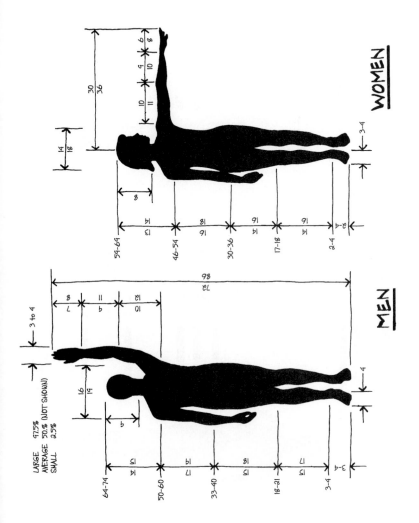

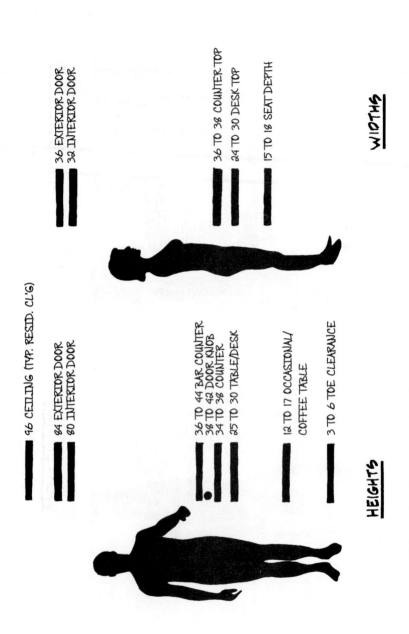

96 CEILING (TYP. RESID. CL'G)

84 EXTERIOR DOOR
80 INTERIOR DOOR

36 TO 44 BAR COUNTER
38 TO 42 DOOR KNOB
34 TO 38 COUNTER
25 TO 30 TABLE/DESK

12 TO 17 OCCASIONAL/
COFFEE TABLE

3 TO 6 TOE CLEARANCE

HEIGHTS

36 EXTERIOR DOOR
32 INTERIOR DOOR

36 TO 38 COUNTER TOP
24 TO 30 DESK TOP

15 TO 18 SEAT DEPTH

WIDTHS

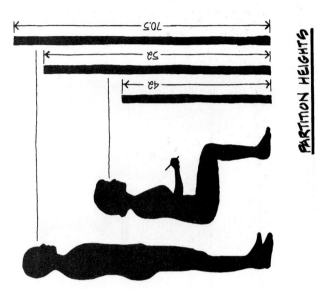

PARTITION HEIGHTS

70.5

52

43

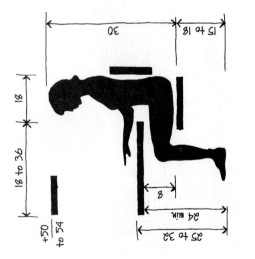

WORKSTATION

30

15 to 18

18

18 to 36

+50 to 54

8

24 min.

35 to 32

37

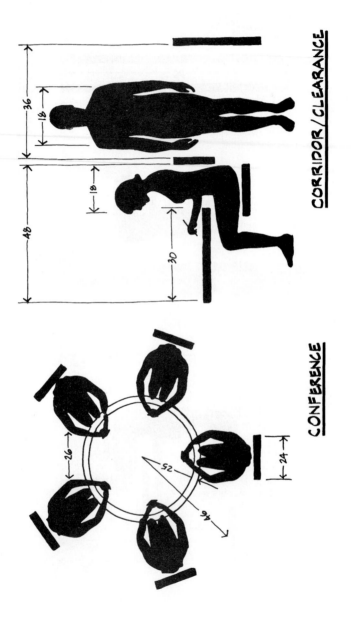

CORRIDOR/CLEARANCE

CONFERENCE

OVERHEAD / UNDER COUNTER REACH

30

OPT. STORAGE
27.7

27

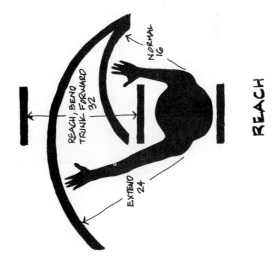

REACH, BEND
TRUNK FORWARD
32

NORMAL
16

EXTEND
24

REACH

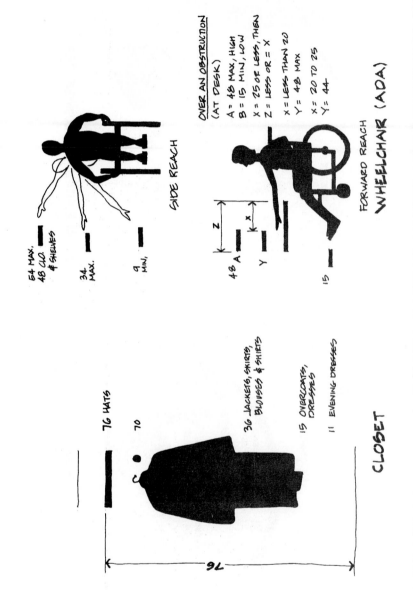

TYPICAL HEIGHTS

STANDING   SEATED

8'-0"	96"	TYP. RESID CEILING
	94	
	92	
	90	
	88	
7'-0"	84" 86	OFFICE DOORS
	82	
	80	RESID. DOORS
	78	SHOWER HEADS
	76	
6'-0"	72" 74	CLOTHES LINES
		NO SEE OVER (HIGH SHELF, MEN)
	70	TOP OF MIRROR
	68	HIGH SHELF (WOMEN)
	66	
	64	MIN CAT WALK CLEARANCE
5'-0"	60" 62	
	58	THERMOSTATS
	56	SEE OVER — MIRROR TOP
	54	GRAB BARS, PHONE DIAL HT. — NO SEE OVER, FL. LAMP (HIGH)
	52	HIGHEST FILE
4'-0"	48" 50	PUSH PLATES — HIGH SHELF
		SHOWER VALVES, WALL SWITCH PLATES
	46	DOOR PUSH BARS — AVE. EYE LEVEL, HIGH FILE, FRONT TAB
	44	HIGH BAR TOP
	42	COUNTERS, DOOR KNOBS (MAX.), HANDRAILS, BAR TOPS, DOOR LOCK — SEE OVER HEIGHT, PHONE DIAL HEIGHT
	40	FLOOR LAMP (LOW)
3'-0"	36" 38	RAILS ON STEPS (MAX.)
		HAND RAILS, COUNTERS, OR. KNOBS — LUNCH COUNTER
	34	RAILS ON STEPS (MIN.) — HIGH FILE, TOP TAB
	32	PANIC BARS — SEWING TABLE
	30	LAV. RIM — STOOL FOR 42" COUNTER, WORK TABLE, DESK
	28	
2'-0"	24" 26	TYPING TABLE, TABLE MIN. KNEE SPACE, CHAIR FOR 42" COUNTER
	22	
	20	
	18	WALL OUTLETS (MAX.) — BED
	16	HIGHEST STEP — WORK CHAIR
1'-0"	12" 14	RUNG SPACING — SEAT (MIN)
		WALL OUTLET (AVE.)
	10	WALL OUTLET (MIN.) — COFFEE TABLE (LOW)
	8	RISER (MAX.)
	6	— TOE SPACE (MAX.)
	4	RISER (MIN.) — TOE SPACE (MIN.)
0'-0"	0" 2	THRESHOLD (1/4 TO 1/2")

NOTES

___ G. SPACE PLANNING

___ 1. <u>General</u>
    ___ *a.* With so many building types, it is interesting that there really are so few "space types" that the interior designer may be involved in. The interior designer is not likely to be involved in building layout (room-to-room or space-to-space relationships, or room/space sizes, although there can be exceptions such as office T.I.). Rather, the interior designer usually inherits a room or space and must do space planning and furniture arrangement within the given conditions. Hopefully, the given conditions allow enough room.

    ___ *b.* This section deals with common spaces to most building types that the interior designer may be involved with. They run throughout all building types. Often, the primary use for the building sets the overall layout of the building in which the interior designer will not be involved. But the auxillary uses may require an interior designer. As an example, a fire station layout is mainly set by apparatus (truck) and equipment storage. But the building will usually have auxiliary spaces (reception, office, living, toilet, sleeping, dining, & cooking) that might require the assistance of an interior designer. This is usually the case. Exceptions to this general rule might be single-family residences or office space, where the designer may be involved with all the rooms and spaces.

    ___ *c.* This section has the following space types:
        ___ (1) General
        ___ (2) Living/Waiting
        ___ (3) Bedrooms/Sleeping
        ___ (4) Dining/Eating
        ___ (5) Kitchens/Cooking
        ___ (6) Toilets/Bathing
        ___ (7) Office/Work
        ___ (8) Retail/Shopping
        ___ (9) Reception/Counter/Circulation
        ___ (10) Group seating (performance, classrooms, etc.)
        ___ (11) Storage.

___ 2. <u>Living/Waiting</u>
    ___ *a.* General
        Planning considerations should include adequate floor and wall space for furniture groupings, window locations, and separation of traffic ways from centers of activity. Ideally there should be no through-traffic. If such traffic is necessary, it should be at one end, with the remaining portion of the room a dead-end space. During social activities, people tend to gather or congregate in relatively small groups. A desirable conversation area is relatively small, approximately *10 feet* in diameter.
    ___ *b.* Overall layouts
        ___ (1) Residential: Use the following layouts for general planning (also see p. 329 for furnishings).

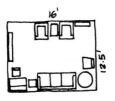

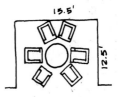

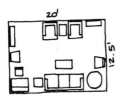

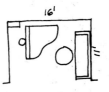

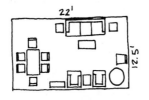

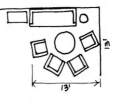

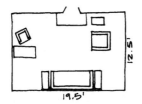

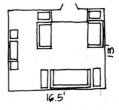

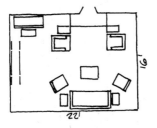

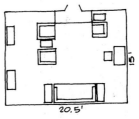

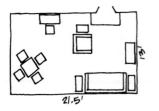

21.5'

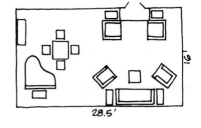

28.5'

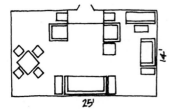

25'

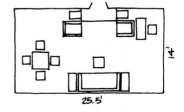

25.5'

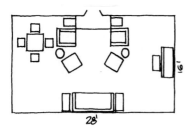

28'

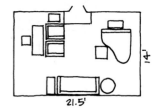

21.5'

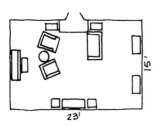

23'

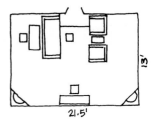

21.5'

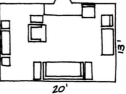

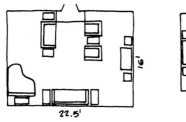

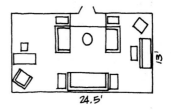

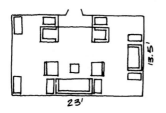

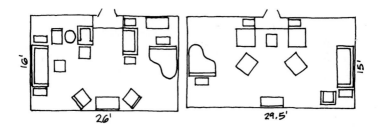

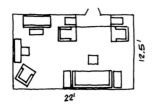

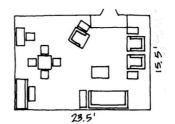

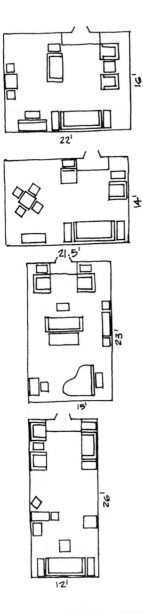

22'

16'

21.5'

16'

21.5'

14'

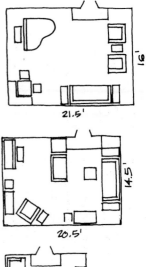

20.5'

14.5'

23'

15'

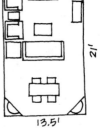

21'

13.5'

26'

12'

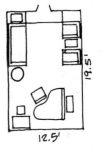

19.5'

12.5'

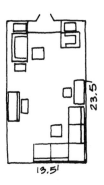

23.5

13.5'

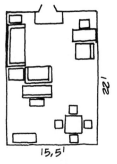

22'

15,5'

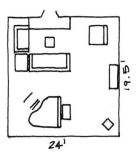

19.5'

24'

21'

12'

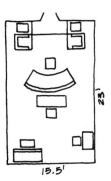

23'

15.5'

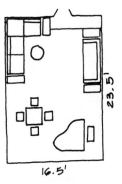

23.5'

16.5'

_____ (2) Public waiting: Much of the information fo residential living areas can be used for public areas. The following layouts depict typical office waiting and public spaces.

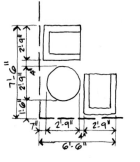

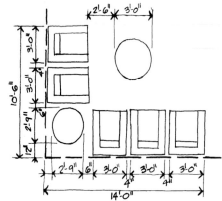

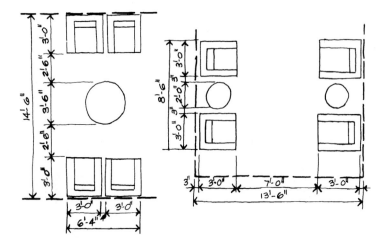

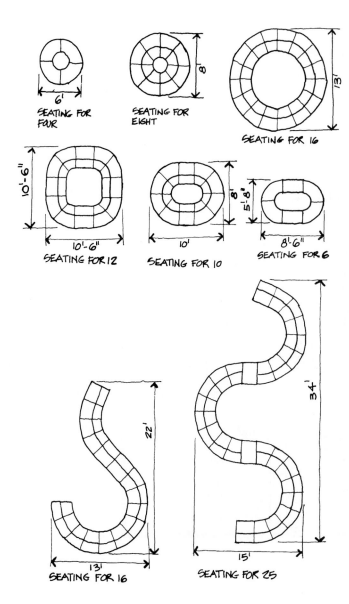

SEATING FOR FOUR

SEATING FOR EIGHT

SEATING FOR 16

SEATING FOR 12

SEATING FOR 10

SEATING FOR 6

SEATING FOR 16

SEATING FOR 25

_____ *c.* Living/waiting details

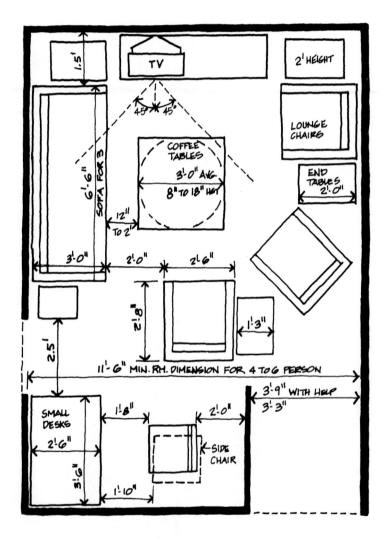

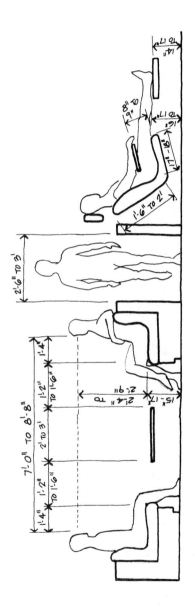

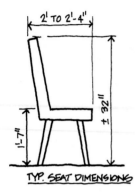

TYP. SEAT DIMENSIONS

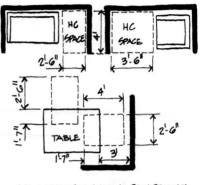

ADA ACCESSIBLE SEATING REQUIREMENTS

___ *d.* Furniture templates:
The following are furniture templates at ¼″ = 1′0″
scale. Use these for space planning of living/waiting
aeras. Dimensions are in inches.

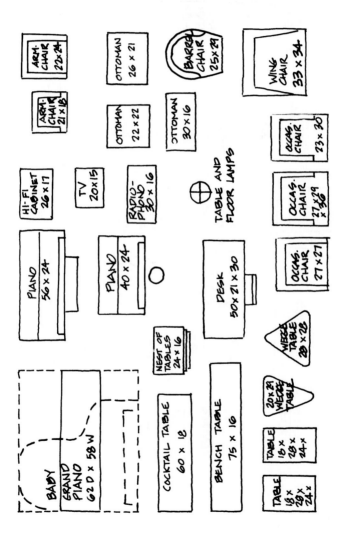

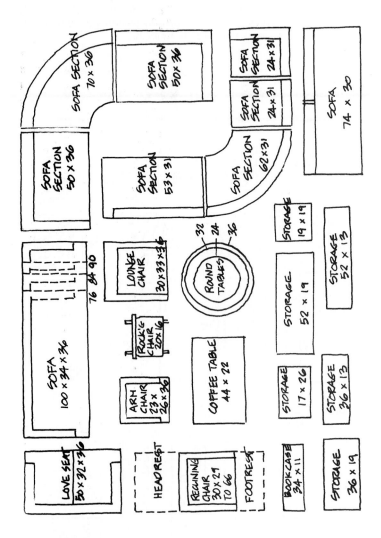

___ 3. <u>Bedroom/Sleeping</u>
    ___ *a.* Overall layouts
        Use the following layouts for general planning.
        ___ (1) Residential layouts

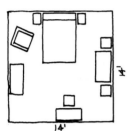
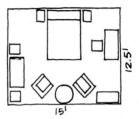

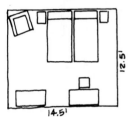
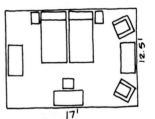

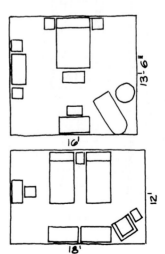

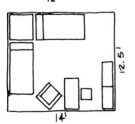

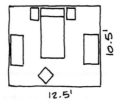

10.5'

12.5'

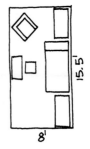

15.5'

8'

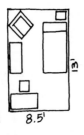

13'

8.5'

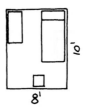

10'

8'

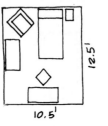

12.5'

10.5'

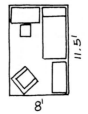

11.5'

8'

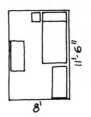

11'-6"

8'

___ (2) Hotel layouts
       For bathrooms, see p. 79

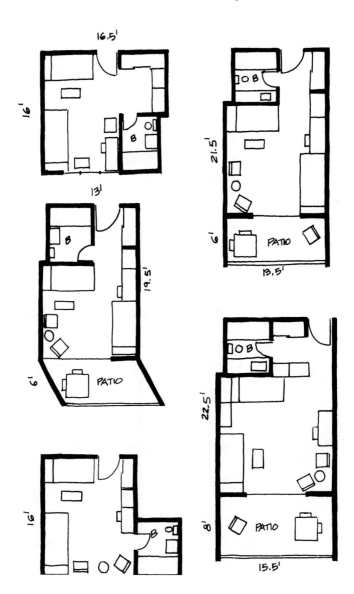

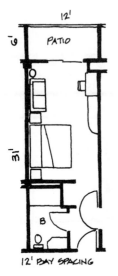

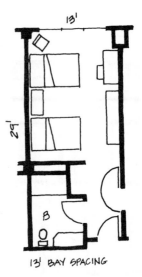

12' BAY SPACING

13' BAY SPACING

14' BAY SPACING

16 BAY SPACING

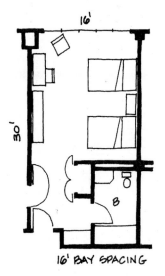

16' BAY SPACING

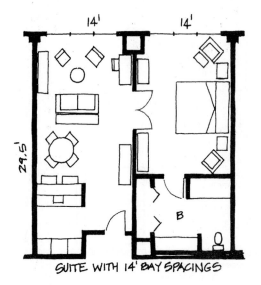

SUITE WITH 14' BAY SPACINGS

b. Details

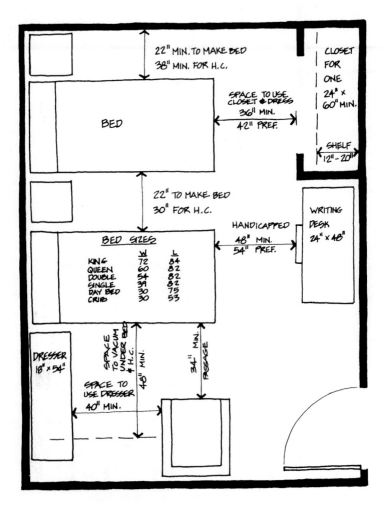

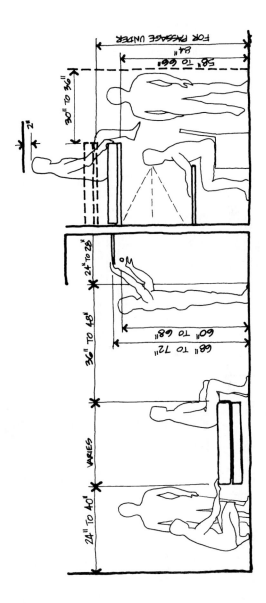

FOR PASSAGE UNDER

84"

58" TO 66"

30" TO 36"

2"

24" TO 28"

36" TO 48"

60" TO 68"

68" TO 72"

VARIES

24" TO 40"

___ *c.* Bedroom templates.
The following furniture templates are at ¼″ = 1′0″
scale. Dimensions are in inches. Use these for layout
of bedroom/sleeping areas.

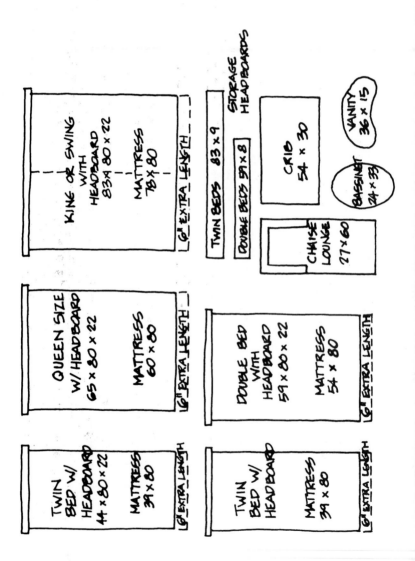

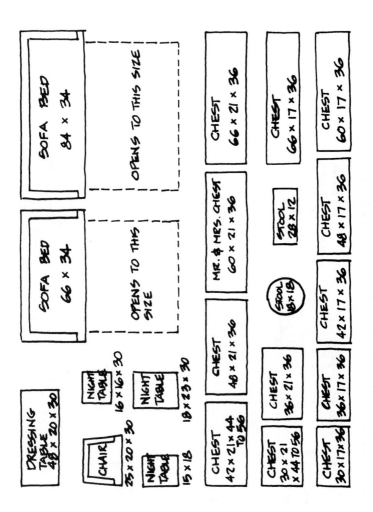

SOFA BED
84 × 34

OPENS TO THIS SIZE

SOFA BED
66 × 34

OPENS TO THIS SIZE

CHEST
66 × 21 × 36

CHEST
66 × 17 × 36

CHEST
60 × 17 × 36

MR. & MRS. CHEST
60 × 21 × 36

STOOL
28 × 12

CHEST
48 × 17 × 36

CHEST
48 × 21 × 36

STOOL
18 × 18

CHEST
42 × 17 × 36

CHEST
36 × 21 × 36

CHEST
36 × 17 × 36

DRESSING TABLE
48 × 20 × 30

NIGHT TABLE
16 × 16 × 30

NIGHT TABLE
18 × 23 × 30

CHAIR
25 × 20 × 30

NIGHT TABLE
15 × 18

CHEST
42 × 21 × 44 TO 56

CHEST
30 × 21 × 44 TO 56

CHEST
30 × 17 × 36

___ 4. <u>Dining/Eating</u>
    ___ *a.* Overall layouts
         Use the following layouts for general planning.
         ___ (1) Residential layouts

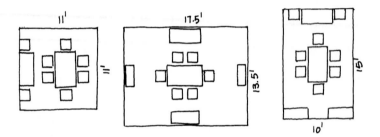

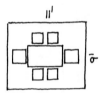
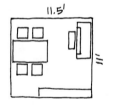
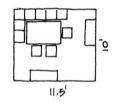

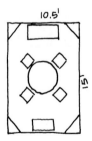
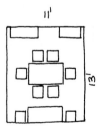
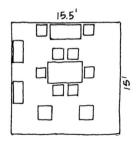

___ (2) Restaurant layouts
    Restaurants usually include:
    ___ (*a*) General public space (waiting and toilets)
    ___ (*b*) Dining area
    ___ (*c*) Kitchen

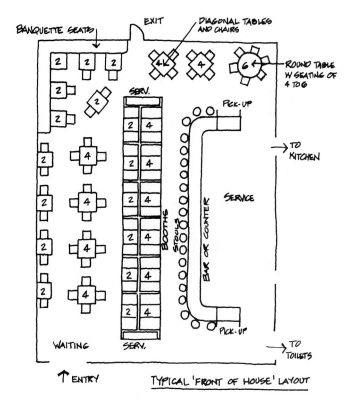

TYPICAL 'FRONT OF HOUSE' LAYOUT

Estimated Areas for Total Restaurant Building

Type of Operation	Area (SF/Seat)
Table Service	25 to 35
Counter Service	20 to 25
Booth Service	20 to 30
Cafeteria Service	20 to 30

Estimated Dining Areas ("Front of House" Only)

Type	Dining Space (SF/Seat)
Table	10 to 20
Counter	15 to 20
Booth	10 to 15
Cafeteria	10 to 15
Banquet	10 to 15

Notes: 1. Toilets are taking more space in restaurants than ever before. See p. 380.
2. For occupancy count for legal exiting, see p. 151.
3. For commercial kitchens ("back of house") see p. 75.

___ *b.* Details

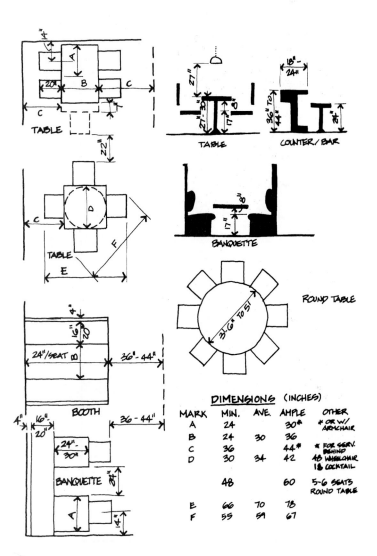

TABLE

TABLE

COUNTER / BAR

TABLE

BANQUETTE

ROUND TABLE

BOOTH

BANQUETTE

DIMENSIONS (INCHES)				
MARK	MIN.	AVE.	AMPLE	OTHER
A	24		30*	* OR W/ ARMCHAIR
B	24	30	36	
C	36		44*	* FOR SERV. BEHIND
D	30	34	42	48 WHEELCHAIR 18 COCKTAIL
	48		60	5-6 SEATS ROUND TABLE
E	66	70	78	
F	55	59	67	

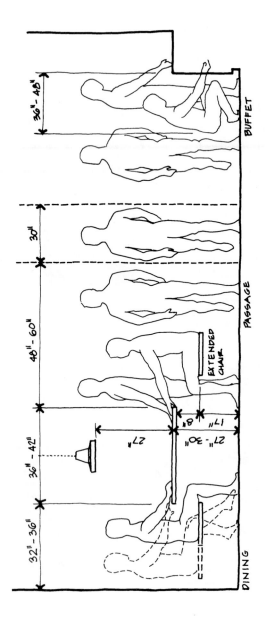

DINING

32" - 36"

36" - 42"

27"

27" - 30"

8"

17"

EXTENDED CHAIR

48" - 60"

PASSAGE

30"

36" - 48"

BUFFET

___ *c.* Dining room templates
The following furniture templates are at ¼″ = 1′0″ scale. Dimensions are in inches. Use them for layout of residential dining areas.

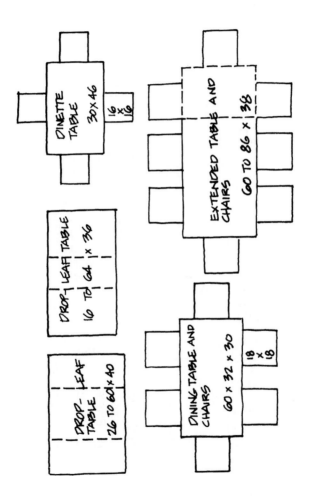

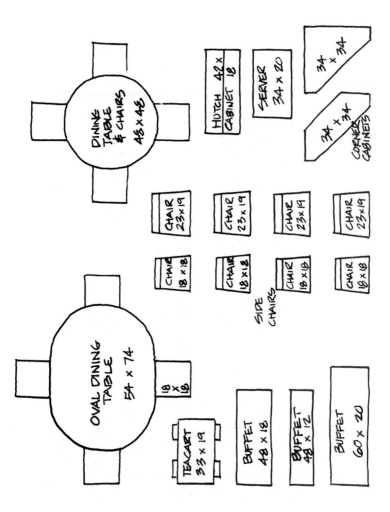

DINING TABLE & CHAIRS 48 x 48

HUTCH CABINET 42 x 18

SERVER 34 x 20

34 x 34

34 x 34

CORNER CABINETS

CHAIR 23 x 19

CHAIR 23 x 19

CHAIR 23 x 19

CHAIR 23 x 19

CHAIR 18 x 18

CHAIR 18 x 18

CHAIR 18 x 18

CHAIR 18 x 18

SIDE CHAIRS

OVAL DINING TABLE 54 x 74

18 x 18

TEACART 33 x 19

BUFFET 48 x 18

BUFFET 48 x 12

BUFFET 60 x 20

72

___ 5. <u>Kitchens/Cooking</u>
    ___ *a.* Overall layouts
        ___ (1) Residential

C	= Cooktop (range/oven)		
D	= Desk	R	= Refrigerator
DR	= Dryer	S	= Sink
DW	= Dishwasher	T	= Table and chairs
F	= Folding	TR	= Trash
I	= Ironing board	W	= Washer
P	= Pantry	WO	= Wall oven

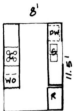

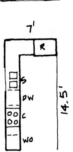

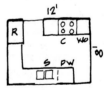

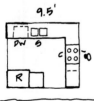

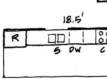

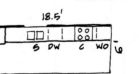

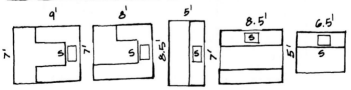

PANTRY TYPES

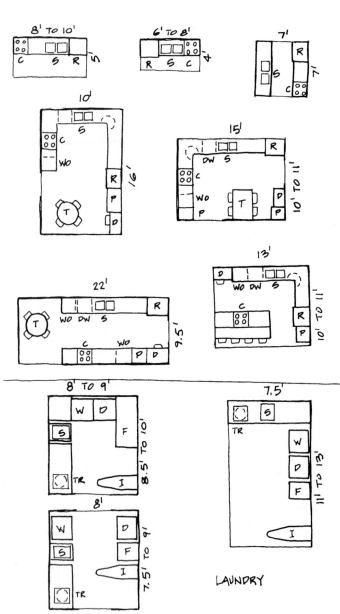

LAUNDRY

___ (2) Commercial restaurant kitchens
 ___ (*a*) Typically kitchens range roughly from one-third to one-half the total area of a restaurant.
 ___ (*b*) For general planning, the following areas are usually included in a restaurant kitchen:

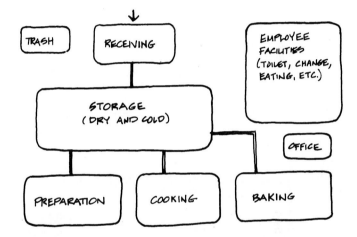

 ___ (*c*) Typical space allocations (%) of kitchens

Receiving	5%
Storage	20
Preparation	15
Cooking	10
Baking	10
Dishwashing	5
Aisles	15
Trash	5
Misc. (employee changing room, eating area, office etc.)	15
	100%

___ *b.* Details (residential)
Also see p. 325 for washers and dryers.

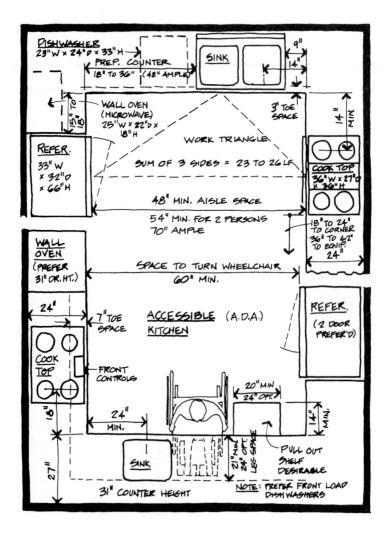

DISHWASHER
23"W x 24"D x 33"H

PREP. COUNTER
18" TO 36" (48" AMPLE)

SINK

9"

14"

WALL OVEN
(MICROWAVE)
25"W x 22"D x
18"H

15" TO 18"

REFER.
33"W
x 32"D
x 66"H

3" TOE
SPACE

14" MIN

WORK TRIANGLE

SUM OF 3 SIDES = 23 TO 26 LF

COOK TOP
36"W x 27"D
x 36"H

48" MIN. AISLE SPACE

54" MIN. FOR 2 PERSONS
70" AMPLE

18" TO 24"
TO CORNER
36" TO 42"
TO EQUIP.
24"

WALL
OVEN
(PREFER
31" OR. HT.)

SPACE TO TURN WHEELCHAIR
60" MIN.

24"

7" TOE
SPACE

ACCESSIBLE (A.D.A.)
KITCHEN

REFER.
(2 DOOR
PREFER'D)

COOK
TOP

FRONT
CONTROLS

20" MIN
24" OPT.

18"

24"
MIN.

14" MIN.

27"

SINK

21" MIN
24" OPT.
LEG SPACE

PULL OUT
SHELF
DESIRABLE

31" COUNTER HEIGHT

NOTE: PREFER FRONT LOAD
DISHWASHERS

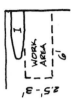

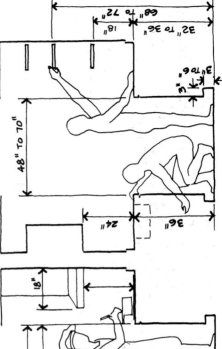

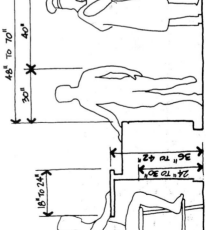

LAUNDRY CLEARANCES

___ *c.* Kitchen templates (residential)
The following furniture templates are at ¼″ = 1′0″ scale. Dimensions are in inches. Use them for layout of residential kitchen areas.

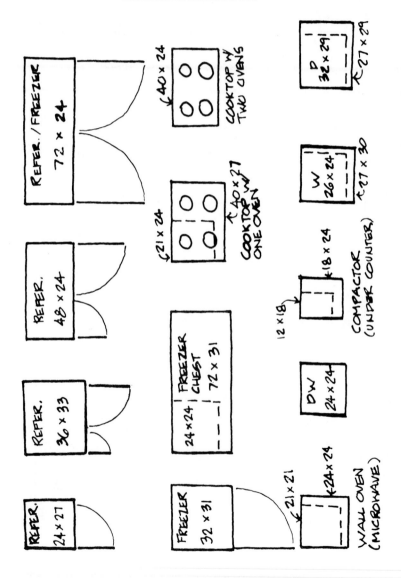

___ 6. <u>Toilets/Bathing</u>
    ___ *a.* Overall layouts
        ___ (1) Residential:

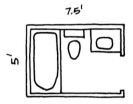

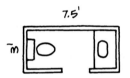

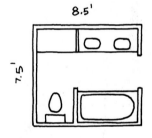

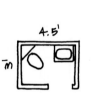

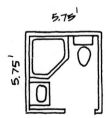

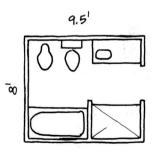

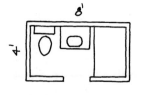

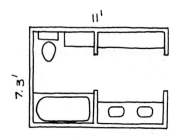

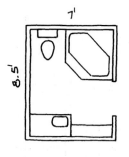

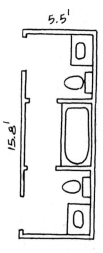

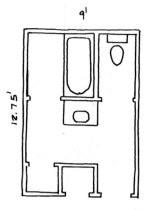

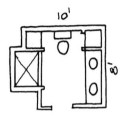

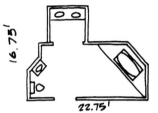

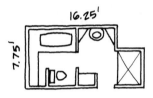

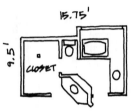

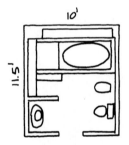

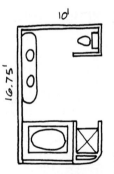

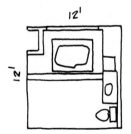

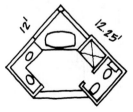

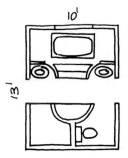

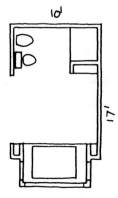

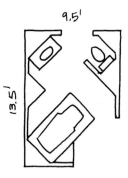

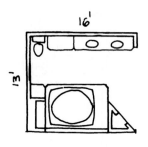

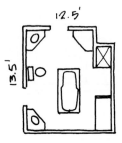

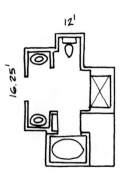

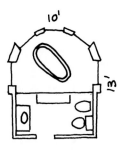

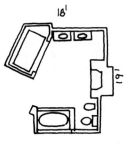

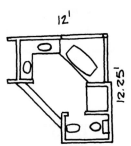

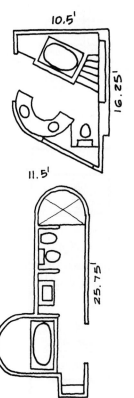

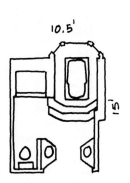

___ (2) Public toilets:

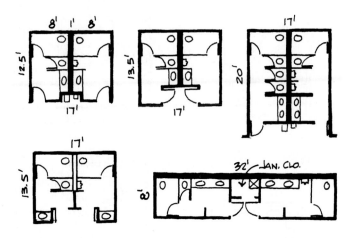

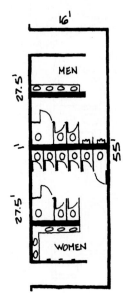

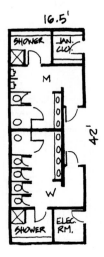

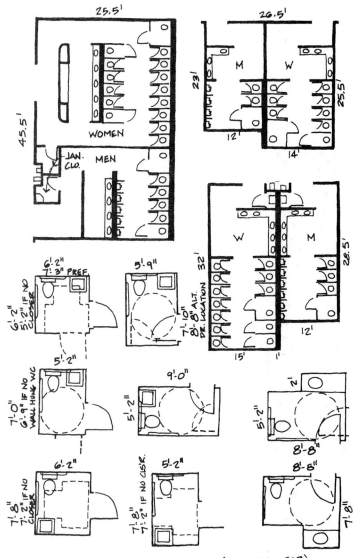

SINGLE USER TOILETS (DIM. ARE CLEAR)

___ *b.*   Toilet details

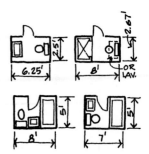

RESIDENTIAL BATHROOMS

WATER CLOSET

BIDET

LAVATORY

SHOWER

TUB R

TUB S

FIXTURE SIZES AND CLEARANCES (INCHES)

FIXTURE	A		B		C		D		E	
	MIN.	LIB.	MIN.	LIB.	MIN.	LIB.	MIN.	LIB.	MIN.	LIB.
WATER C.	27	31	19	21	12	18	15	22	18	34 - 36
BIDET	25	27	14	14	12	18	15	22	18	34 - 36
LAVATORY	16	21	18	30	2	6	14	22	18	30
SHOWER	32	36	34	36	2	8	18	34		
TUB R	60 STD	72	30 STD	42	2	8	18 - 20	30 - 34	2	8
TUB S	38		39		2	4				

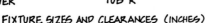

NOTE: FOR H.C. ACCESSIBILITY, SEE FOLLOWING PAGES.

TOILET ROOMS

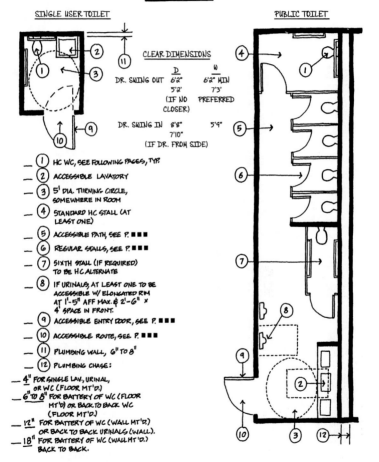

SINGLE USER TOILET

PUBLIC TOILET

CLEAR DIMENSIONS

	D	W
DR. SWING OUT	6'2"	6'2" MIN
	5'2'	7'3'
	(IF NO CLOSER)	PREFERRED
DR. SWING IN	8'8"	5'9"
	7'10"	
	(IF DR. FROM SIDE)	

1. HC WC, SEE FOLLOWING PAGES, TYP.
2. ACCESSIBLE LAVATORY
3. 5' DIA. TURNING CIRCLE, SOMEWHERE IN ROOM
4. STANDARD HC STALL (AT LEAST ONE)
5. ACCESSIBLE PATH, SEE P. ■ ■ ■
6. REGULAR STALLS, SEE P. ■ ■ ■
7. SIXTH STALL (IF REQUIRED) TO BE HC ALTERNATE
8. IF URINALS, AT LEAST ONE TO BE ACCESSIBLE W/ ELONGATED RIM AT 1'-5" AFF MAX. & 2'-6" × 4' SPACE IN FRONT.
9. ACCESSIBLE ENTRY DOOR, SEE P. ■ ■ ■
10. ACCESSIBLE ROUTE, SEE P. ■ ■ ■
11. PLUMBING WALL, 6" TO 8"
12. PLUMBING CHASE:

__ 4" FOR SINGLE LAV., URINAL, OR WC (FLOOR MT'D.)

__ 6" TO 8" FOR BATTERY OF WC (FLOOR MT'D) OR BACK TO BACK WC (FLOOR MT'D.)

__ 12" FOR BATTERY OF WC (WALL MT'D.) OR BACK TO BACK URINALS (WALL).

__ 18" FOR BATTERY OF WC (WALL MT'D.) BACK TO BACK.

ACCESSIBLE TOILET STALLS (ADA)

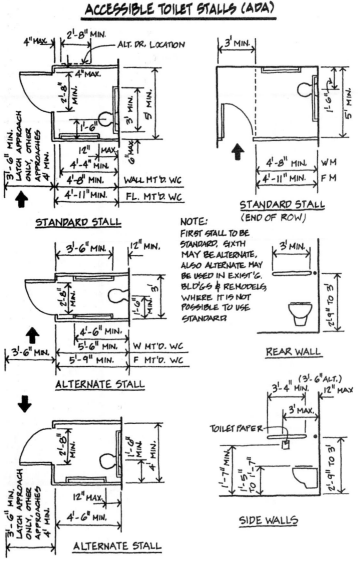

ACCESSIBLE FIXTURES (ADA)

WATER CLOSETS

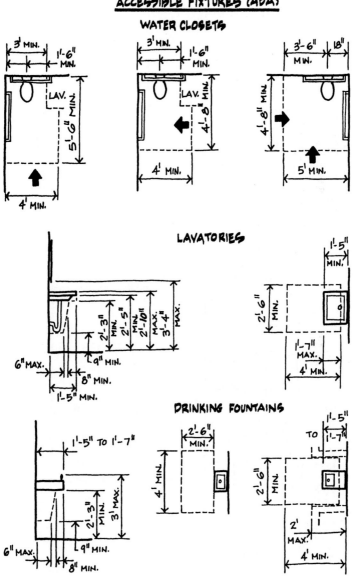

LAVATORIES

DRINKING FOUNTAINS

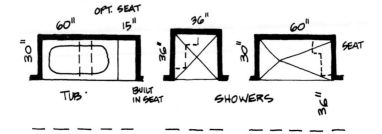

ACCESSIBLE TUBS AND SHOWERS

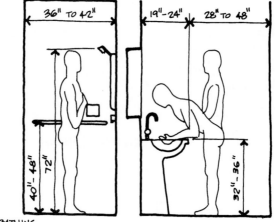

BATHING

___ *c.* Toilet and bathroom templates
The following fixture templates are at ¼" = 1'0"
scale. Use them for layout of toilet and bathrooms.

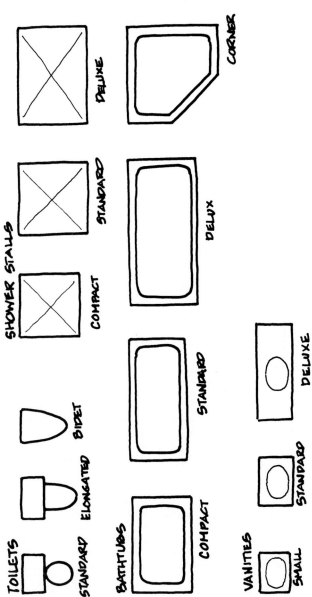

___ 7. <u>Office/Work</u>
    ___ *a.* General Planning
        ___ (1) Desks should be spaced at a distance of 6 feet from the front of desk behind. Increase to 7 feet when in rows of two.
        ___ (2) Private office desk should face door.
        ___ (3) Employees performing close work should have the best lighting.
        ___ (4) Hang coats and jackets at work areas, not in special rooms.
        ___ (5) Heavy equipment should be located against walls or columns to avoid overloading floor.
        ___ (6) Circulation:
            ___ (*a*) Do not obstruct aisle or corridors for fire exiting.
            ___ (*b*) Aisles between rows of desks (secondary aisles) should be 36 inches wide.
            ___ (*c*) Aisles which carry a moderate amount of traffic should be 48 inches wide.
            ___ (*d*) Aisles leading to main exits should be 60 inches wide.
        ___ (7) Group large office functions by department:
            ___ (*a*) Management
            ___ (*b*) Finance
            ___ (*c*) Sales
            ___ (*d*) General services (central files, etc.)
            ___ (*e*) Technical services
            ___ (*f*) Production
        ___ (8) Study organization chart: The arrangement of the office functions will actually be a projection of the organization chart of the firm, located with respect for the flow of work and the physical requirements of each department.
        ___ (9) Ten guidelines for location of departments:
            ___ (*a*) Convenience to public
            ___ (*b*) Flow of work
            ___ (*c*) Equally used
            ___ (*d*) Centralized functions
            ___ (*e*) Confidential areas
            ___ (*f*) Conference rooms
            ___ (*g*) Freight elevators

___ (*h*) Shipping dock
___ (*i*) Service facilities (eating, lounge, medical, etc.)
___ (*j*) Passenger elevators
___ (10) Areas:

    ___ (*a*) Space allowance:

		SF
___	1. Top executive	400–600
___	2. Manager	150–200
___	3. Assistant manager	100–125
___	4. Supervisor	80–100
___	5. Operator, 60-inch desk	50–60
___	6. Operator, 55-inch desk	50–55
___	7. Operator, 50-inch desk	45
___	8. Standard letter file	6
___	9. Standard legal file	7
___	10. Letter lateral file	6.5
___	11. Legal lateral file	7.5

    ___ (*b*) In general office area, an allotment of 100 SF/person for clerical work is liberal, 65 SF/person is economical, 80 SF/person is average.

    ___ (*c*) Private office: 100 to 300 SF is typical.

    ___ (*d*) Semiprivate office: 150 to 400 SF is typical.

    ___ (*e*) Rooms based on 15 people:

        ___ 1. Reception: 400 SF
        ___ 2. Waiting or interviewing: 200 SF
        ___ 3. Conference room: 500 SF
        ___ 4. Add approx. 10 SF for each additional person.

___ (11) Office layout can be done by *module,* ranging from 4 × 4 feet to 6 × 6 feet, adjustable in 4 to 6 inch increments. In layout of private offices, controlling factors are minimum practical layout, reconciled with exterior window and wall design. Walls need to meet at exterior window *mullions.* Also, *structural column* locations effect layout. Column spacing is usually at 25, 30, or 35 ft. centers.

___ (12) *Efficiency of layout* is measured by ratio of rentable space to total space. Average efficiency is about *70%*. Maximum possible is about 85%. The nonrentable space consists of elevators, stairs, toilets, lobbies, corridors, shafts, janitor's closets, and so forth. These are often in the central service core.

___ (13) *Floor-to-floor height* is usually about *12'*. (11' to 14'). Finished ceiling height is usually 8' to 8½'.

___ *b.* Overall layouts:

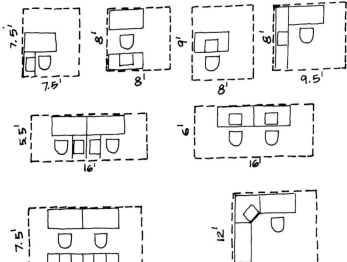

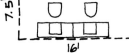

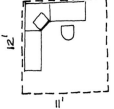

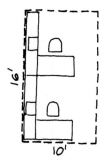

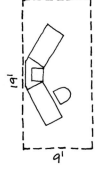

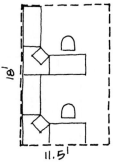

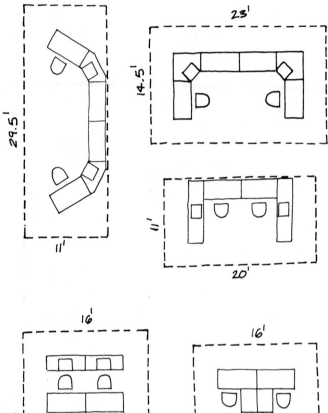

OPEN OFFICE SYSTEMS FURNITURE

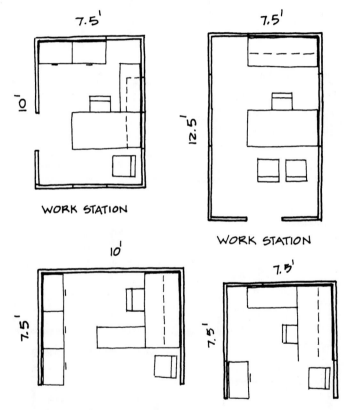

WORK STATION

WORK STATION

SECRETARIAL STATION

CLERICAL STATION

ENCLOSED OFFICE

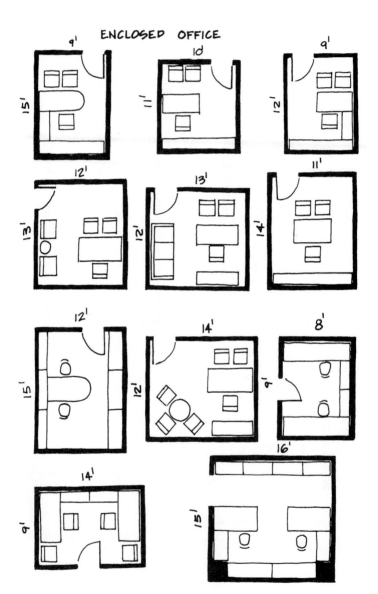

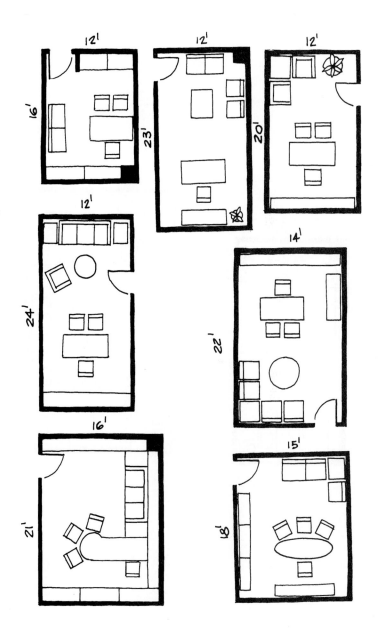

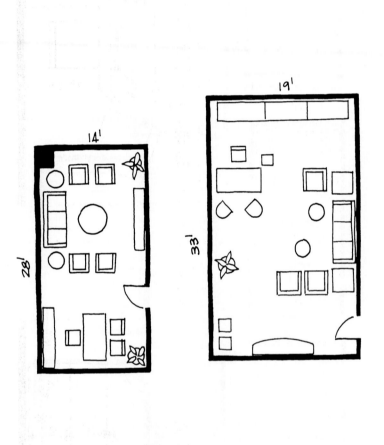

___ *c.* Details:

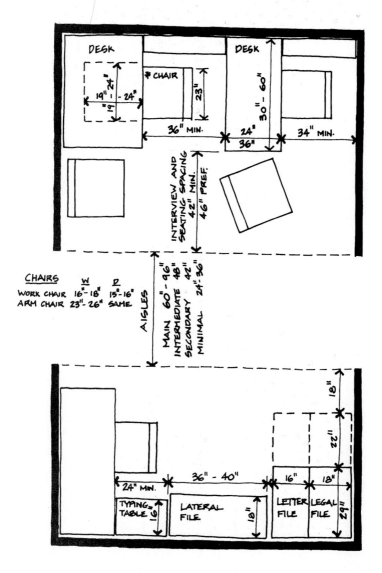

CHAIRS

	W	D
WORK CHAIR	16"-18"	15"-16"
ARM CHAIR	23"-26"	SAME

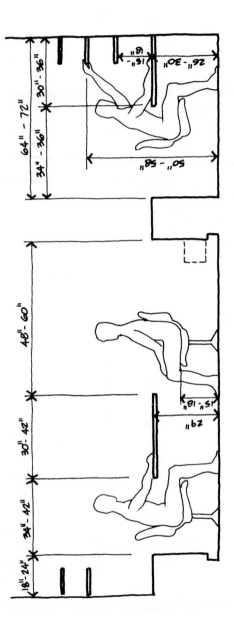

___ *d.* Office furniture templates:

The following office furniture templates are at ¼″ = 1′0″ scale. Use them to do office layouts.

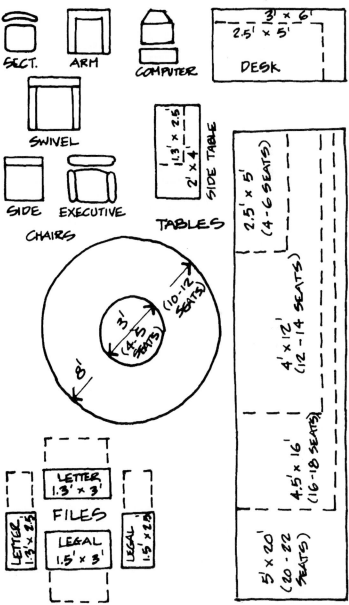

___ 8. <u>Retail/Shopping</u>
    ___ *a.* General
        ___ (1) Shops with one customer aisle only are usually 12 to 15 feet wide by 50 to 60 feet deep in large cities and 15 to 18 feet wide by 60 to 80 feet deep in smaller cities.

        ___ (2)

Aisle widths	Minimum	Desirable
Clerks	1'–8"	2' to 2'-3"
Main	4' to 6'	5'-6" to 7' up to 11'
Secondary		3' to 3'-6"

        ___ (3) Many retail stores are planned on a 4-foot module to accommodate standard retail fixtures.

        ___ (4) Divisions
            ___ (*a*) Entry/store front
            ___ (*b*) Retail
            ___ (*c*) Rear (stockroom, dressing rooms, office, repair, etc.) Size will vary; see sketches.

        ___ (5) Types of layouts:

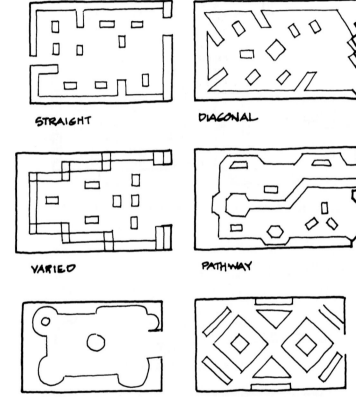

STRAIGHT

DIAGONAL

VARIED

PATHWAY

CURVED

GEOMETRIC

___ *b.*   Overall layouts:

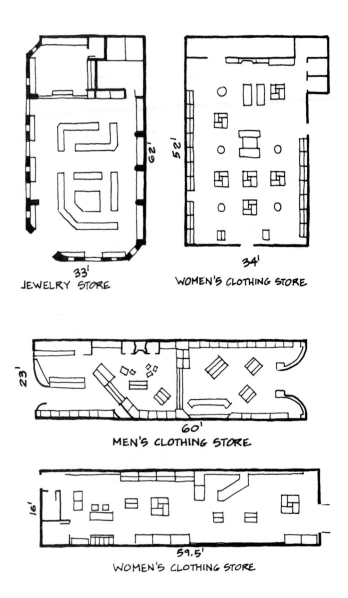

JEWELRY STORE

WOMEN'S CLOTHING STORE

MEN'S CLOTHING STORE

WOMEN'S CLOTHING STORE

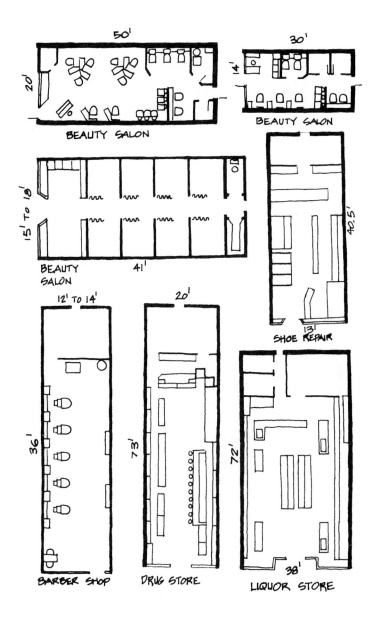

BEAUTY SALON

BEAUTY SALON

BEAUTY SALON

SHOE REPAIR

BARBER SHOP

DRUG STORE

LIQUOR STORE

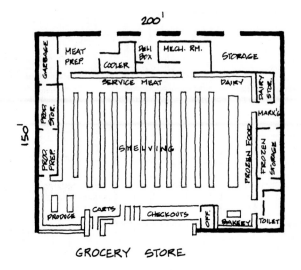

GROCERY STORE

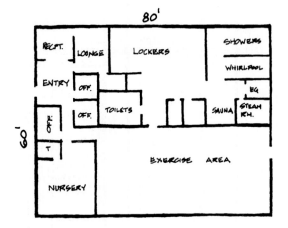

HEALTH STUDIO

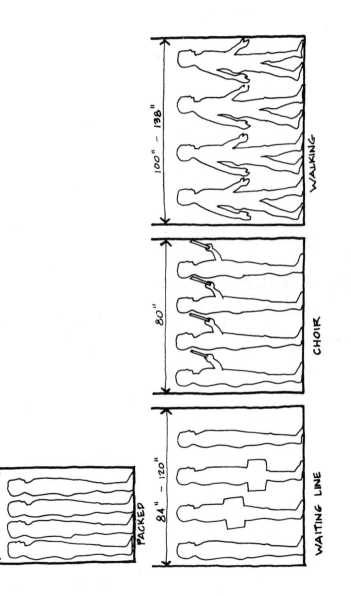

PACKED
49" – 74"

CHOIR
80"

WALKING
100" – 138"

WAITING LINE
84" – 120"

___ 10. <u>Group Seating</u>
    ___ *a.* Auditorium or theater fixed seating: Allow 7 to 12 SF (7½ SF average) per seat, including aisles and crossovers. This is sufficiently accurate for preliminary planning.

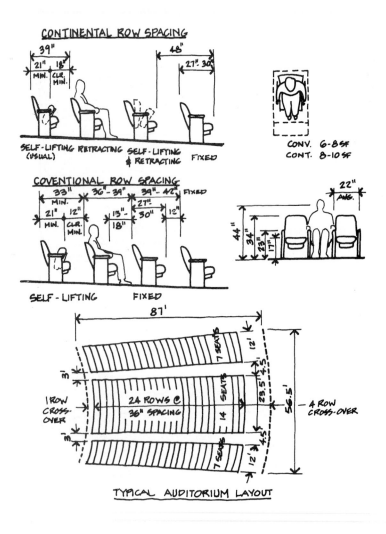

TYPICAL AUDITORIUM LAYOUT

___ *b.* Classroom with individual desks and chairs:

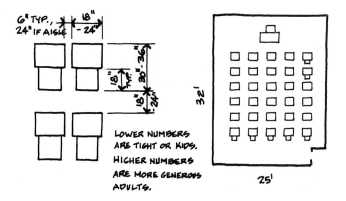

6" TYP.,
24" IF AISLE

18"
- 24"

18" TYP.

30 - 36"

18" - 24"

32'

25'

LOWER NUMBERS
ARE TIGHT OR KIDS.
HIGHER NUMBERS
ARE MORE GENEROUS
ADULTS.

___ *c.* Group seating, tables, and chairs:

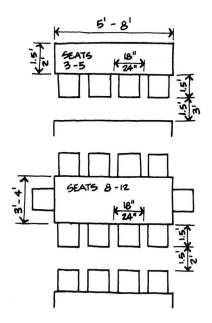

5' - 8'

1.5' - 2'

SEATS
3 - 5

18"
24"

1.5' - 3'
1.5'

ONE WAY VIEW

SEATS 8 - 12

3' - 4'

18"
24"

1.5' - 2'
1.5'

NO DIRECTION

___ 11. <u>Storage</u>
    ___ *a.* Commercial: See p.104
    ___ *b.* Residential:
        ___ (1) *<u>Shelving:</u>* Standard shelving sizes are 6″, 8″, 10″, 12″, and 18″ deep. Shelving can be either fixed or adjustable.
        ___ (2) *<u>Drawers:</u>* 16 to 24″ deep; 12 to 36″ wide; and 2 to 8″ high. May be of wood, metal, or molded plastic.
        ___ (3) Storage requirements:
            ___ (*a*) *<u>Bedroom:</u>* 4 to 6 feet of hanging space per person. Allow 8 LF of hanging space when shared by 2 people. The average rod space per garment is about 2″ for women's clothing, 2¼″ for men's clothing, and 4″ for heavy coats. Recommended rod heights are 68″ for long rods, 63″ for adult clothing, and 32″ for children's clothing. The shelf is normally located 2″ above the rod, with another shelf 12″ higher.
            ___ (*b*) *<u>Linen:</u>* Shelves 12 to 18″ deep. Provide minimum 9 SF for 1- to 2-bedroom house and 12 SF for 3–4-bedroom house.
            ___ (*c*) *<u>Bathroom:</u>* A mirrored wall cabinet of 4 to 6″ deep is typical, plus drawers in vanity.
            ___ (*d*) Front entry closet for coats.
            ___ (*e*) Cleaning equipment: Utility closet a minimum of 24″ wide.
            ___ (*f*) Kitchen.
            ___ (*g*) Other:
                ___ 1. Books: Shelves 8″ (85%), 10″ (10%), and 12″ (5%) deep. Vertical spacing varies from 8 to 16″ (10 to 12″ most typical). Horizontally, books average 7 to 8 volumes per LF of shelf.
                ___ 2. Magazines.
                ___ 3. Card tables and chairs: 30–36″ sq. and 2 to 3″ thick

when folded. Folded chairs
average 30″ × 16″ × 3″.
___ 4. Phonograph records: 14″ ×
         15″.
___ 5. Games.
___ 6. Movie and slide projectors
         and screens.
___ 7. Toys.
___ 8. Sports equipment.
___ 9. Tools.
___ 10. Bulk: Usually outside, in
         garage, or in attic.
___ (4) Closets: Standard closet depth is 24 to 30″
         for clothing and 16 to 20″ for linens. Types:
         ___ (a) Reach-in (24″ minimum)
         ___ (b) Edge-in (additional 18″)
         ___ (c) Walk-in

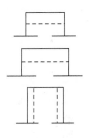

___ (5) Details:

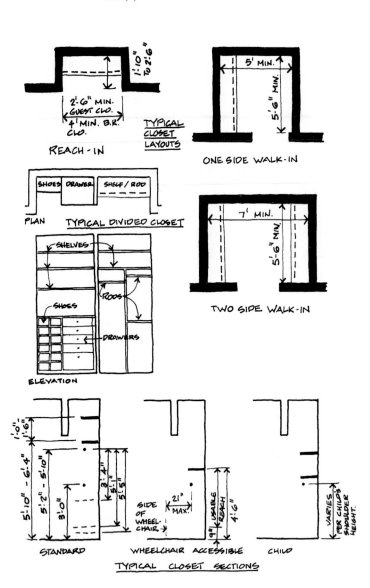

REACH-IN

TYPICAL CLOSET LAYOUTS

ONE SIDE WALK-IN

TYPICAL DIVIDED CLOSET

PLAN

TWO SIDE WALK-IN

ELEVATION

TYPICAL CLOSET SECTIONS

STANDARD   WHEELCHAIR ACCESSIBLE   CHILD

NOTES

NOTES

__ H. PRACTICAL MATH AND TABLES

(13) (30) (49)

__ 1. <u>General:</u> Interior designers seldom have to be involved in higher mathematics, but they continually need to do simple math *well.*

    __ *a.* For rough estimating (such as in this book) an accuracy of more than 90 to 95% is seldom required.

    __ *b.* Try to have a rough idea of what the answer should be, before making the calculation (i.e., does the answer make sense?).

    __ *c.* Round numbers off and don't get bogged down in trivia.

    __ *d.* For final exact numbers that are important (such as final building areas), go slow, and recheck calculations at least once.

__ 2. <u>Decimals of a Foot</u>

		<u>Decimals of an Inch</u>	
1″ = .08′	7″ = .58′	⅛″ = 0.125″	⅝″ = 0.625″
2″ = .17′	8″ = .67′	¼″ = 0.250″	¾″ = 0.750″
3″ = .25′	9″ = .75′	⅜″ = 0.375″	⅞″ = 0.875″
4″ = .33′	10″ = .83′	½″ = 0.50″	1″ = 1.0″
5″ = .42′	11″ = .92′		
6″ = .50′	12″ = 1.0′		

__ 3. <u>Simple Algebra</u>

One unknown and two knowns

$A = B/C$
$B = A \times C$
$C = B/A$

Example: $3 = 15/5$
$15 = 3 \times 5$
$5 = 15/3$

__ 4. <u>Ratios and Proportions</u>

One unknown and three knowns (cross multiplication)

$$\frac{A}{B} = \frac{C}{D}$$

Example: $\dfrac{X}{5} \diagup\!\!\!\!\diagdown \dfrac{10}{20}$ $20 X = 5 \times 10$

$$A \times C = B \times D \qquad X = \frac{5 \times 10}{20} = 2.5 \qquad X = 2.5$$

__ 5. <u>Percent Increases or Decreases</u>

50% increase = ½ increase, use × 1.5

100% increase = double, use × 2.0

200% increase = triple, use × 3.0

Example: 20 increases to 25

To find percent increase: 25–20 = 5 [amount of increase]

    5/20 = 0.25 or 25% increase

___ 6. <u>Slopes, Gradients, and Angles</u>
   (see p. 123)

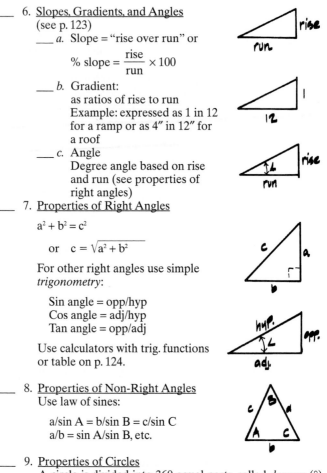

   ___ *a.* Slope = "rise over run" or

   $$\% \text{ slope} = \frac{\text{rise}}{\text{run}} \times 100$$

   ___ *b.* Gradient:
   as ratios of rise to run
   Example: expressed as 1 in 12
   for a ramp or as 4″ in 12″ for
   a roof

   ___ *c.* Angle
   Degree angle based on rise
   and run (see properties of
   right angles)

___ 7. <u>Properties of Right Angles</u>

   $a^2 + b^2 = c^2$

   or $c = \sqrt{a^2 + b^2}$

   For other right angles use simple
   trigonometry:

   Sin angle = opp/hyp
   Cos angle = adj/hyp
   Tan angle = opp/adj

   Use calculators with trig. functions
   or table on p. 124.

___ 8. <u>Properties of Non-Right Angles</u>
   Use law of sines:

   $a/\sin A = b/\sin B = c/\sin C$
   $a/b = \sin A/\sin B$, etc.

___ 9. <u>Properties of Circles</u>
   A circle is divided into 360 equal parts, called *degrees* (°).
   One degree is an angle at the center of a circle which cuts
   off an arc that is $\frac{1}{360}$ of the circumference. Degrees are subdivided into 60 minutes ('). Minutes are subdivided into 60
   seconds (″). See p. 128.

___ 10. <u>Equivalents of Measure</u>
   Use the three bar graphs on p. 128 for quick metric con-
   versions.

___ 11. <u>Geometric Figures</u>
   Use the formulas on pp. 129 to calculate areas and
   volumes.

___ 12. <u>Units and Conversions</u>
Use the tables on pp. 131–138 to convert units.

Table of Slopes, Grades, Angles

% Slope	Inch/ft	Ratio	Deg. from horiz.
1	⅛	1 in 100	
2	¼	1 in 50	
3	⅜		
4	½	1 in 25	
5	⅝	1 in 20	3
6	¾		
7	⅞		
8	approx. 1	approx. 1 in 12	
9	1⅛		
10	1¼	1 in 10	6
11	1⅜	approx. 1 in 9	
12	1½		
13	1⅝		
14	1¾		
15			8.5
16	1⅞		
17	2	approx. 2 in 12	
18	2⅛		
19	2¼		
20	2⅜	1 in 5	11.5
25	3	3 in 12	14
30	3.6	1 in 3.3	17
35	4.2	approx. 4 in 12	19.25
40	4.8	approx. 5 in 12	21.5
45	5.4	1 in 2.2	24
50	6	6 in 12	26.5
55	6⅝	1 in 1.8	28.5
60	7¼	approx. 7 in 12	31
65	7¾	1 in 1½	33
70	8⅜	1 in 1.4	35
75	9	1 in 1.3	36.75
100	12	1 in 1	45

Trigonometry Tables

Deg	Sin	Cos	Tan	Deg	Sin	Cos	Tan	Deg	Sin	Cos	Tan
1	.0175	.9998	.0175	31	.5150	.8572	.6009	61	.8746	.4848	1.8040
2	.0349	.9994	.0349	32	.5299	.8480	.6249	62	.8829	.4695	1.8807
3	.0523	.9986	.0524	33	.5446	.8387	.6494	63	.8910	.4540	1.9626
4	.0698	.9976	.0699	34	.5592	.8290	.6745	64	.8988	.4384	2.0503
5	.0872	.9962	.0875	35	.5736	.8192	.7002	65	.9063	.4226	2.1445
6	.1045	.9945	.1051	36	.5878	.8090	.7265	66	.9135	.4067	2.2460
7	.1219	.9925	.1228	37	.6018	.7986	.7536	67	.9205	.3907	2.3559
8	.1392	.9903	.1405	38	.6157	.7880	.7813	68	.9272	.3746	2.4751
9	.1564	.9877	.1584	39	.6293	.7771	.8098	69	.9336	.3584	2.6051
10	.1736	.9848	.1763	40	.6428	.7660	.8391	70	.9397	.3420	2.7475
11	.1908	.9816	.1944	41	.6561	.7547	.8693	71	.9455	.3256	2.9042
12	.2079	.9781	.2126	42	.6691	.7431	.9004	72	.9511	.3090	3.0777
13	.2250	.9744	.2309	43	.6820	.7314	.9325	73	.9563	.2924	3.2709
14	.2419	.9703	.2493	44	.6947	.7193	.9657	74	.9613	.2756	3.4874
15	.2588	.9659	.2679	45	.7071	.7071	1.0000	75	.9659	.2588	3.7321
16	.2756	.9613	.2867	46	.7193	.6947	1.0355	76	.9703	.2419	4.0108
17	.2924	.9563	.3057	47	.7314	.6820	1.0724	77	.9744	.2250	4.3315
18	.3090	.9511	.3249	48	.7431	.6691	1.1106	78	.9781	.2079	4.7046
19	.3256	.9455	.3443	49	.7547	.6561	1.1504	79	.9816	.1908	5.1446
20	.3420	.9397	.3640	50	.7660	.6428	1.1918	80	.9848	.1736	5.6713
21	.3584	.9336	.3839	51	.7771	.6293	1.2349	81	.9877	.1564	6.3138
22	.3746	.9272	.4040	52	.7880	.6157	1.2799	82	.9903	.1392	7.1154
23	.3907	.9205	.4245	53	.7986	.6018	1.3270	83	.9925	.1219	8.1443
24	.4067	.9135	.4452	54	.8090	.5878	1.3764	84	.9945	.1045	9.5144
25	.4226	.9063	.4663	55	.8192	.5736	1.4281	85	.9962	.0872	11.4301
26	.4384	.8988	.4877	56	.8290	.5592	1.4826	86	.9976	.0698	14.3007
27	.4540	.8910	.5095	57	.8387	.5446	1.5399	87	.9986	.0523	19.0811
28	.4695	.8829	.5317	58	.8480	.5299	1.6003	88	.9994	.0349	28.6363
29	.4848	.8746	.5543	59	.8572	.5150	1.6643	89	.9998	.0175	57.2900
30	.5000	.8660	.5774	60	.8660	.5000	1.7321	90	1.000	.0000	∞

Note: Deg = degrees of angle; Sin = sine; Cos = cosine; Tan = tangent.

____ 13. <u>Perspective Sketching</u>

Use the following simple techniques of using 10′ cubes and lines at 5′ with diagonals for quick perspective sketching: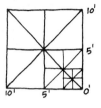

____ a. The sketches shown on p. 126 show two techniques:

The *first* establishes diagonal Vanishing Points (VP) on the Horizon Line (HL) at certain distances from the VPs, also on the HL. 10′ cubes are established by projecting diagonals to the VPs. The *second* technique has 10′ cubes and lines at the 5′ half-points. Diagonals through the half-points continue the 5′ and 10′ module to the VPs. The vertical 5′ roughly equals eye level, and establishes the HL. Half of 5′ or 2.5′ is a module for furniture height and width.

____ b. The sketch shown on p. 127 illustrates the most common way people view buildings. That is, close up, at almost a one-point perspective. To produce small sketches, set right vertical measure at ½″ apart. Then, about 10½″ to left, set vertical measure at ⅜″ apart. This will produce a small sketch to fit on 8½ × 11 paper. Larger sketches can be done using these proportions.

PERSPECTIVE SKETCHING

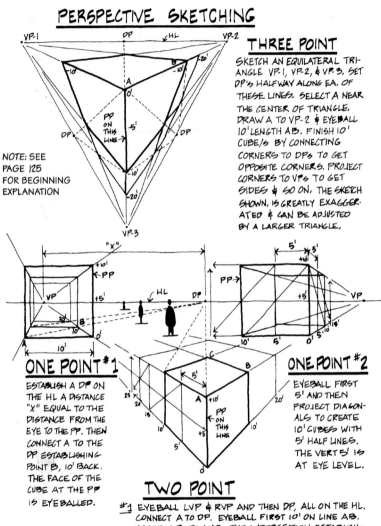

THREE POINT

SKETCH AN EQUILATERAL TRI-
ANGLE VP-1, VP-2, & VP-3. SET
DP's HALFWAY ALONG EA. OF
THESE LINES. SELECT A NEAR
THE CENTER OF TRIANGLE.
DRAW A TO VP-2 & EYEBALL
10' LENGTH AB. FINISH 10'
CUBE/s BY CONNECTING
CORNERS TO DPs TO GET
OPPOSITE CORNERS. PROJECT
CORNERS TO VP's TO GET
SIDES & SO ON. THE SKETCH
SHOWN, IS GREATLY EXAGGER-
ATED & CAN BE ADJUSTED
BY A LARGER TRIANGLE.

NOTE: SEE
PAGE 125
FOR BEGINNING
EXPLANATION

ONE POINT #1

ESTABLISH A DP ON
THE HL A DISTANCE
"X" EQUAL TO THE
DISTANCE FROM THE
EYE TO THE PP. THEN
CONNECT A TO THE
DP ESTABLISHING
POINT B, 10' BACK.
THE FACE OF THE
CUBE AT THE PP
IS EYEBALLED.

ONE POINT #2

EYEBALL FIRST
5' AND THEN
PROJECT DIAGON-
ALS TO CREATE
10' CUBES WITH
5' HALF LINES.
THE VERT 5' IS
AT EYE LEVEL.

TWO POINT

#1 EYEBALL LVP & RVP AND THEN DP, ALL ON THE HL.
CONNECT A TO DP. EYEBALL FIRST 10' ON LINE AB.
CONNECT B TO LVP. THE INTERSECTION ESTABLISH-
ES POINT C, 10' BACK, & SO ON.

#2 5' DIAGONALS CAN ALSO BE USED BY EYEBALLING
THE FIRST 5'.

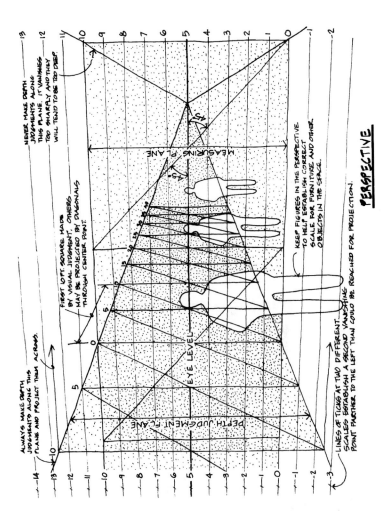

PERSPECTIVE

NEVER MAKE DEPTH JUDGMENTS ALONG THIS PLANE. IT VANISHES TOO SHARPLY AND THEY WILL TEND TO BE TOO DEEP.

FIRST 10 FT. SQUARE MADE BY VISUAL JUDGMENT. OTHERS MAY BE PROJECTED BY DIAGONALS THROUGH CENTER POINT.

MEASURING PLANE

EYE LEVEL

DEPTH JUDGMENT PLANE

ALWAYS MAKE DEPTH JUDGMENTS ALONG THIS PLANE AND PROJECT THEM ACROSS.

KEEP FIGURES IN THE PERSPECTIVE TO HELP ESTABLISH CORRECT SCALE FOR FURNITURE AND OTHER OBJECTS IN THE SPACE.

LINES OF TICKS AT TWO DIFFERENT SCALES ESTABLISH A SECOND VANISHING POINT FURTHER TO THE LEFT THAN REACHED FOR PROJECTION.

29

127

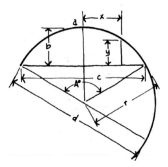

Circumference $= 6.28318\,r = 3.14159\,d$
Diameter $= 0.31831$ circumference
Area $= 3.14159\,r^2 = \pi r^2$

Arc $\quad a = \dfrac{\pi r A^\circ}{180^\circ} = 0.017453\,r A^\circ$

Angle $A^\circ = \dfrac{180^\circ d}{\pi r} = 57.29578\,\dfrac{d}{r}$

Radius $r = \dfrac{4b^2 + c^2}{8b}$

Chord $c = 2\sqrt{2br - b^2} = 2r\sin\dfrac{A}{2}$

Rise $\quad b = r - \tfrac{1}{2}\sqrt{4r^2 - c^2} = \dfrac{c}{2}\tan\dfrac{A}{4}$

$\qquad\quad = 2r\sin^2\dfrac{A}{4} = r + y - \sqrt{r^2 - x^2}$

$\quad y = b - r + \sqrt{r^2 - x^2}$

$\quad x = \sqrt{r^2 - (r + y - b)^2}$

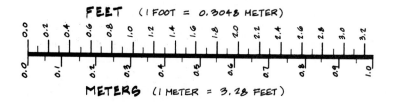

FEET (1 FOOT = 0.3048 METER)

METERS (1 METER = 3.28 FEET)

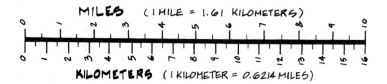

MILES (1 MILE = 1.61 KILOMETERS)

KILOMETERS (1 KILOMETER = 0.6214 MILES)

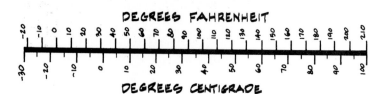

DEGREES FAHRENHEIT

DEGREES CENTIGRADE

GEOMETRIC FIGURES

PLANE SHAPES (TWO-DIMENSIONAL)

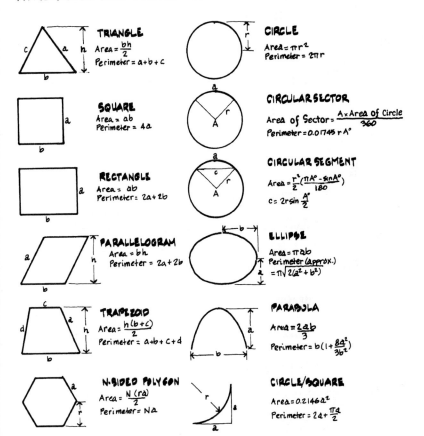

TRIANGLE
Area $= \dfrac{bh}{2}$
Perimeter $= a + b + c$

SQUARE
Area $= ab$
Perimeter $= 4a$

RECTANGLE
Area $= ab$
Perimeter $= 2a + 2b$

PARALLELOGRAM
Area $= bh$
Perimeter $= 2a + 2b$

TRAPEZOID
Area $= \dfrac{h(b+c)}{2}$
Perimeter $= a + b + c + d$

N-SIDED POLYGON
Area $= \dfrac{N(ra)}{2}$
Perimeter $= Na$

CIRCLE
Area $= \pi r^2$
Perimeter $= 2\pi r$

CIRCULAR SECTOR
Area of Sector $= \dfrac{A \times \text{Area of Circle}}{360}$
Perimeter $= 0.01745\, r\, A^\circ$

CIRCULAR SEGMENT
Area $= \dfrac{r^2}{2}\left(\dfrac{\pi A^\circ - \sin A^\circ}{180}\right)$
$c = 2r \sin \dfrac{A^\circ}{2}$

ELLIPSE
Area $= \pi ab$
Perimeter (approx.)
$= \pi \sqrt{2(a^2 + b^2)}$

PARABOLA
Area $= \dfrac{2ab}{3}$
Perimeter $= b\left(1 + \dfrac{8a^2}{3b^2}\right)$

CIRCLE/SQUARE
Area $= 0.2146a^2$
Perimeter $= 2a + \dfrac{\pi a}{2}$

GEOMETRIC FIGURES

SOLID BODIES (THREE-DIMENSIONAL)

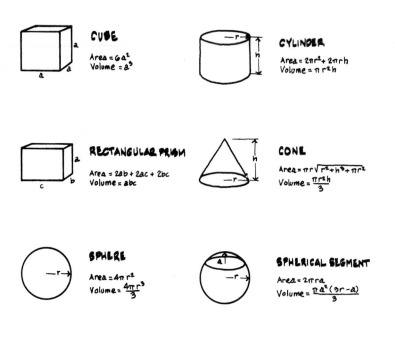

CUBE

Area = $6a^2$
Volume = a^3

CYLINDER

Area = $2\pi r^2 + 2\pi rh$
Volume = $\pi r^2 h$

RECTANGULAR PRISM

Area = $2ab + 2ac + 2bc$
Volume = abc

CONE

Area = $\pi r \sqrt{r^2 + h^2} + \pi r^2$
Volume = $\dfrac{\pi r^2 h}{3}$

SPHERE

Area = $4\pi r^2$
Volume = $\dfrac{4\pi r^3}{3}$

SPHERICAL SEGMENT

Area = $2\pi ra$
Volume = $\dfrac{\pi a^2 (3r - a)}{3}$

ELLIPSOID

Volume = $\dfrac{\pi abc}{3}$

PARABOLOID

Volume = $\dfrac{\pi r^2 h}{2}$

LENGTHS

METERS m	INCHES in.	FEET ft.	YARD yd.	RODS r.	CHAINS ch.	MILES, U.S. STATUTE	MILES, U.S. NAUTICAL	KILO-METERS km
1	39.37	3.28	1.09	0.199	0.05	$0.0^{3}6214$	$0.0^{3}5396$	0.001
0.025	1	0.083	0.028	$0.0^{2}51$	$0.0^{2}13$	$0.0^{4}158$	$0.0^{4}137$	$0.0^{2}54$
0.305	12	1	0.333	0.06	0.015	$0.0^{3}189$	$0.0^{3}165$	$0.0^{3}305$
0.914	36	3	1	0.18	0.045	$0.0^{3}568$	$0.0^{3}493$	$0.0^{3}914$
5.029	198	16.5	5.5	1	0.25	$0.0^{2}313$	$0.0^{2}271$	$0.0^{2}503$
20.117	792	66	22	4	1	0.013	0.0109	0.020
1609.35	63360	5280	1760	320	80	1	0.868	1.609
1853.25	72962.5	6080.2	2026.7	368.5	92.12	1.15	1	1.853
1000	39370	3280.8	1093.6	198.8	49.71	0.621	0.540	1

* 1 METER (m) = 10 DECIMETERS (dm) = 100 CENTIMETERS (cm) = 1000 MILLIMETERS (mm)
NOTE: NOTATIONS 2, 3, 4, ETC., INDICATE THE NUMBER OF ZEROS.
EXAMPLE: 1 METER = $0.0^{3}6214$ = 0.0006214 STATUTE MILES.

AREAS

SQUARE METERS SM	SQUARE INCHES SI	SQUARE FEET SF	SQUARE YARDS SY	SQUARE RODS SR	ACRES AC	HECTARES HA	SQUARE MILES STATUTE	SQUARE KILOMETER SQ KM
1	1550.0	10.76	1.196	0.039	0.0^3247	0.0001	0.0^6386	0.0^51
0.0^365	1	0.0^269	0.0^377	0.0^626	0.0^616	0.0^765	0.0^925	0.0^965
0.093	144	1	0.111	0.0^237	0.0^423	0.0^593	0.0^736	0.0^793
0.836	1296	9	1	0.333	0.0^321	0.0^484	0.0^632	0.0^684
25.293	39204	272.25	30.25	1	0.006	0.0^325	0.0^598	0.0^426
4046.87	6272640	43560	4840	160	1	0.405	0.0^216	0.0^241
10000	15499969	107639	11959.9	395.37	2.47104	1	0.0^239	0.01
2589999		27878400	3097600	1024000	640	259	1	2.59
1000000		10763867	1195985	39736.6	247.104	100	0.386	1

VOLUMES

CUBIC DECIMETER OR LITERS	CUBIC INCHES	CUBIC FEET	CUBIC YARDS	U.S. QUARTS		U.S. GALLONS		U.S. BUSHELS
				LIQUID	DRY	LIQUID	DRY	
1	61.02	0.035	$0.^2013$	1.057	0.908	0.264	0.227	0.028
0.016	1	$0.^3058$	$0.^421$	0.017	0.015	$0.^2043$	$0.^2072$	$0.^247$
28.32	1728	1	0.037	29.92	25.714	7.481	6.429	0.804
764.56	46656	27	1	807.90	694.28	201.97	173.57	21.70
0.946	57.75	0.033	$0.^2124$	1	0.859	0.25	0.215	0.027
1.1012	67.20	0.039	$0.^2144$	1.1637	1	0.291	0.25	0.031
3.786	231	0.134	$0.^2495$	4	3.437	1	0.859	0.107
4.405	268.8	0.196	$0.^2576$	4.655	4	1.164	1	0.125
35.24	2150.4	1.244	0.0461	37.24	32	9.309	8	1

U.S. DRY MEASURE : 1 BUSHEL = 4 PECKS = 8 GALLONS = 32 QUARTS = 64 PINTS
U.S. LIQUID MEASURE = 1 GALLON = 4 QUARTS = 8 PINTS = 92 GILLS = 128 FLUID OUNCES
1 U.S. GALLON = 0.83268 IMPERIAL GALLON

WEIGHTS

KILOGRAMS kg	GRAINS	OUNCES		POUNDS		TONS		
		TROY	AVOIR	TROY	AVOIR	NET (SHORT) 2000 lbs	GROSS (LONG) 2240 lbs	METRIC 1000 kg
1	15432.4	32.15	35.27	2.679	2.205	$0.{}^{2}1102$	$0.{}^{3}984$	0.001
$0.{}^{4}648$	1	$0.{}^{2}0208$	$0.{}^{3}23$	$0.{}^{3}174$	$0.{}^{3}143$	$0.{}^{7}714$	$0.{}^{7}638$	$0.{}^{7}648$
0.031	480	1	1.097	0.083	0.069	$0.{}^{4}343$	$0.{}^{4}306$	$0.{}^{4}311$
0.024	437.5	0.911	1	0.076	0.063	$0.{}^{4}313$	$0.{}^{4}279$	$0.{}^{4}284$
0.373	5760	12	13.166	1	0.823	$0.{}^{3}411$	$0.{}^{3}367$	$0.{}^{3}373$
0.454	7000	14.58	16	1.215	1	0.0005	$0.{}^{3}446$	$0.{}^{3}454$
907.185	14000000	29166.7	32000	2430.56	2000	1	0.893	0.907
1016.05	15680000	32666.7	35840	2722.22	2240	1.12	1	1.016
1000	15432356	32150.7	35274	2679.23	2204.62	1.102	0.984	1

1 LONG HUNDREDWEIGHT (CWt.) = 1/20 TON = 4 QUARTERS = 8 STONES = 112 LBS = 50.8 Kg

DENSITIES

GRAMS PER CU. CENTIMETER g/cm³	POUNDS PER CU. INCH lb./in.³	POUNDS PER CU. FOOT lb./ft³	POUNDS PER CU. YARD lb./yd³	KILOGRAMS PER CU. METER kg/m²	POUNDS PER BUSHEL, U.S.	POUNDS PER GALLON, DRY, U.S.	POUNDS PER GALLON, LIQUID, U.S	KILOGRAMS PER HECTOLITER kg/hl
1	0.036	62.43	1685.56	1000	77.689	9.711	8.345	100
27.68	1	1728	46656	27679.7	2150.4	268.8	231	2767.97
0.016	$0.0^{3}579$	1	27	16.02	1.24	0.156	0.134	1.602
$0.0^{3}59$	$0.0^{4}21$	0.037	1	0.593	0.046	$0.0^{2}576$	$0.0^{2}495$	0.059
0.001	$0.0^{4}36$	0.062	1.686	1	0.078	$0.0^{2}91$	$0.0^{2}83$	0.10
0.013	$0.0^{3}47$	0.804	21.696	12.87	1	0.125	0.107	1.287
0.103	$0.0^{2}37$	6.429	173.57	102.97	8	1	0.859	10.297
0.119	$0.0^{2}43$	7.481	201.97	119.83	9.31	1.194	1	11.98
0.01	$0.0^{3}36$	0.624	16.86	10	0.777	0.097	0.083	1

PRESSURE

PASCALS N/m²	BARS 10⁵N/m²	POUNDS f PER IN²	ATMOS-PHERES	COLUMNS OF MERCURY (0°C, g=9.807 m/s²)		COLUMNS OF WATER (15°C, g=9.807 m/s²)	
				cm	in	cm	in
1	0.0⁴1	0.0³145	0.0⁴1	0.0³75	0.0³295	0.0102	0.004
100000	1	14.5	0.99	75	29.53	1020.7	401.8
6894.8	0.0689	1	0.068	5.17	2.04	70.37	27.7
101326	1.01	14.696	1	76	29.92	1034	407.1
1333	0.013	0.193	0.013	1	0.39	13.61	5.357
3386	0.034	0.49	0.033	2.54	1	34.56	13.61
97.98	0.0³98	0.014	0.0³97	0.073	0.029	1	0.39
248.9	0.0²25	0.036	0.0²25	0.187	0.073	2.54	1

POWER

HORSE-POWER	KILO-WATTS	METRIC HORSE-POWER	kgf-m PER SEC.	FT-LBF PER SEC.	KILO-CALORIES PER SEC.	B.T.U. PER SEC.
1	0.746	1.014	76.04	550	0.178	0.707
1.341	1	1.36	102.0	737.6	0.239	0.948
0.986	0.736	1	75	542.5	0.176	0.697
0.013	$0.0^{2}98$	0.013	1	7.23	$0.0^{2}23$	$0.0^{2}93$
$0.0^{2}18$	$0.0^{2}14$	$0.0^{2}18$	0.138	1	$0.0^{3}32$	$0.0^{2}13$
5.615	4.187	5.692	426.9	3088	1	3.968
1.415	1.055	1.434	107.6	778.2	252.0	1

137

ENERGY OR WORK

JOULES (NEWTON-METER)	KILOGRAM-METERS	FOOT-POUNDS	KILOWATT HOURS	METRIC HORSE-POWER-HOURS	HORSE-POWER-HOURS	LITER-ATMOSPHERES	KILO-CALORIES	BRITISH THERMAL UNITS
1	0.102	0.738	$0.^{6}278$	$0.^{6}378$	$0.^{6}37$	$0.^{2}987$	$0.^{3}24$	$0.^{3}948$
9,807	1	7.233	$0.^{6}272$	$0.^{6}370$	$0.^{6}37$	0.0968	$0.^{2}234$	$0.^{2}93$
1.356	0.138	1	$0.^{6}377$	$0.^{6}512$	$0.^{6}505$	0.0134	$0.^{3}324$	0.0013
3600000	367100	2655000	1	1.36	1.34	35528	859.9	3412
2648000	270000	1952900	0.736	1	0.986	26131	632.4	2510
2684500	273750	1980000	0.746	1.014	1	26493	641.2	2544
101.33	10.33	74.74	$0.^{4}28$	$0.^{4}38$	$0.^{4}38$	1	0.024	0.096
4186.8	426.9	3088	$0.^{2}116$	$0.^{2}158$	$0.^{2}156$	41.32	1	3.968
1055	107.6	778.2	$0.^{3}29$	$0.^{3}399$	$0.^{3}393$	10.41	0.252	1

EXAMPLE (DECIMALS)

PROBLEM: CONVERT 5'-3" TO A DECIMAL NUMBER.

SOLUTION: SEE PAGE 121 (ITEM 2).
3" = .25', SO: 5' + .25' = <u>5.25'</u>

EXAMPLE (DECIMALS)

PROBLEM: CONVERT ¼" TO DECIMALS OF AN INCH.

SOLUTION: SEE PAGE 121 (ITEM 2).   ¼" = <u>0.25"</u>

EXAMPLE: (SIMPLE ALGEBRA)

PROBLEM: A ROOM OF 15' x 15' MUST BE
LAYED OUT IN A QUARTER GRID.
WHAT IS THE GRID DIMENSION?

SOLUTION: SEE PAGE 121 (ITEM 3).
15' ÷ 4 = <u>3.75'</u> OR 3'-9" GRID = X

EXAMPLE: (PROPORTIONS)

PROBLEM: A 20' LONG ROOM HAS A SLOPING
CEILING WITH A RATIO OF 1 HIGH
TO 12 LONG. IF THE LOW WALL IS 8' HIGH,
WHAT IS THE HEIGHT OF THE FAR HIGH WALL?

SOLUTION:
SEE PAGE 121 (ITEM 4).
$\frac{A}{B} = \frac{C}{D}$ OR $\frac{1}{12} = \frac{X}{20}$ CROSS MULTIPLY
12X = 1 x 20
X = 20 ÷ 12 OR 1.67'
THE HIGH WALL IS: 8' + 1.67' = <u>9.67'</u>
OR APPROX. 9'-8"

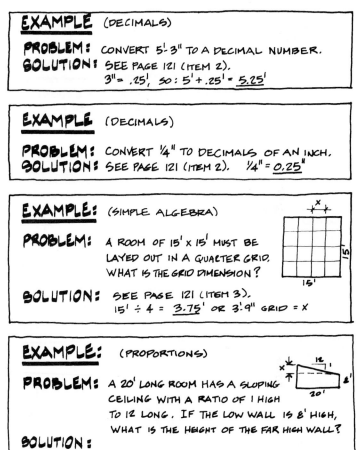

EXAMPLE: (PERCENTAGE)

PROBLEM: THE ORIGINAL PROGRAM FOR A TENANT IMPROVEMENT CALLED FOR A 5000 SF SPACE. IT WAS LATER INCREASED TO 8500 SF. WHAT IS THE % INCREASE IN SIZE?

SOLUTION:

SEE PAGE 121 (ITEM 5).

8500 SF − 5000 SF = 3500 SF INCREASE

3500 SF ÷ 5000 SF = 0.7 OR 70% INCREASE

EXAMPLE: (SLOPE)

PROBLEM: A RAMP IS 3' HIGH AND 28' LONG. WHAT IS THE SLOPE?

SOLUTION:

SEE PAGE 122 (ITEM 6).

$\% \text{ SLOPE} = \dfrac{\text{RISE}}{\text{RUN}} = \dfrac{3'}{28'} = 0.107'$ OR 10.7% SLOPE

EXAMPLE: (RIGHT ANGLES)

PROBLEM: A CEILING SLOPES AN ADDITIONAL 15' ABOVE THE NORMAL 8' HEIGHT. WHAT IS THE LENGTH OF CEILING, IF THE ROOM IS 50' LONG?

SOLUTION:

SEE PAGE 122 (ITEM 7).

$c = \sqrt{a^2 + b^2} = \sqrt{15^2 + 50^2} = \underline{52.2'}$

EXAMPLE: (CONVERSION)

PROBLEM: CONVERT A 835 SF APARTMENT INTO SQUARE METERS.

SOLUTION:

REFERRING TO PAGE 132, 1SF = 0.093 SM.
THEREFORE : 835 SF × 0.093 SM/SF = <u>77.7 SM</u>

EXAMPLE: (DECIMALS, CONVERSION)

PROBLEM: CONVERT 5'- 3 1/4" TO MILLIMETERS.

SOLUTION:

REFER TO PAGE 121 TO CONVERT TO FEET
IN DECIMALS : 1/4" = 0.25". INCHES = 3 + .25.
CONVERT DIMENSIONS TO FEET IN DECIMELS:
1/4 OF DIFFERENCE BETWEEN 3" (.25') AND
4" (.33') = 0.08' ÷ 4 = 0.02'. THEREFORE,
5' + .25' + 0.02' (1/4") = 5.27'

REFER TO PAGE 131 TO CONVERT TO METERS :
1 FT = 0.305 M. THEREFORE, 5.27' × 0.308
= 1.607 M. SINCE 1M = 1000MM (SEE
BOTTOM OF PAGE 131), 1.607 × 1000
= <u>1607 MILLIMETERS</u>

NOTES

___ I. BUILDING LAWS

___ 1. <u>Zoning</u> (45)

When doing a tenant improvement in or a remodel of an existing building, where the use is changing, the interior designer will need to check with the local zoning or planning department. An example of change of use is changing an office to a restaurant. Issues that may need to be resolved are:

___ *a.* Zone
___ *b.* Allowable use
___ *c.* Prohibited uses or special-use permit
___ *d.* Restrictions on operation of facility
___ *e.* Maximum building coverage
___ *f.* Floor area ratio
___ *g.* Restrictions due to adjacent zone(s)
___ *h.* Required parking
___ *i.* Required loading zone
___ *j.* Parking layout restrictions
___ *k.* Signage (exterior)
___ *l.* Special submittals required for approval and/or hearings
___ *m.* Although not part of the zoning ordinance, private covenants, conditions, and restrictions (CC&Rs) that "run" with the land should be checked.
___ *n.* The interior designer may need to retain an architect or civil engineer for this type of work.

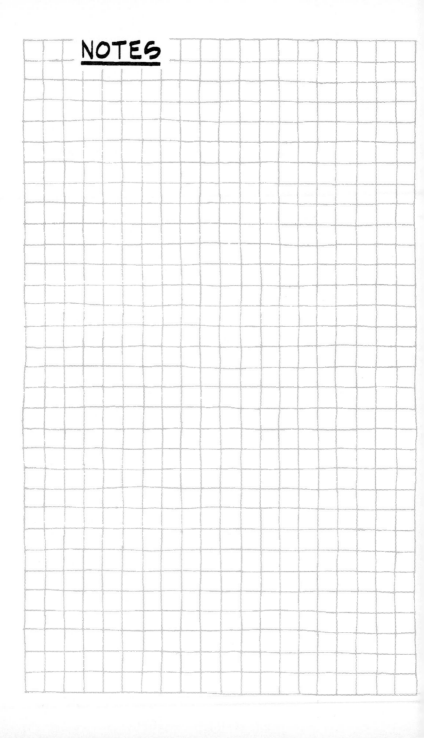

NOTES

___ 2. <u>Code Requirements for Residential</u> (27)
<u>Construction</u> (1997 UBC)

Use the following checklist for single-family residences:
___ *a.* Location on lot
    ___ (1) Openings must be 3' from property line.
    ___ (2) Walls less than 3' must be 1-hour construction.
___ *b.* Separation between abutting dwelling units must be a min. of 1-hour construction.
___ *c.* Windows and ventilation
    ___ (1) Habitable rooms must have natural light by exterior windows with area of at least $\frac{1}{10}$ floor area, but min. of 10 SF.
    ___ (2) Bath and laundry-type rooms must have ventilation by operable exterior windows with area of not less than $\frac{1}{20}$ floor area. Min. of 1.5 SF.
    ___ (3) Habitable rooms must have natural ventilation by operable exterior windows with area of not less than $\frac{1}{20}$ floor area. Min. of 5 SF.
    ___ (4) In lieu of natural ventilation, mechanical ventilation may be used:
        ___ (*a*) In habitable rooms, 2 air changes per hour, 15 C.F.M., min.
        ___ (*b*) In bath and laundry-type rooms, 5 air changes per hour.
        ___ (*c*) The point of discharge must be at least 3' from any building opening.
        ___ (*d*) Bathrooms with lavatory and WC only may have circulating fan.
    ___ (5) Any room may be considered as a portion of an adjoining room when $\frac{1}{2}$ of area of the common wall is open and provides an opening of at least $\frac{1}{10}$ of floor area of interior room, or 25 SF, whichever is greater.
    ___ (6) Eaves over windows shall not be less than 30" from side and rear property lines.
___ *d.* Ceiling heights
    ___ (1) Habitable rooms, 7'6" min.
    ___ (2) Other rooms, 7'0" min.
    ___ (3) Where exposed beams are used, height is to bottom when spacing less than 48"; otherwise, it is measured to the top.

___ (4) At sloped ceilings, the min. ceiling height is required at only ½ the area, but never less than 5′ height.

___ (5) At furred ceilings, the min. ceiling height is required at only ⅔ the area, but furred ceiling to be at 7′0″ min.

___ *e.* Sanitation

___ (1) Room with WC shall be separated from food preparation or storage area by a tight-fitting door.

___ (2) Every dwelling unit (DU) shall have a kitchen with a sink.

___ (3) Every DU shall have a bath with a WC, lavatory, bathtub, or shower.

___ (4) Every sink, lavatory, bathtub, or shower shall have hot and cold running water.

___ *f.* Room dimensions

___ (1) At least one room shall have at least 120 SF.

___ (2) Other habitable rooms, except kitchens, shall have at least 70 SF and shall be not less than 7′ in any dimension.

___ (3) Each WC shall be located in a clear space at least 30″ wide and have at least 24″ clearance in front.

___ *g.* Fire warning system

___ (1) Each dwelling must have smoke detectors in each sleeping room and the corridor to sleeping rooms, at each story (close proximity to stairways), and basement.

___ (2) In new construction, smoke detectors are to be powered by building wiring but equipped with backup battery.

___ (3) If additions or alterations (exceeding $1000) or sleeping rooms are being added, the entire building shall have smoke detectors.

___ (4) In existing buildings, smoke detectors may be solely battery-operated.

___ *h.* Exits

___ (1) Doors

___ (*a*) At least one entry door shall be 3′ wide by 6′8″ high.

___ (*b*) There must be a floor or landing at each side of each door, not more than 1″ below door and sloped not greater than 2%.

    ___ (c) At interior stairs, doors may open at the top step; if door swings away from step and step or landing is not lower than 8″, the landing must be the width of stair or door and 36″ deep.

___ (2) Emergency exits

    ___ (a) Sleeping rooms below 4th floor, and basements shall have at least one operable window.

    ___ (b) The windows shall be operable from the inside and have a min. clear opening of 5.7 SF (24″ high min., 20″ wide min.) and sill shall not be higher than 44″ above floor.

    ___ (c) Windows below grade shall have a window well. The window must be 9 SF clear opening min. and 36″ min. dimension. When well is 44″ deep, or more, provide ladder or steps.

    ___ (d) Bars, grilles, or grates may be installed provided they are operable from inside, and the building has smoke detectors.

___ i. Stairs

___ (1) Rise: 4″ min., 7″ max., except stairs serving occupant load of less than 10, rise = 8″ max., tread = 9″ min.

___ (2) Run: 11″ min.

___ (3) Variation in treads and risers = ⅜″ max.

___ (4) Winders: require tread at 12″ out from narrow side, but always no less than 6″ at any point.

___ (5) Spiral stairs limited to 400 SF of area served with 26″ min. clear width. Tread at 12″ from center to be 7½″. Max. riser = 9½″.

___ (6) Handrails

    ___ (a) At least one, at open side, continuous and terminations to posts or walls

    ___ (b) Height: 34″ to 38″ above tread nosing

    ___ (c) Clearance from walls: 1½″

    ___ (d) Width of grip: 1¼″ to 2″

___ (7) Headroom: 6′8″ min.

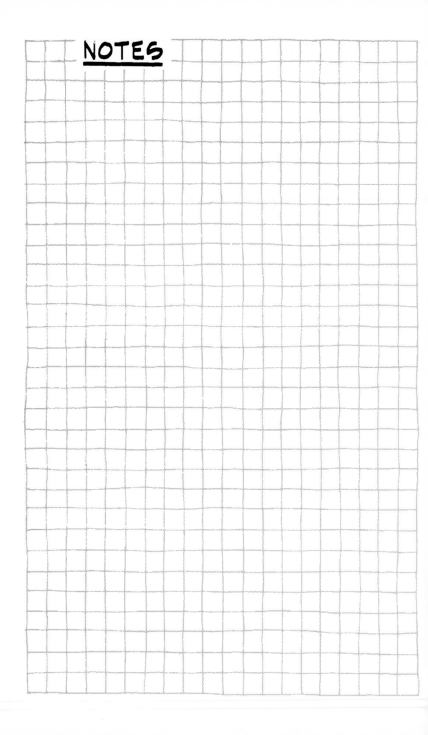

NOTES

___ 3. <u>Building Code (Based on 1997 UBC)</u>　(1)(4)(10)(25)

Note: Generally, the 1994 UBC is the same, except where noted.

Configuring a tenant improvement or interior remodel in an existing building that meets fire safety code require-ments is one of the interior designer's first responsibilities. The interior designers should acquire plans of the existing building. They will probably identify the code basics (occu-pancy type, construction type, occupancy load for exiting, whether the building is sprinklered, etc.). Because the inte-rior designer may not be familiar with all of the intricacies of the code, he or she should work closely with the building official or an architect. This handbook uses only the Uni-form Building Code (UBC) as a guide. However, all other model codes in the U.S. are similar in approach.

___ *a.* *Occupant Load:* Determining the occupant load from UBC Table 10-A will (in some cases) help determine the occupancy classification. When start-ing a project, a listing of interior program areas by name, along with their floor area, occupant classifi-cation, and occupant load should be compiled. Total the occupant load to help determine the final over-all occupancy classification and the exiting require-ments.

___ *b.* *Occupancy Classification:* The building code clas-sifies buildings by occupancy in order to group simi-lar life-safety problems together. Table 3-A of the UBC provides a concise definition of all occupancy classifications.

___ *c.* *Construction type:* The inerior designer should be aware of the building's construction type as this might affect interior work. Construction types are based on whether the building construction materi-als are combustible or noncombustible, and on the number of hours that a wall, column, beam, floor, or other structural element can resist fire. Wood is an example of a material that is combustible. Steel and concrete are examples of noncombustible materials. Steel, however, will lose structural strength as it begins to soften in the heat of a fire.

There are two ways that construction can be resis-tant to fire. First it can be *fire-resistive*—built of a monolithic, noncombustible material like concrete or masonry. Second, it can be *protected*—encased in a noncombustible material such as steel columns or wood studs covered with gypsum plaster, wallboard, and so forth.

The following are the construction types per the UBC:

___ *Type I and Type II (fire-resistive)* construction is noncombustible, built from concrete, masonry, and/or steel, and is used when substantial hourly ratings (4 to 2 hours) are required.

___ *Type II, 1-hour, and unprotected (N)* construction is also of the same materials as above, but the hourly ratings are less. Light steel framing would fit into this category.

___ *Type III, 1-hour, and unprotected (N)* construction has noncombustible exterior walls of masonry or concrete, and interior walls of any allowable material including wood.

___ *Type IV* construction is combustible *heavy timber* framing. It achieves its rating from the large size of the timber (2″ thickness, min., actual). The outer surface chars, creating a fire-resistant layer that protects the remaining wood. Exterior walls must be of noncombustible materials.

___ *Type V, 1-hour, and unprotected (N)* construction is of light wood framing.

Note: **As the type number goes up, the cost of construction goes down, so you generally want to use the lowest construction type (highest number) the code allows.**

___ *d.* *Fireproofing:* See UBC Table 6-A for specific requirements of each construction type. See table below on how to achieve ratings.

___ (1) Thicknesses (in inches) of fire resis-
tive structural materials will give
hourly ratings:

ITEM	NON-COMBUSTIBLE						HEAVY TIMBER	LIGHT WOOD FRAME
	4 HR.	3 HR.	2 HR.	1½ HR.	1 HR.	0 HR.		
STEEL, STRUCTURAL * LT. GA. JOISTS STUDS	←	SEE NOTE 2, BELOW			SEE NOTE 3c	→		↑
CONCRETE, COLUMNS WALLS SLABS	6-8"	14" 6½" 6.2"	12" 6" 5"	10" 5" 4.3"	8" 3½" 3½"			
POST TENSION FLOOR PRE-CAST CONC.COL BEAMS WALLS SLABS PLANKS TEE BMS		6.2" 12" 9½" 6½" 6.2" 8"+2" TOPG.	5" 10" 7" 6" 5" 8" 3.25"	4.25" 8" 7" 5" 4.3" 8" 2.75"	3½" 6" 4" 3.5" 3.5" 3" 1.75"	← TOPPINGS		
BRICK, MASONRY WALLS VAULTS & DOMES (RISE NOT LESS THAN 1/12 SPAN)	6-8"	8" 8"	6" 8"	6" 6"	4" 4"			SEE NOTE 2, BELOW
C.M.U. MASONRY WALLS	8" SOLID	8"	8"	6"	4"			
WOOD: COLUMNS, FLOOR ROOF BEAMS, FLOOR ROOF TRUSSES, FLOOR ROOF							8×8 6×8 6×10 4×6 8×8 4×6	
WOOD DECK, FLOOR ROOF							3"+1" 1⅛"-2"	↓

* At 20' above floor, open steel structure does not need fire protection.

___ (2) Fire-resistive materials may be
applied to structural members to
protect from fire. Use the above
table, as well as the following:
___ Concrete: $1'' \approx 2$ hr; $2''$ to $3'' \approx 4$ hr.
___ Solid masonry: $2'' \approx 1$ hr; add $1''$/hr to $4'' \approx 4$ hr.
___ Plaster: $1'' \approx 1$ hr, add $1''$/hr.
___ Vermiculite (spray-on): $1'' \approx 4$ hr.

___ Gypsum wallboard: 2 layers ½"
type "X" or 1 layer of ⅝" type
"X" ≈ ¾ to 1 hr.

**Costs: Spray-on vermiculite: $0.75 to 1.00/SF
surface/inch thickness**

___ (3) Flame spread: The UBC requires
finish materials to resist the spread
of fire as follows:
  ___ (*a*) Maximum   flame-spread
  class

Occupancy Group	Enclosed Vertical Exitways	Other Exitways(1)	Rooms or Areas
A	I	II	II (2)
B	I	II	III
E	I	II	III
H	I	II	III (3)
I-1.1, I-1.2, I-2	I	I (4)	II (5)
I-3	I	I (4)	I (5)
M	I	II	III
R-1	I	II	III
R-3	III	III	III (6)
S-1, S-2	II	II	III
S-3, S-4, S-5	I	II	III
U	No restrictions		

Notes: (1) Finish classification is not applicable to interior walls and
ceilings of exterior exit balconies.
(2) In Group A, Division 3 and 4 Occupancies, Class III may be
used.
(3) Over 2 stories shall be Class II.
(4) In Group I, Divisions 2 and 3 Occupancies, Class II may be
used.
(5) Class III may be used in administrative spaces.
(6) Flame-spread provisions are not applicable to kitchens and
bathrooms of Group R, Division 3 Occupancies.
  ___ (*b*) Flame-spread classification

Class	Flame-spread index
I	0 to 25
II	26 to 75
III	76 to 200

___ (c) Use following finishes to meet above requirements
___ For woods, see p. 251
___ Aluminum: flame-spread index of 5 to 10
___ Masonry or Concrete: 0
___ Gypsum wallboard: 10 to 25
___ Carpet: 10 to 600
___ Mineral-fiber sound-absorbing panels: 10 to 25
___ Vinyl tile: 10 to 50
___ Chemically treated wood fiberboard: 20 to 25

___ (4) Fire Loads: Interior building contents that will start or contribute to a fire. These typically range from 10 (residential) to 50 PSF (office), and can be reduced 80 to 90% by use of metal storage containers for paper.

___ e. *Required occupancy separations:* For hourly ratings, these are determined from UBC Table 3-B. Most buildings will have some mix of occupancies. If one of the occupancies is a minor area and subservient to the major one, the whole building can often be classified as the major occupancy. It will then have to meet the requirements of the more restrictive occupancy, but no separating walls will be necessary.

Some buildings will have different occupancies, none of which is the dominant one. UBC Table 3-B gives the required fire resistance of the walls and/or floors that separate the occupancies. Openings through separation walls must meet the following criteria:

___ For *4-hour walls,* no opening allowed.
___ For *3-hour walls,* openings must not exceed 25% of the length of the wall, and no one opening may be larger than 120 SF.
___ For *2-hour walls,* openings to be 1½-hour protected.

___ For *1-hour walls,* openings to be 1-hour protected.

___ f. *Sprinkler requirements:* The interior designer should note if the existing building does or does not have sprinklers. If they exist, they will almost always be legally required for the tenant improvement or remodel. If they do not exist and the occupancy type is being changed, they may be required. Also, local ordinances may require sprinklers over and above what the model code says.

A sprinkler system is the most effective way to provide fire safety in a building. The UBC requires fire sprinklers in the following situations:

___ *A occupancies* that are: drinking establishments greater than 5000 SF; multitheater complexes; amusement buildings (unless small and temporary); and theaters with/legitimate stages, over 1000 SF, and any "smoke protected" assembly seating.

___ *E-1 occupancies,* except for: each classroom that has at least 1 exit door at ground level; assembly rooms having ½ of required exits at ground level; or where 2-hour separation walls divide the building into 20,000 SF (or less) compartments.

___ *F occupancies* that are woodworking shops of over 2500 SF that generate combustible dust.

___ *H occupancies,* Division 1, 2, 3, 6, and 7 or Division 4 more than 3000 SF.

___ *I occupancies.*

___ *M occupancies* where any floor exceeds 12,000 SF or total area exceeds 24,000 SF, or 3 stories or more in height.

___ *R-1 occupancies* that are: apartments, three or more stories with 16 or more DUs; congregate residences, three or more stories with 20 or more occupants; or hotels, three or more stories or with 20 or more DUs.

___ *Basements* for Group A (greater than 1500 SF) or E-1 occupancies, greater than 1500 SF.

___ *Exhibition, display, or retail sales areas:* Group A or B-2, greater than 12,000 SF; Group B-2, greater than 24,000 SF on all floors or more than three stories in height.

___ *Stairs,* at enclosed usable space above and below for Group A-2, 2.1, 3, 4, and E-1 occupancies.

___ *All occupancies without sufficient fire department access through outside wall at basement or floor in excess of 1500 SF* (Group R-3 and Group U excluded). Sufficient access is 20 SF of openings with a minimum dimension of 30″ per 50 LF of wall. If these openings are only on one side, the floor dimension cannot exceed 75′ from the opening. Furthermore, sprinklers are required in buildings with a floor level of 30 or more occupants that is located 55′ above the lowest level of fire truck access.

___ *Miscellaneous:* Rubbish and linen chutes; nitrate film storerooms; and combustible-fiber storage vaults.

See p. 381 for sprinkler installations.

___ g. *Area separation walls:* One building can be divided into what the code considers separate buildings through the use of area separation walls. The allowable floor area criteria are then applied individually to each of the separate areas. The following criteria apply to area separation walls:

___ Type I and Type II FR require 4 hours.

___ Type II—1 hour and N require 2 hours.

___ Type III—1 hour and N require 4 hours

___ Type IV—Require 4 hours

___ Type V—1 hour and N require 2 hours.

The total width of openings cannot exceed 25% of the length of the wall and must be protected by a fire assembly with a 3-hour rating for a 4-hour wall or a 1½-hour rating for a 2-hour wall. Area separation walls must extend from the foundation to a point 30″ above the roof, unless the roof has a 1-hour rating. See p. 266 for fire doors.

___ h. *Exiting and stairs:* At the conceptual stage of architectural design, the most important aspect of the building code requirements is the number and distribution of exits.

A *means of egress* is a continuous path of travel from any point in a building or structure to the open air outside at ground level. It consists of three separate and distinct parts:

_____ 1. the exit access
_____ 2. the exit
_____ 3. the exit discharge

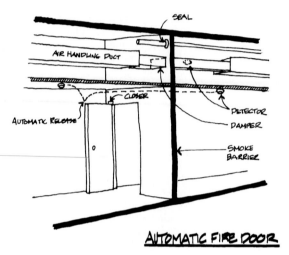

AUTOMATIC FIRE DOOR

The *exit access* leads to an exit. A minimum of two exits is almost always required (see UBC Table 10-A).

_____ 1. Hall or corridor width is to be no less than 44″. It can be 36″ for fewer than 50 people.

_____ 2. Dead-end corridors are limited to 20′ long.

_____ 3. When more than one exit is required, the occupant should be able to go toward either exit from any point in the corridor system.

_____ 4. Corridors used for exit access usually require 1-hour construction.

_____ 5. Maximum travel distance from any point to an exit is *200′* (150′ in 1994 UBC) for a non-sprinklered building or *250′* (200′ in 1994 UBC) for a sprinklered building. This distance can be *increased by 100′* if the corridor meets all the requirements of this section. Some occupancies require less travel distance.

_____ 6. Handrails or fully open doors cannot extend more than 7″ into the corridor.

___ 7. Doors at their worst extension into the corridor cannot obstruct the required width by more than half.

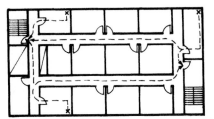

EXIT ACCESS ON UPPER OFFICE FLOOR — — ➤

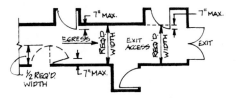

The *exit* is that portion of a means of egress that is separated from the area of the building from which escape is made, by walls, floors, doors, or other means that provide the protected path necessary for the occupants to proceed with safety to a public space. The most common form the exit takes is an enclosed stairway. In a single-story building the exit is the door opening to the outside.

After determining occupant load (Table 10-A, UBC) for spaces, rooms, floors, etc., use the following guidelines:

___ 1.   Almost all buildings need 2 exits (see UBC Table 10-A). In more than one story, stairs become part of an exit. Elevators are not exits.

___ 2.   An occupant load of 501 to 1000 requires 3 exits.

___ 3.   An occupant load of 1001 or more requires 4 exits.

___ 4. In buildings 4 stories and higher and in Types 1 and 2 FR construction, the exit stairs are required to have 2-hour enclosure; otherwise, 1 hour is acceptable.

___ 5. When 2 exits are required, they have to be separated by a distance equal to half the diagonal dimension of the floor and/or room the exits are serving (measured in straight lines). See sketch below.

___ 6. Where more than two exits are required, two of them need to be separated by at least half the diagonal dimension. The others are spaced to provide good access from any direction.

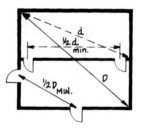

___ 7. May exit from room through one adjoining room only (except rooms with occupant loads of 10 or less), provided adjoining rooms (other than DUs) are not kitchens, storerooms, toilets, closets, and so forth. Foyers, lobbies, and reception rooms are not considered adjoining rooms and can always be exited through.

___ 8. The total exit width required (in inches) is determined by multiplying the occupant load by *0.3* for *stairs* (0.7 for H-1, 2, 3, 7 and 0.4 for I-2 occupancies) and *0.2* for *other exits* (except 0.4 for H-1, 2, 3, and 7). This width should be divided equally among the required number of exits.

___ 9. Total occupant load for calculating exit stair width is defined as the sum of the occupant load on the floor in question. The maximum exit stair width calculated is maintained for the entire exit. See sketch on p. 162.

___ 10. Minimum exit door width is 36″ with 32″ clear opening. Maximum door width is 48″.

___ 11. The width of exit stairs and of landings between flights of stairs must all be the same and must meet the minimum exit stair width requirements as calculated, or 44″ minimum width for an occupant load of 50 or more, or 36″ minimum width for 49 or less, whichever is greater

___ 12. Doors must swing in the direction of travel when serving a hazardous area or when serving an occupant load of 50 or more.

___ A _horizontal exit_ is a way of passage through a 2-hour fire wall into another area of the same building or into a different building that will provide refuge from smoke and fire. Horizontal exits cannot provide more than half of the required exit capacity, and any such exit must discharge into an area capable of holding the occupant capacity of the exit. The area is calculated at 3 SF/occupant. In institutional occupancies the area needed is 15 SF/ambulatory person, and 30 SF/nonambulatory person.

___ _Exit discharge_ is that portion of a means of egress between the termination of an exit and a public way. The most common form this takes is the door out of an exit stairway opening onto a public street. Exits can discharge through a courtyard with 1-hour walls that connects the exit with a public way. In type B occupancy office buildings (and I-1.1 hospitals and nursing homes), 50% of the exits can discharge through a street floor lobby area if the entire street floor is sprinklered and the path through the lobby is unobstructed and obvious.

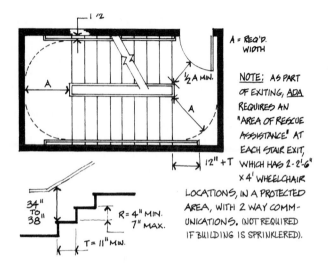

A = REQ'D. WIDTH

NOTE: AS PART OF EXITING, ADA REQUIRES AN "AREA OF RESCUE ASSISTANCE" AT EACH STAIR EXIT, WHICH HAS 2-2'-6" X 4' WHEELCHAIR LOCATIONS, IN A PROTECTED AREA, WITH 2 WAY COMMUNICATIONS. (NOT REQUIRED IF BUILDING IS SPRINKLERED).

½ A MIN.

12" + T

34" TO 38"

R = 4" MIN. 7" MAX.

T = 11" MIN.

___ *Smokeproof enclosures* for exits are required in any tall building with floors 75′ above the lowest ground level where fire trucks have access. A smokeproof enclosure is an exit stair that is entered through a vestibule that is ventilated by either natural or mechanical means such that products of combustion from a fire will be limited in their penetration of the exit-stair enclosure. Smokeproof enclosures are required to be 2-hour construction. They must discharge directly to the outside, or directly through a 2-hour exit passageway to the outside. In a *sprinklered* building, mechanically pressurized and vented stairways can be substituted for smokeproof enclosures.

Code Requirements for Stairs

		Riser	
UBC requirements	Tread min.	Min.	Max.
General (including HC)	11″	4″	7″
Private Stairways (occ. <10)	9″		8″
Winding—Min. required T at 12″			
from narrow side*	6″ at any point		
Spiral—at 12″ from column*	7½″		
Only permitted in R-3 dwellings and R-1 private apartments*			
Rules of thumb for stairs:			
Interior	2R + T = 25		
Exterior	2R + T = 26		

*Requires handrails for ramps >1:15.

Code Requirements for Ramp Slopes

Type	Max. slope	Max. rise	Max. run
UBC, required for accessible			
access	1:12*	5′	
UBC others	1:8*	5′	
Assembly with fixed seats	1:5		
HC, new facilities	1:12*	2.5′	30′
HC, existing facilities	1:10*	6″	5′
	1:8*	3″	2′
HC, curb ramps	1:10	6″	5′

*Requires handrails for ramps >1:15.

    ___ *i.*   *Interior walls and partitions:* Based on the construction type requirements shown on UBC Table 6-A, *determine hourly ratings of interior bearing walls and partitions.* Where required to be noncombustible, they are usually metal studs or masonry. Where allowed to be combustible, the framing may be of wood but the clading is rated (usually ⅝″ Type X gypsum board). The typical 1-hour partition is of wood (or metal) studs with rated gypsum board each side.

        ___ (1) Sometimes fire-retardant treated wood framing is allowed in noncombustible construction types.

___ (2) Wood panels or similar light construction up to ¾ height of room (when higher must enclose top with glass) are usually allowed.

___ (3) Light-transmitting plastic may be used as or in interior partitions.

___ (4) Folding portable or movable partitions do not need to be rated but their surfaces need to conform to flame-spread requirements (see p. 154). These should not block any exiting.

TABLE 3-A—DESCRIPTION OF OCCUPANCIES BY GROUP AND DIVISION[1]

GROUP AND DIVISION	SECTION	DESCRIPTION OF OCCUPANCY
A-1		A building or portion of a building having an assembly room with an occupant load of 1,000 or more and a legitimate stage.
A-2		A building or portion of a building having an assembly room with an occupant load of less than 1,000 and a legitimate stage.
A-2.1	303.1.1	A building or portion of a building having an assembly room with an occupant load of 300 or more without a legitimate stage, including such buildings used for educational purposes and not classed as a Group E or Group B Occupancy.
A-3		Any building or portion of a building having an assembly room with an occupant load of less than 300 without a legitimate stage, including such buildings used for educational purposes and not classed as a Group E or Group B Occupancy.
A-4		Stadiums, reviewing stands, and amusement park structures not included within other Group A Occupancies.
B	304.1	A building or structure, or a portion thereof, for office, professional or service-type transactions, including storage of records and accounts; eating and drinking establishments with an occupant load of less than 50.
E-1		Any building used for educational purposes through the 12th grade by 50 or more persons for more than 12 hours per week or four hours in any one day.
E-2	305.1	Any building used for educational purposes through the 12th grade by less than 50 persons for more than 12 hours per week or four hours in any one day.
E-3		Any building or portion thereof used for day-care purposes for more than 6 persons.
F-1		Moderate-hazard factory and industrial occupancies include factory and industrial uses not classified as Group F, Division 2 Occupancies.
F-2	306.1	Low-hazard factory and industrial occupancies include facilities producing noncombustible or nonexplosive materials that during finishing, packing, or processing do not involve a significant fire hazard.
H-1		Occupancies with a quantity of material in the building in excess of those listed in Table 3-D that present a high explosion hazard as listed in Section 307.1.1.
H-2	307.1	Occupancies with a quantity of material in the building in excess of those listed in Table 3-D that present a moderate explosion hazard or a hazard from accelerated burning as listed in Section 307.1.1.
H-3		Occupancies with a quantity of material in the building in excess of those listed in Table 3-D that present a high fire or physical hazard as listed in Section 307.1.1.

(Continued)

TABLE 3-A—DESCRIPTION OF OCCUPANCIES BY GROUP AND DIVISION[1] (Continued)

H-4		Repair garages not classified as Group S, Division 3 Occupancies.
H-5		Aircraft repair hangars not classified as Group S, Division 5 Occupancies and heliports.
H-6	307.1 and 307.11	Semiconductor fabrication facilities and comparable research and development areas when the facilities in which hazardous production materials are used, and the aggregate quantity of material is in excess of those listed in Table 3-D or 3-E.
H-7	307.1	Occupancies having quantities of materials in excess of those listed in Table 3-E that are health hazards as listed in Section 307.1.1.
I-1.1		Nurseries for the full-time care of children under the age of 6 (each accommodating more than 5 children), hospitals, sanitariums, nursing homes with nonambulatory patients and similar buildings (each accommodating more than 5 patients).
I-1.2	308.1	Health-care centers for ambulatory patients receiving outpatient medical care which may render the patient incapable of unassisted self-preservation (each tenant space accommodating more than 5 such patients).
I-2		Nursing homes for ambulatory patients, homes for children 6 years of age or over (each accommodating more than 5 persons).
I-3		Mental hospitals, mental sanitariums, jails, prisons, reformatories, and buildings where personal liberties of inmates are similarly restrained.
M	309.1	A building or structure, or a portion thereof, for the display and sale of merchandise, and involving stocks of goods, wares or merchandise, incidental to such purposes and accessible to the public.
R-1	310.1	Hotels and apartment houses, congregate residences (each accommodating more than 10 persons).
R-3		Dwellings, lodging houses, congregate residences (each accommodating 10 or fewer persons).
S-1		Moderate hazard storage occupancies including buildings or portions of buildings used for storage of combustible materials not classified as Group S, Division 2 or Group H Occupancies.
S-2	311.1	Low-hazard storage occupancies including buildings or portions of buildings used for storage of noncombustible materials.
S-3		Repair garages where work is limited to exchange of parts and maintenance not requiring open flame or welding, and parking garages not classified as Group S, Division 4 Occupancies.
S-4		Open parking garages.
S-5		Aircraft hangars and helistops.
U-1	312.1	Private garages, carports, sheds and agricultural buildings.
U-2		Fences over 6 feet (1829 mm) high, tanks and towers.

[1]For detailed descriptions, see the occupancy definitions in the noted sections.

TABLE 3-B—REQUIRED SEPARATION IN BUILDINGS OF MIXED OCCUPANCY[1] (HOURS)

	A-1	A-2	A-2.1	A-3	A-4	B	E	F-1	F-2	H-1	H-2	H-3	H-4,5	H-6,7[2]	I	M	R-1	R-3	S-1	S-2	S-3	S-5	U-1[3]
A-1		N	N	N	N	3	N	3	3		4	4	4	4	3	3	1	1	3	3	4	3	1
A-2			N	N	N	1	N	1	1		4	4	4	4	3	1	1	1	1	1	3	1	1
A-2.1				N	N	1	N	1	1		4	4	4	4	3	1	1	1	1	1	3	1	1
A-3					N	N	N	N	N		3	4	4	3	2	N	1	1	N	N	3	1	1
A-4						1	N	1	1		4	4	4	4	3	1	1	1	1	1	3	1	1
B							1	N[5]	N		1	1	1	1	2	N	1	1	N	N	1	1	1
E								1	1		3	4	4	3	1	1	1	1	1	1	3	1	1
F-1									1		1	1	1	1	3	N[5]	1	1	N	N	1	1	1
F-2											2	1	1	1	2	1	1	1	N	N	1	1	1
H-1	NOT PERMITTED IN MIXED OCCUPANCIES. SEE SECTION 307.2.9																						
H-2												1	1	1	2	2	4	4	2	2	2	2	1
H-3													1		1	1	3	3	1	1	1	1	1
H-4,5														1	1	1	3	3	1	1	1	1	1
H-6,7[2]															4	1	4	4	1	1	1	1	3
I																2	1	1	2	2	4	3	1
M																		1	1[4]	1[4]	1	1	1
R-1																		N	3	1	3	1	1
R-3																			1	1	1	1	1
S-1																				1	1	1	1
S-2																					1	1	N
S-3																						1	1
S-4	OPEN PARKING GARAGES ARE EXCLUDED EXCEPT AS PROVIDED IN SECTION 311.2																						
S-5																							N

N—No requirements for fire resistance.

[1]For detailed requirements and exceptions, see Section 302.4.

[2]For special provisions on highly toxic materials, see the Fire Code.

[3]For agricultural buildings, see also Appendix Chapter 3.

[4]See Section 309.2.2 for exception.

[5]For Group F, Division 1 woodworking establishments with more than 2,500 square feet (232.3 m^2), the occupancy separation shall be one hour.

TABLE 6-A—TYPES OF CONSTRUCTION—FIRE-RESISTIVE REQUIREMENTS (In Hours)

For details, see occupancy section in Chapter 3, type of construction sections in this chapter and sections referenced in this table.

BUILDING ELEMENT	TYPE I	TYPE II			TYPE III		TYPE IV	TYPE V	
	Noncombustible						Combustible		
	Fire-resistive	Fire-resistive	1-Hr.	N	1-Hr.	N	H.T.	1-Hr.	N
1. Bearing walls—exterior	4 Sec. 602.3.1	4 Sec. 603.3.1	1	N	4 Sec. 604.3.1	4 Sec. 604.3.1	4 Sec. 605.3.1	1	N
2. Bearing walls—interior	3	2	1	N	1	N	Sec. 605.3.1	1	N
3. Nonbearing walls—exterior	4 Sec. 602.3.1	4 Sec. 603.3.1	1 Sec. 603.3.1	N	4 Sec. 604.3.1	4 Sec. 604.3.1	4 Sec. 605.3.1	1	N
4. Structural frame[1]	3 Sec. 602.5	2	1	N	1	N	1 or H.T.	1	N
5. Partitions—permanent	1[2]	1[2]	1[2]	N	1	N	1 or H.T.	1	1
6. Shaft enclosures[3]	2	2	1	1	1	1	1	1	1
7. Floors and floor-ceilings	2	2	1	N	1	N	H.T.	1	N
8. Roofs and roof-ceilings	2 Sec. 602.5	1 Sec. 603.5	1 Sec. 603.5	N	1	N	H.T.	1	N
9. Exterior doors and windows	Sec. 602.3.2	Sec. 603.3.2	Sec. 603.3.2	Sec. 603.3.2	Sec. 604.3.2	Sec. 604.3.2	Sec. 605.3.2	Sec. 606.3	Sec. 606.3
10. Stairway construction	Sec. 602.4	Sec. 603.4	Sec. 603.4	Sec. 603.4	Sec. 604.4	Sec. 604.4	Sec. 605.4	Sec. 606.4	Sec. 606.4

N—No general requirements for fire resistance.
H.T.—Heavy timber.

[1] Structural frame elements in an exterior wall that is located where openings are not permitted, or where protection of openings is required, shall be protected against external fire exposure as required for exterior bearing walls or the structural frame, whichever is greater.

[2] Fire-retardant-treated wood (see Section 207) may be used in the assembly, provided fire-resistance requirements are maintained. See Sections 602 and 603.

[3] For special provisions, see Sections 304.6, 306.6 and 711.

TABLE 10-A—MINIMUM EGRESS REQUIREMENTS[1]

USE[2]	MINIMUM OF TWO MEANS OF EGRESS ARE REQUIRED WHERE NUMBER OF OCCUPANTS IS AT LEAST	OCCUPANT LOAD FACTOR[3] (square feet) × 0.0929 for m²
1. Aircraft hangars (no repair)	10	500
2. Auction rooms	30	7
3. Assembly areas, concentrated use (without fixed seats) Auditoriums Churches and chapels Dance floors Lobby accessory to assembly occupancy Lodge rooms Reviewing stands Stadiums	50	7
Waiting area	50	3
4. Assembly areas, less-concentrated use Conference rooms Dining rooms Drinking establishments Exhibit rooms Gymnasiums Lounges Stages	50	15
Gaming: keno, slot machine and live games area	50	11
5. Bowling alley (assume no occupant load for bowling lanes)	50	4
6. Children's homes and homes for the aged	6	80
7. Classrooms	50	20
8. Congregate residences	10	200
9. Courtrooms	50	40
10. Dormitories	10	50
11. Dwellings	10	300
12. Exercising rooms	50	50
13. Garage, parking	30	200

(Continued)

TABLE 10-A—MINIMUM EGRESS REQUIREMENTS[1] (Continued)

14. Health care facilities—		
Sleeping rooms	8	120
Treatment rooms	10	240
15. Hotels and apartments	10	200
16. Kitchen—commercial	30	200
17. Library—		
Reading rooms	50	50
Stack areas	30	100
18. Locker rooms	30	50
19. Malls (see Chapter 4)	—	—
20. Manufacturing areas	30	200
21. Mechanical equipment room	30	300
22. Nurseries for children (day care)	7	35
23. Offices	30	100
24. School shops and vocational rooms	50	50
25. Skating rinks	50	50 on the skating area; 15 on the deck
26. Storage and stock rooms	30	300
27. Stores—retail sales rooms		
Basements and ground floor	50	30
Upper floors	50	60
28. Swimming pools	50	50 for the pool area; 15 on the deck
29. Warehouses[5]	30	500
30. All others	50	100

[1] Access to, and egress from, buildings for persons with disabilities shall be provided as specified in Chapter 11.

[2] For additional provisions on number of exits from Groups H and I Occupancies and from rooms containing fuel-fired equipment or cellulose nitrate, see Sections 1018, 1019 and 1020, respectively.

[3] This table shall not be used to determine working space requirements per person.

[4] Occupant load based on 5 persons for each alley, including 15 feet (4572 mm) of runway.

[5] Occupant load for warehouses containing approved high rack storage systems designed for mechanical handling may be based on the floor area exclusive of the rack area rather than the gross floor area.

EXAMPLE:

PROBLEM: A TENANT IMPROVEMENT IS TO GO INTO A NEW "SHELL" OFFICE BUILDING. THE BUILDING IS 12 STORIES HIGH. EXISTING PLANS SHOW: 40 000 SF PER FLOOR; OCCUPANCY CLASS = B (OFFICE); AND CONSTRUCTION TYPE = II FR.

THE TENANT IMPROVEMENT IS TO BE A 10000 SF CAFETERIA WITH 25% KITCHEN AND 75% DINING.

WHAT ARE THE BASIC CODE REQUIREMENTS?

SOLUTION:

1. DETERMINE OCCUPANT LOAD AND EXITS:
   SEE PAGE 151 AND TABLE 10-A.

SPACE	AREA	FACTOR	OCCUPANTS	REQR'S
DINING:	7500 SF ÷	15	= 500	2 EXITS
KITCHEN:	2500 SF ÷	200	= 13	
			513 OCC.	

2. DETERMINE OCCUPANCY TYPE:
   SEE PAGE 151 AND TABLE 3-A.
   OCC. CLASS = A-2.1 (MORE THAN 300 OCCUPANTS)

3. SEPARATION OF MIXED OCCUPANCIES:
   SEE PAGE 155 AND TABLE 6-A.
   B TO A-2.1 = 1 HR.

4. WALLS:
   SEE PAGE 163 INTERIOR NON-BEARING PARTITIONS ARE TO BE NON-COMBUSTIBLE, 1 HR RATED PER TABLE 6-A FOR THE II FR CONSTRUCTION TYPE OF THE OVERALL BUILDING. THIS IS USUALLY METAL STUDS WITH A LAYER OF 5/8" (TYPE X) GYPBOARD ON EACH SIDE.

—CONTINUED—

5. FLAME SPREAD OF SURFACES :
   SEE PAGE 154

OCCUPANCY	VERTICAL EXITWAYS	OTHER	EXITWAYS
A	I	II	II

   I = 0 TO 25 FLAME SPREAD INDEX.
   II = 26 TO 75 FLAME SPREAD INDEX.
   SEE PAGE 155 FOR FINISH OPTIONS.

<u>NOTES</u>

NOTES

___ 4. <u>Accessibility (ADA requirements)</u> ⟨20⟩

___ *a.* *General:* This section concerns accessibility for the disabled as required by *ADA, the Americans with Disabilities Act* (Title 3, the national civil rights law), in nongovernment buildings (Title 2 applies to government buildings). Local or state laws may (in part) be more restrictive regarding alterations and new buildings. For each item under consideration, *the more restrictive law applies.*

___ *b.* *ADA* applies to:

   ___ (1) <u>*Places of public accommodation*</u> (excluding private homes, and clubs, as well as churches). Often buildings will have space for both the general public and space for employees only.

   ___ (2) <u>*Commercial facilities*</u> (employees only) requirements are less restrictive, requiring only an accessible entry, exit, and route through each type of facility function. Only when a disabled employee is hired (under Title 1) do more restrictive standards apply.

___ *c.* <u>*Existing buildings*</u> are to comply by removing "architectural barriers," as much as possible, when this is "readily achievable" (not requiring undue expense, hardship, or loss of space). This effort, in theory, is to be ever ongoing until all barriers are removed. When barriers can't be readily removed, "equivalent facilitation" is allowed. Priorities of removal are:

   ___ (1) Entry to places of public accommodation

   ___ (2) Access to areas where goods and services are made available to the public

   ___ (3) Access to restroom facilities

   ___ (4) Removal of all other barriers

___ *d.* <u>*Alterations*</u> to existing buildings require a higher standard. To the maximum extent possible, the altered portions are to be made accessible. If the altered area is a "primary function" of the building, then an accessible "path of travel" must be provided from the entry to the area (including public restrooms, telephones, and drinking fountains) with exemption only possible when cost of the path exceeds 20% of the cost to alter the primary function.

___ *e.* <u>*New buildings or facilities*</u> must totally comply, with the only exceptions being situations of "structural impracticability."

___ *f.* <u>*See Index, p. 459,*</u> for a complete list of *ADA* requirements.

ACCESSIBLE ROUTE PER A.D.A.
(INTERIOR AND EXTERIOR)

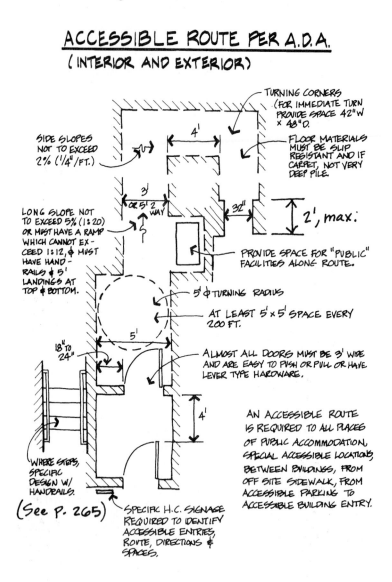

TURNING CORNERS
(FOR IMMEDIATE TURN
PROVIDE SPACE 42"W
× 48"D.

FLOOR MATERIALS
MUST BE SLIP
RESISTANT AND IF
CARPET, NOT VERY
DEEP PILE.

SIDE SLOPES
NOT TO EXCEED
2% (1/4"/FT.)

4'

3'
OR 5' 2
WAY

32"

2', max.

LONG SLOPE NOT
TO EXCEED 5% (1:20)
OR MUST HAVE A RAMP
WHICH CANNOT EX-
CEED 1:12, & MUST
HAVE HAND-
RAILS & 5'
LANDINGS AT
TOP & BOTTOM.

PROVIDE SPACE FOR "PUBLIC"
FACILITIES ALONG ROUTE.

5' ⌀ TURNING RADIUS

AT LEAST 5' × 5' SPACE EVERY
200 FT.

5'

18" to
24"

5'

ALMOST ALL DOORS MUST BE 3' WIDE
AND ARE EASY TO PUSH OR PULL OR HAVE
LEVER TYPE HARDWARE.

4'

AN ACCESSIBLE ROUTE
IS REQUIRED TO ALL PLACES
OF PUBLIC ACCOMMODATION,
SPECIAL ACCESSIBLE LOCATIONS,
BETWEEN BUILDINGS, FROM
OFF SITE SIDEWALK, FROM
ACCESSIBLE PARKING TO
ACCESSIBLE BUILDING ENTRY.

WHERE STEPS,
SPECIFIC
DESIGN W/
HANDRAILS.

(See P. 265)

SPECIFIC H.C. SIGNAGE
REQUIRED TO IDENTIFY
ACCESSIBLE ENTRIES,
ROUTE, DIRECTIONS &
SPACES.

NOTES

<u>NOTES</u>

The interior designer usually is working with an existing building which has already set energy requirements (especially for external climatic loads). However, tenant improvements or remodels do affect internal loads. Use this section as a guide to energy conservation.

___ 1. Building Type

All buildings produce internal heat. All buildings are affected by external loads (heating or cooling) based on the climate, and internal loads (heat from equipment, lights, people, etc.). Large commercial buildings tend to be internally dominated. Residences or small commercial buildings tend to be the exact opposite.

___ 2. Human Comfort

The comfort zone may be roughly defined as follows: Most people in the temperate zone, sitting indoors in the shade in light clothing, will feel tolerably comfortable at temperatures ranging from *70° to 80°F* as long as the relative humidity lies between *20 and 50%*. As humidity increases, they will begin to become uncomfortable at lower and lower temperatures until the relative humidity reaches *75 to 80%,* when discomfort at any temperature sets in. But if they are sitting in a draft, the range of tolerable temperature shifts upward, so that temperatures of *85°F* may be quite comfortable in the *20 to 50%* relative humidity range, if local air is moving at *200 ft/min*. Indoor air moving more slowly than *50 ft/min* is generally unnoticed, while flows of *50 to 100 ft/min* are pleasant and hardly noticed. Breezes from *100 to 200 ft/min* are pleasant, but one is constantly aware of them, while those from *200 to 300 ft/min* are at first slightly unpleasant, then annoying and drafty.

___ 3. Checklist for Passive Building Design (Strategies for Energy Conservation):

Note: Many of the following items conflict, so it is impossible to choose all.

  _X_   Cold climate or winter
     _X_   Hot climate or summer

Indoor/outdoor rooms

  ___ ___   *a.* Provide outdoor semiprotected areas for year-round climate moderation.

  ___   *b.* Provide solar-oriented interior zone for maximizing heat.

  ___ ___   *c.* Plan specific rooms or functions to coincide with solar orientation (i.e., storage on "bad"

<u>Cold   Hot</u>

orientation such as west, living on "good" orientation such as south).

Solar walls and windows

____   *d.* Use high-capacitance materials to store solar heat gain. Best results are by distributing "mass" locations throughout interior. On average, provide 1 to 1¼ CF of concrete or masonry per each SF of south-facing glass. For an equivalent effect, 4 times more mass is needed when not exposed to sun. Do not place carpeting on these floor areas.

____   *e.* This same "mass effect" can be used in reverse in hot, dry (clear sky) climates. "Flush" building during cool night to pre-cool for next day. Be sure to shade the mass.

____   *f.* Maximize south-facing glazing (with overhangs as needed). On average, south-facing glass should be 10 to 25% of floor area. For north latitude/cold climates this can go up to 50%. For south latitude/hot climates this strategy may not be appropriate.

Thermal envelope

____ ____ *g.* Provide air shafts for natural or mechanically assisted house-heat recovery. This can be recirculated warm air at high ceilings or recovered heat from chimneys.

____   *h.* Centralize heat sources within building interior (fireplaces, furnaces, hot water heater, cooking, laundry, etc.). Lower-level positioning for these is most desirable.

____   *i.* Put heat sources (HW, laundry, etc.) outside building.

____ ____ *j.* Use vestibule or exterior "wind shield" at entryways. Orient away from undesirable winds.

____ ____ *k.* Locate low-use spaces, storage, utility, and garage areas to provide buffers. Locate at "bad" orientations (i.e., on north side in cold climate or west side in hot climate).

____ ____ *l.* Subdivide interior to create separate heating and cooling zones. One example is separate living and sleeping zones.

____ ____ *m.* Minimize window and door openings (usually N, E, and W).

Cold Hot

___ ___ *n.* Provide ventilation openings for air flow to and from specific spaces and appliances. See p. 311 for fireplaces.

Natural ventilation

___ *o.* Use "open plan" interior to promote natural ventilation air flow.

___ *p.* Provide vertical air shafts to promote interior air flow.

___ *q.* Use double roof and wall construction for ventilation within the building shell.

___ *r.* Orient door and window openings to facilitate natural ventilation from prevailing breezes. For best results:

Windows on opposite sides of rooms.
Inlets and outlets of equal size giving maximum air change.
A smaller inlet increases air speed.

___ 4. Checklist for Active Building Design (Strategies for Energy Conservation)

___ *a.* Whenever possible, use fans in lieu of compressors, as they use about 80% less energy. In residential construction this may take the form of "whole-house" fans. See *o*, below.

___ *b.* Design for natural lighting in lieu of artificial lighting. In hot climates or summers, avoid direct sun.

___ *c.* Use high-efficiency lighting (50–100 lumens per watt). See Part 16A. Provide switches or controls to light only areas needed and to take advantage of daylighting.

___ *d.* Use gas rather than electric when possible, as this can be up to 75% less expensive.

___ *e.* Use efficient equipment and appliances

___ (1) Microwave rather than convection ovens.

___ (2) Refrigerators rated 5–10 kBtu/day or 535–1070 kwh/yr.

___ *f.* If fireplaces, use high-efficiency type with tight-fitting high-temperature glass, insulated, and radiant-inducing boxed with outside combustion air. See p. 311.

___ *g.* Use night setback and load-control devices.

___ *h.* Use multizone HVAC.

___ *i.* Locate ducts in conditioned space or tightly seal and insulate.

___ *j.* Insulate hot and cold water pipes (R = 1 to 3).

___ *k.* Locate air handlers in conditioned space.

___ *l.* Install thermostats away from direct sun and supply grilles.

___ *m.* Use heating equipment with efficiencies of 70% for gas and 175% for electric, or higher.

___ *n.* Use cooling equipment with efficiencies of SEER = 10, COP = 2.5 or higher.

___ *o.* Use "economizers" on commercial HVAC to take advantage of good outside temperatures.

___ *p.* In dry, hot climates, use evaporative cooling.

___ *q.* Use gas or solar in lieu of electric hot water heating. Insulate hot water heaters.

___ *r.* For some building types and at some locations, utilities have peak load rates, such as on summer afternoons. These peak rates should be identified and designed for. Therefore, designing for peak loads may be more important than yearly energy savings. In some cases saving energy and saving energy cost may not be the same.

__ K. ACOUSTICS ② ③ ④ ⑩

Note: Also see acoustical treatment, p. 292, and wall assemblies, p. 359.

There are both positive and negative functions to consider in acoustic design.

The positive function is to ensure that the reverberation characteristics of a building are appropriate to their function. See 1 below.

On the negative side, the task is to make certain that unwanted outside noises are kept out of quiet areas of the building. See 2 below.

__ 1. Room Acoustics
Sound can be likened to light. *Sound control* uses reflection and diffusion to enhance acoustics in such spaces as auditoriums and sound studios, and absorption for noise control in more typical spaces such as offices.

__ *a.* <u>*Reflection:*</u> The geometry of the room is important in effective sound control. Large concave surfaces concentrate sound and should usually be avoided, while convex surfaces disperse sound.

__ *b.* <u>*Diffusion*</u> promotes uniform distribution of continuous sound and improves "liveness" (very important in performing arts). It is increased by objects and surface irregularities. Ideal diffusing surfaces neither absorb nor reflect sound but scatter it.

__ *c.* <u>*Absorption*</u> (see table on p. 191) provides the most effective form of noise control. Sound pressure waves travel at the speed of sound (1100 fps), which is a slow enough velocity that reflections of the original sound-wave form can interfere with perception of the original, intended signal. *Reverberation time* is the measure of this problem.

Sound of any kind emitted in a room will be absorbed or reflected off the room surfaces. Soft materials absorb sound energy. Hard materials reflect sound energy back into the space. The reflected sound can reinforce the direct sound and enhance communication if the room size and room surfaces are configured appropriately. Annoying reverberations (echoes) occur in rooms *more than 30 feet long.* Echoes are stronger when the reflecting surface is highly reflective and is concave toward the listener.

The room volume and surface characteristics will determine the reverberation time for the room. *Reverberation time* is the time in seconds or portions of a second that it takes for a sound to decay through 60 decibels. It is calculated as follows:

$$RT = \frac{0.05 \times \text{room volume (cf)}}{\text{average absorption of room}}$$

Desirable room reverberation times are:

Office and commercial spaces	0.5 seconds
Rooms for speech	1.0 seconds
Rooms for music	1.5 seconds
Sports arenas	2.0 seconds

The *absorption,* also called *noise reduction coefficient (NRC),* of a surface is the product of the acoustic coefficient for the surface multiplied by the area of the surface. The sound absorption of a room is the sum of the sound absorptions of all the surfaces in the room. *The higher the coefficient, the more sound absorbed, with 1.0 (complete absorption) being the highest possible value.* Generally, a material with a coefficient below *0.2* is considered to be reflective and above *0.2* to be absorbing. Some common acoustic coefficients are:

1½″ glass fiber ceiling panels	1.0
Carpet and pad	0.6
Acoustic tile (no paint)	0.8
Cloth-upholstered seats	0.6
An audience	0.8
Concrete	0.02
Gypsum board	0.05
Glass	0.09
Tile	0.01
Fabric	0.30

The average absorption coefficient of a room should be at least *0.2.* Average absorption above *0.5* is usually not desirable, nor is it economically justified. A lower value is suitable for large rooms; and larger values for controlling sound in small or noisy rooms. Although absorptive materials can be placed anywhere, ceiling treatment is more effective in large rooms, while wall treatment is more effective in small rooms. If additional absorptive material is being added to a room to improve it, the total absorption should be increased at least *3 times* to bring absorption to between *0.2 and 0.5.* An increase of *10 times* is about the practical limit. Each doubling of the absorption in a room reduces reverberation time by one-half.

EXAMPLE:
WHAT IS THE ABSORPTION COEFFICIENT AND REV. TIME FOR A 20' x 10' x 9'H
OFFICE WITH CARPET FLOOR, A.T.C., & GYPB'D. WALL (BUT 1/3 OF WHICH HAS
SOUND ABSORPTION MATERIAL)?

ABSORPTION COEFFICIENT:

FLOOR	0.6 x 200 =	120
2/3 WALL	0.05 x 356 =	18
1/3 WALL	0.8 x 178 =	142
CEILING	0.8 x 200 =	160
		440

$$\text{AVER. COEF. OF ABSORPTION} = \frac{\text{TOTAL ABSORP.}}{\text{TOTAL RM. SURF.}} = \frac{440}{20 \times 9 \times 2 + 10 \times 9 \times 2 + 10 \times 20 \times 2}$$

$$= \frac{440}{940 \text{ SF}} = .47 \text{ O.K.}$$

$$\text{REVERBERATION TIME} = \frac{0.05 \times (10 \times 20 \times 9)}{440} = 0.2 < 0.5, \text{ SO O.K.}$$

    ___ d. *Other factors affecting acoustics:*

        ___ (1) If a corridor is appreciably higher than it is wide, some absorptive material should be placed on the walls as well as the ceiling, especially if the floor is hard. If the corridor is wider than its height, ceiling treatment is usually enough.

        ___ (2) Acoustically critical rooms require an appropriate volume of space. Rooms for speech require 120 CF per audience seat. Rooms for music require 270 CF per audience seat.

___ (3) "Ray diagramming" can be a useful tool in sound control. As with light, the reflective angle of a sound wave equals its incident angle. In like manner, concave shapes focus sound and convex shapes disperse sound.

___ 2. <u>Sound Isolation</u>

Sound travels through walls and floors by causing building materials to vibrate and then broadcast the noise into the quiet space. There are two methods of setting up the vibration: through structure-borne sound, and air-borne sound.

Structure-borne sound is the vibration of building materials caused by vibrating pieces of equipment, or by walking on hard floors.

Airborne sound is a pressure vibration in the air. When it hits a wall, the wall materials are forced to vibrate. The vibration passes through the materials of the wall. The far side of the wall then passes the vibration back into the air.

___ *a. <u>Sound Isolation Guidelines:</u>*

___ (1) Choose a quiet, protected site. Orient building with doors and windows away from noise.

___ (2) Use site barriers such as walls or landscaping (dense tree lines or hedges).

___ (3) Avoid placing noisy areas near quiet areas. Areas with similar noise characteristics should be placed next to each other. Place bedrooms next to bedrooms and living rooms next to living rooms.

___ (4) As the distance from the sound source increases, pressure at the listener's ear will decrease by the inverse square law (as with light). Therefore, separate sound sources by distance.

___ (5) Orient spaces to minimize transmission problems. Space windows of adjoining apartments the maximum possible distance apart. Place noisy areas back-to-back. Place closets between noisy and quiet areas.

___ (6) Massive materials (concrete or masonry) are the best noise-isolation materials.

___ (7) Choose quiet mechanical equipment. Use vibration isolation, sound-absorbing duct lining, and resilient pipe connections. Design for low flow velocities in pipes and ducts.

___ (8) Reducing structure-borne sound from walking on floors is achieved by carpet (with padding, improves greatly).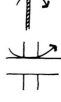

___ (9) Avoid flanking of sound over ceilings.

___ (10) Avoid flanking of sound at wall and floor intersections.

___ (11) Wall and floor penetrations (such as electrical boxes) can be a source of sound leakage. A 1-square-inch wall opening in a 100-SF gypsum-board partition can transmit as much sound as the entire partition.

___ (12) Many sound leaks can be plugged in the same manner as is done for air leaks, by caulking.

___ (13) Walls and floors are classified by *Sound Transmission Class (STC),* which is a measure of the reduction of loudness provided by various barriers. The higher the number, the better. In determining the required STC rating of a barrier, the following rough guidelines may be used:

STC Effect on Hearing

25	Normal speech clearly heard through barrier.
30	Loud speech can be heard and understood fairly well. Normal speech can be heard but barely understood.
35	Loud speech is unintelligible but can be heard.
42–45	Loud speech can be heard only faintly. Normal speech cannot be heard.
46–50	Loud speech not audible. Loud sounds other than speech can be heard only faintly, if at all.

See p. 192 for recommended STC room barriers.

Rough Estimating of STC Ratings

Note: See p. 359 for detailed wall assemblies.

When the wall or floor assembly produces less sound isolation than desired, the following modifications can be made. Select the appropriate wall or floor assembly. To improve the rating, select modifications (largest number, + ½ next largest, + ½ next largest, etc):

Light frame walls

Base design	*STC Rating*
Wood studs w/ ½″ gyp'bd.	32
Metal studs w/ ⅝″ gyp'bd.	39
Modification	*Added STC*
Staggered Studs	+9
Double-surface skin	+3 to +5
Absorption insulation	+5

Heavy walls

The greater the density, the higher the rating. Density goes up in the following order: CMU, brick, concrete.

Base Design	*STC Rating*
4-inch CMU, brick, concrete	37–41, 42
6-inch	42, 46
8-inch	47, 49, 51
12-inch	52, 54, 56
Modification	*Added STC*
Furred-out surface	+7 to +10
Add plaster, ½″	+2 to +4
Sand-filled cores	+3

Wood floors

Base Design	STC Rating
½-in plyw'd, subfloor with oak floor, no ceiling	25

Modification	Added STC
Add carpet	+10
⅝-inch gyp'bd. ceiling	+10
Add resilient damping board	+7
Add absorbtion insul.	+3

Concrete floors

Base Design	STC Rating
4-, 6-, 8-inch thick concrete	41, 46, 51

Modification	Added STC
Resil. Susp. Ceiling	+12
Add sleepers	+7
Add absorption insul.	+3

Glass

¼″ float	26
double glaze	32

Doors

wood HC	26
SC	29
metal	30
special acoustical	35 to 38

Costs: Sound attenuation blankets: 1″ thick = $3.75 (10% L and 90% M). Add $2 per added inch up to 3″.

EXAMPLE:
ROUGHLY ESTIMATE HOW TO GET S.T.C. = 45 FOR AN OFFICE WALL PART-
ITION MADE OF WOOD STUDS AND GYPB'D.

FROM ABOVE, A WOOD STUD PARTITION W/ ½" GYPB'D. IS ...... S.T.C.= 32

ADD STAGGERED STUDS FOR FULL CREDIT	+9
ADD DOUBLE GYPB'D. FOR ½ CREDIT, BOTH SIDES: ½ × 5 =	+2.5
ADD ABSORPTION BATTS BETWEEN STUDS: 1/2 × 5 =	+2.5
TOTAL =	46.0

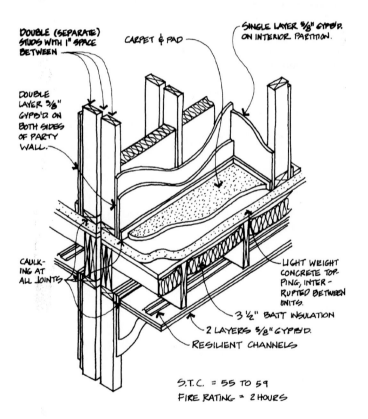

SINGLE LAYER ⅝" GYPB'D.
ON INTERIOR PARTITION.

DOUBLE (SEPARATE)
STUDS WITH 1" SPACE
BETWEEN

CARPET & PAD

DOUBLE
LAYER ⅜"
GYPB'D ON
BOTH SIDES
OF PARTY
WALL.

CAULK-
ING AT
ALL JOINTS

LIGHT WEIGHT
CONCRETE TOP-
PING, INTER-
RUPTED BETWEEN
UNITS.

3 ½" BATT INSULATION

2 LAYERS ⅝" GYPB'D.

RESILIENT CHANNELS

S.T.C. = 55 TO 59
FIRE RATING = 2 HOURS

PARTY WALL DETAIL

(4)

USE OF ABSORPTION IN COMMON OCCUPANCIES			
ROOM OCCUPANCY	CEILING TREATMENT	WALL TREATMENT	SPECIAL
AUDITORIUMS, CHURCHES, THEATERS, CONCERT HALLS, RADIO, RECORDING AND T.V. STUDIOS, SPEECH & MUSIC ROOMS			●
BOARDROOMS, TELECONFERENCING	●	●	
CLASSROOMS	●	○	
COMMERCIAL KITCHENS	●		
COMPUTER AND BUSINESS MACHINE ROOMS	●		
CORRIDORS AND LOBBIES	○		
GYMNASIUMS, ARENAS, & RECREATIONAL SPACES	●	●	
HEALTH CARE PATIENT ROOMS	●		
LABORATORIES	●		
LIBRARIES	●		
MECHANICAL EQUIPMENT ROOMS			●
MEETING AND CONFERENCE ROOMS	●	○	
OPEN OFFICE PLAN	●	●	
PRIVATE OFFICES	●		
RESTAURANTS	●	○	
SCHOOLS & INDUSTRIAL SHOPS, FACTORIES	●	●	
STORES AND COMMERCIAL SHOPS	●		

● STRONGLY RECOMMENDED
○ ADVISABLE

SOUND ISOLATION CRITERIA ④

SOURCE ROOM OCCUPANCY	RECEIVER ROOM ADJACENT	SOUND ISOLATION REQUIREMENT (MINIMUM) FOR ALL PATHS BETWEEN SOURCE AND RECEIVER
EXECUTIVE AREAS, DOCTOR'S SUITES, PERSONNEL OFFICES, LARGE CONFERENCE ROOMS, CONFIDENTIAL PRIVACY REQUIREMENTS	ADJACENT OFFICES AND RELATED SPACES	STC 50-55
NORMAL OFFICES, REGULAR CONFERENCE ROOMS FOR GROUP MEETINGS, NORMAL PRIVACY REQMTS.	ADJACENT OFFICES & SIMILAR ACTIVITIES	STC 45-50
LARGE GENERAL BUSINESS OFFICES, DRAFTING AREAS, BANKING FLOORS	CORRIDORS, LOBBIES, DATA PROCESSING, SIMILAR ACTIVITIES	STC 40-45
SHOP AND LABORATORY OFFICES IN MANUFACT'G USING LABORATORY OR TEST AREAS, NORM. PRIV.	ADJACENT OFFICES, TEST AREAS, CORRID.	STC 40-45
MECHANICAL EQUIPMENT ROOMS	ANY SPACE	STC 50-60+
MULTIFAMILY DWELLINGS (a) BEDROOMS	NEIGHBORS (SEPARATE OCCUPANCY) BEDROOMS BATHROOMS KITCHENS LIVING ROOMS CORRIDORS	STC 48-55 STC 52-58 STC 52-58 STC 50-57 STC 52-58
(b) LIVING ROOMS	LIVING ROOMS BATHROOMS KITCHENS	STC 48-55 STC 50-57 STC 48-50
SCHOOL BUILDINGS (a) CLASSROOMS	ADJACENT CLASS ROOMS LABORATORIES CORRIDORS	STC 50 STC 50 STC 45
(b) LARGE MUSIC OR DRAMA AREA	ADJACENT MUSIC OR DRAMA AREA	STC 60
(c) MUSIC PRACTICE ROOMS	MUSIC PRACTICE RMS.	STC 55
INTERIOR OCCUPIED SPACES	EXTERIOR OF BLDG.	STC 35-60
THEATERS, CONCERT HALLS, LECTURE HALLS, RADIO AND T.V. STUDIOS	ANY AND ALL ADJACENT	USE QUALIFIED ACOUSTICAL CONSULTANT.

NOTES

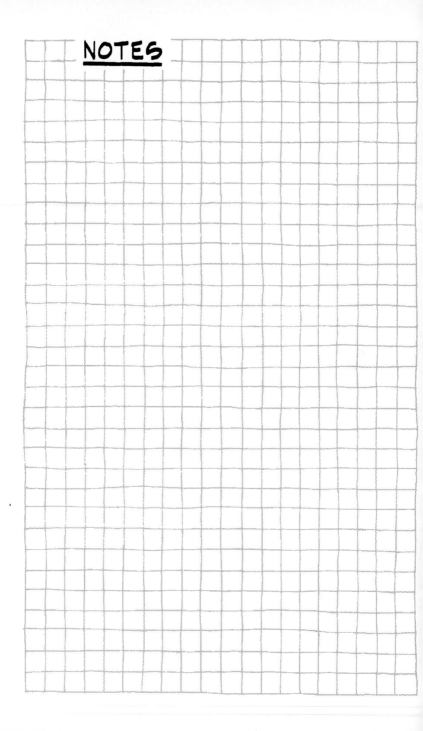

NOTES

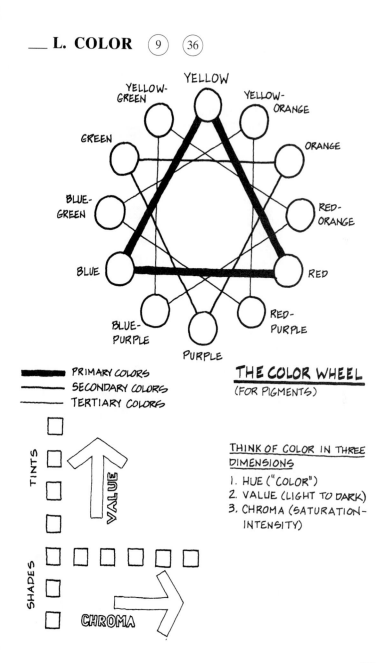

THE COLOR WHEEL
(FOR PIGMENTS)

— PRIMARY COLORS
— SECONDARY COLORS
— TERTIARY COLORS

THINK OF COLOR IN THREE
DIMENSIONS
1. HUE ("COLOR")
2. VALUE (LIGHT TO DARK)
3. CHROMA (SATURATION-
   INTENSITY)

___ 1. <u>Basic Color Schemes</u>

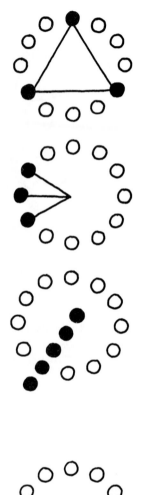

   ___ *a.* <u>*Triadic schemes.*</u>
Made from any three hues that are equidistant on the color wheel.

   ___ *b.* <u>*Analogous or related schemes.*</u> Consist of hues that are side by side.

   ___ *c.* <u>*Monochromatic schemes.*</u> Use only one color (hue) in a range of values and intensities, coupled with neutral blacks or whites.

   ___ *d.* <u>*Complementary schemes.*</u> Use contrast by drawing from exact opposites on the color wheel. Usually one of the colors is dominant while the other is used as an accent. Usually vary the amount and brightness of contrasting colors.

2

SITE FURNISHINGS

NOTES

CAST ALUM. SIDE CHAIR W/
CUSHION, # 2830 - 1000,
"LAFAYETTE" SERIES BY
BROWN JORDAN $500

OVAL ALUM. SIDE CHAIR
W/ MESH SLING, # 1890 - 2000,
"LEGEND MESH" BY BROWN
JORDAN.   COST: $390

TABLE OF METAL STAND W/
GLASS TOP, "ELAN" BY BROWN
JORDAN
  COST: $600

UMBRELLA FOR TABLE TOP,
1666 - 3600, "ELAN" BY
BROWN JORDAN
COST: $220

METAL CHAIR
CT 3001 - BS - 21
BY LANDSCAPE FORMS
COST: $470

METAL CHAIR
VN 3001 - BA - 22
BY LANDSCAPE FORMS
COST: $330

METAL BENCH
SC 3005 - BS - 72
BY LANDSCAPE FORMS
COST: $1600

METAL BENCH
SC 3005 - FS - 72
BY LANDSCAPE FORMS
COST: $1380

ALUM. & TEAK ARMCHAIR,
'MILANO' SERIES, # A547182
BY SMITH & HAWKEN
COST: $435

ALUM. & TEAK BENCH
'MILANO', # A547208
BY SMITH & HAWKEN
COST: $675

STEAMER CHAIR, WOOD
W/ CUSHION, # A496950,
BY SMITH & HAWKEN
COST: $995

RATTAN CHAIR W/ CUSHION,
A381822, BY SMITH &
HAWKEN
COST: $225

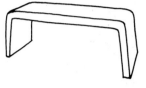

CONCRETE BENCH, 'CLASSIC' SERIES, 'DESIGN CAST' BY PHX. PRECAST PRODUCTS. COST: $145

CONCRETE BENCH, 'SCOTTSDALE' SERIES, 'DESIGN CAST' BY PHX. PRECAST PRODUCTS. COST: $195

CONC. ASH RECEPTICLE, # PSAR 1624, 16" x 24", 'DESIGN CAST' BY PHX. PRECAST PRODUCTS. COST: $70

CONC. WASTE RECEPTACLE, # RSWR 3032, 30" x 32', 30 GAL RIBBED BY PHX. PRECAST PRODUCTS. COST: $265

CONC. PARK WASTE REC., # PSWR 2426, 24" x 26" BY PHX. PRECAST PRODUCTS. COST: $195

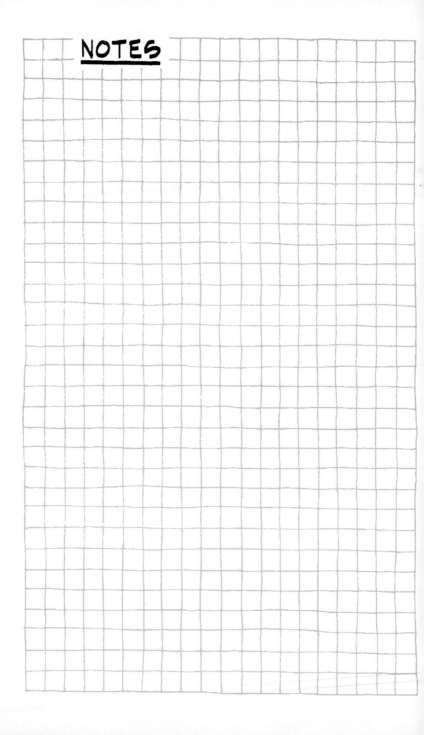

NOTES

3

CONCRETE FINISHES

<u>NOTES</u>

___ A. GENERAL

Since concrete is usually used for the structural frame and floors of buildings, the interior designer is seldom concerned with this material. However, there may be occasions where the interior designer may have need to specify concrete finishes. This may occur where working with an architect for exterior or interior walls or possibly remodeling a one-story interior where a new special slab on grade is to be done.

Concrete walls and floors are usually covered. When they are left exposed, and with special finish treatments, this can have a desirable visual effect.

___ B. FLOORS (SLAB ON GRADE)

Exposed concrete horizontal surfaces are usually left to the exterior of the building, but they can also be used inside for special effects. Possible finishes are:

___ 1. Steel Trowel
   Normal floor finish prior to a floor covering being installed. Slippery when wet. May be left exposed inside industrial spaces, with a hardener.

___ 2. Broom Finish
   Roughens surface to increase slip resistance. Usually used on outside walks.

___ 3. Exposed Aggregate
   Although usually used for outside walks and patios, can be used inside for special effect. Aggregate is usually ¾″ to 1½″ river run smooth rock of different colors.
   Costs: Add $0.85 to $1.90/SF to cost of slab.

___ 4. Colored Concrete
   Can be an integral concrete mix or hand-cast on surface.
   Costs: Add $0.80 to $3.30/SF to cost of slab.

___ 5. Joint Patterns
   For visual effect by sawing joints.
   Costs: Cutting 1″ deep joints: add $1.25/LF to cost of slab.

___ 6. Simulated Colored Concrete Patterns
   Brick, stone, or other decorative textures and materials can be replicated on surface.
   Costs: Stamp patterns: Add $9.50 to $47.50/SF to cost of slab.

__ C. WALLS

__ 1. Colored concrete, chemical retardant, or exposed aggregate
   Costs: Chemical retardation (exposed aggregate): Add $0.70/SF to cost of wall.

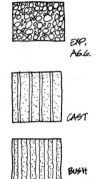

__ 2. Cast with Different Moldings
   Costs: Add $2.50 to $6.00/SF to cost of wall.

__ 3. Treating or Tooling the Concrete Surface
   Done in final stages of hardening.
   Costs: Add $1.30 to $3.20/SF to cost of wall.

__ D. CEILINGS

When ceilings are of exposed concrete, they are usually the exposed underside of the floor or roof, above.

__ 1. Exposed Plank
   Sometimes used in hotels, these ceilings are often too low to put a drop ceiling under. The surface often has acoustical spray applied.

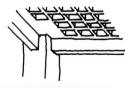

__ 2. Waffle Slabs
   Sometimes used in public buildings, these ceilings are often high and are intended to be left exposed as a design element.

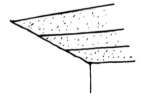

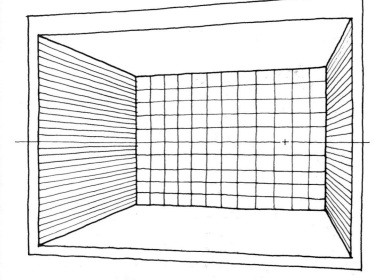

4 MASONRY

NOTES

___ A. MASONRY MATERIALS AND FINISHES

___ 1. <u>General:</u> Masonry, like concrete, is seldom used by the interior designer. Nevertheless, there may be occasions where masonry walls may be needed in a remodel. For masonry floors, see p. 294.

Masonry consists of:

    ___ *a.* Brick
        ___ (1) Fired
        ___ (2) Unfired ("adobe")
    ___ *b.* Concrete block (concrete masonry units or CMU)
    ___ *c.* Stone
    ___ *d.* Glass block

___ 2. <u>Bond Joints</u> ────────────────┐
___ 3. <u>Bond Patterns</u> ──────────┐   │

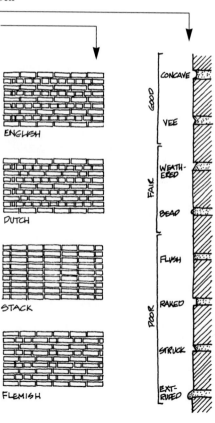

___ 4. <u>Coatings:</u> Must be (see p. 300)
       ___ (1) "Bridgeable" (seal cracks)
       ___ (2) Breathable (do not trap vapor)

___ 5. <u>Brick</u>
   ___ *a.* *Types*
       ___ (1) Common (building)
       ___ (2) Face
           ___ (*a*) FBX Select
           ___ (*b*) FBS Standard
           ___ (*c*) FBA Architectural
       ___ (3) Clinker
       ___ (4) Glazed
       ___ (5) Fire
       ___ (6) Cored
       ___ (7) Sand-lime (white, yellow)
       ___ (8) Pavers
   ___ *b.* *Weatherability*
       ___ (1) NW—Negligible weathering; for indoor or sheltered locations.
       ___ (2) MW—Moderate weather locations.
       ___ (3) SW—Severe weather locations and/or earth contact.
   ___ *c.* *Positions*

STRETCHER HEADER SOLDIER ROWLOCK STRETCHER ROWLOCK HEADER

___ *d.* *Sizes:* (modular brick based on 4″ module with ⅜″ joint)

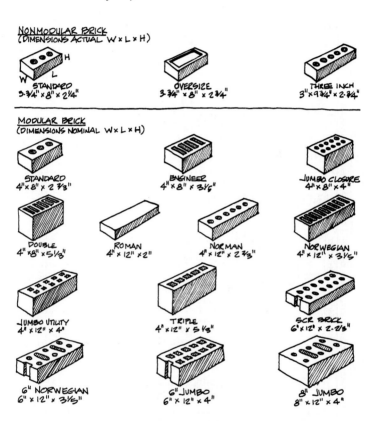

NONMODULAR BRICK
(DIMENSIONS ACTUAL W × L × H)

STANDARD
3-¾″ × 8″ × 2¼″

OVERSIZE
3-¾″ × 8″ × 2¾″

THREE INCH
3″ × 9¾″ × 2-¾″

MODULAR BRICK
(DIMENSIONS NOMINAL W × L × H)

STANDARD
4″ × 8″ × 2⅔″

ENGINEER
4″ × 8″ × 3⅕″

JUMBO CLOSURE
4″ × 8″ × 4″

DOUBLE
4″ × 8″ × 5⅓″

ROMAN
4″ × 12″ × 2″

NORMAN
4″ × 12″ × 2⅔″

NORWEGIAN
4″ × 12″ × 3⅕″

JUMBO UTILITY
4″ × 12″ × 4″

TRIPLE
4″ × 12″ × 5⅓″

SCR BRICK
6″ × 12″ × 2-⅔″

6″ NORWEGIAN
6″ × 12″ × 3⅕″

6″ JUMBO
6″ × 12″ × 4″

8″ JUMBO
8″ × 12″ × 4″

___ *e.* *Coursing:* See p. 218.
___ *f.* **Costs: Standard brick wall, running bond w/rein-forcing (25%M & 75%L) (Variations of +5%, −20%):**

4″, single wythe, veneer:	**$9.50/SF**
8″, double wythe, cavity-filled:	**$20.00/SF**
12″, triple wythe, cavity-filled:	**$30.00/SF**

For other bonds, add 15 to 30%

BRICK COURSING

COURSE	NONMODULAR						MODULAR				
	2 1/4" THICK BRICKS		2 5/8" THICK BRICKS		2 3/4" THICK BRICKS		NOMINAL THICKNESS (HEIGHT) OF BRICK				
	3/8" JOINT	1/2" JOINTS	3/8" JOINT	1/2" JOINT	3/8" JOINT	1/2" JOINT	2"	2 2/3"	3 1/5"	4"	5 1/3"
1	2 5/8"	2 3/4"	3"	3 1/8"	3 1/8"	3 1/4"	2"	2 11/16"	3 3/16"	4"	5 5/16"
2	5 1/4"	5 1/2"	6"	6 1/4"	6 1/4"	6 1/2"	4"	5 5/16"	6 3/8"	8"	10 11/16"
3	7 7/8"	8 1/4"	9"	9 3/8"	9 3/8"	9 3/4"	6"	8"	9 5/8"	1'-0"	1'-4"
4	10 1/2"	11"	1'-0"	1'-0 1/2"	1'-0 1/2"	1'-1"	8"	10 11/16"	1'-0 13/16"	1'-4"	1'-9 5/16"
5	1'-1 1/8"	1'-1 3/4"	1'-3"	1'-3 5/8"	1'-3 5/8"	1'-4 1/4"	10"	1'-1 5/16"	1'-4"	1'-8"	2'-2 11/16"
6	1'-3 3/4"	1'-4 1/2"	1'-6"	1'-6 3/4"	1'-6 3/4"	1'-7 1/2"	1'-0"	1'-4"	1'-7 3/16"	2'-0"	2'-8"
7	1'-6 3/8"	1'-7 1/4"	1'-9"	1'-9 7/8"	1'-9 7/8"	1'-10 3/4"	1'-2"	1'-6 11/16"	1'-10 3/8"	2'-4"	3'-1 5/16"
8	1'-9"	1'-10"	2'-0"	2'-1"	2'-1"	2'-2"	1'-4"	1'-9 5/16"	2'-1 5/8"	2'-8"	3'-6 11/16"
9	1'-11 5/8"	2'-0 3/4"	2'-3"	2'-4 1/8"	2'-4 1/8"	2'-5 1/4"	1'-6"	2'-0"	2'-4 13/16"	3'-0"	4'-0"
10	2'-2 1/4"	2'-3 1/2"	2'-6"	2'-7 1/4"	2'-7 1/4"	2'-8 1/2"	1'-8"	2'-2 11/16"	2'-8"	3'-4"	4'-5 5/16"
11	2'-4 7/8"	2'-6 1/4"	2'-9"	2'-10 3/8"	2'-10 3/8"	2'-11 3/4"	1'-10"	2'-5 5/16"	2'-11 3/16"	3'-8"	4'-10 11/16"
12	2'-7 1/2"	2'-9"	3'-0"	3'-1 1/2"	3'-1 1/2"	3'-3"	2'-0"	2'-8"	3'-2 3/8"	4'-0"	5'-4"
13	2'-10 1/8"	2'-11 3/4"	3'-3"	3'-4 5/8"	3'-4 5/8"	3'-6 1/4"	2'-2"	2'-10 11/16"	3'-5 5/8"	4'-4"	5'-9 5/16"
14	3'-0 3/4"	3'-2 1/2"	3'-6"	3'-7 3/4"	3'-7 3/4"	3'-9 1/2"	2'-4"	3'-1 5/16"	3'-8 13/16"	4'-8"	6'-2 11/16"
15	3'-3 3/8"	3'-5 1/4"	3'-9"	3'-10 7/8"	3'-10 7/8"	4'-0 3/4"	2'-6"	3'-4"	4'-0"	5'-0"	6'-8"
16	3'-6"	3'-8"	4'-0"	4'-2"	4'-2"	4'-4"	2'-8"	3'-6 11/16"	4'-4 3/16"	5'-4"	7'-1 5/16"
17	3'-8 5/8"	3'-10 3/4"	4'-3"	4'-5 1/8"	4'-5 1/8"	4'-7 1/4"	2'-10"	3'-9 5/16"	4'-6 3/8"	5'-8"	7'-6 11/16"
18	3'-11 1/4"	4'-1 1/2"	4'-6"	4'-8 1/4"	4'-8 1/4"	4'-10 1/2"	3'-0"	4'-0"	4'-9 5/8"	6'-0"	8'-0"
19	4'-1 7/8"	4'-4 1/4"	4'-9"	4'-11 3/8"	4'-11 3/8"	5'-1 3/4"	3'-2"	4'-2 11/16"	5'-0 13/16"	6'-4"	8'-5 5/16"
20	4'-4 1/2"	4'-7"	5'-0"	5'-2 1/2"	5'-2 1/2"	5'-5"	3'-4"	4'-5 5/16"	5'-4"	6'-8"	8'-10 11/16"
21	4'-7 1/8"	4'-9 3/4"	5'-3"	5'-5 5/8"	5'-5 5/8"	5'-8 1/4"	3'-6"	4'-8"	5'-7 3/16"	7'-0"	9'-4"
22	4'-9 3/4"	5'-0 1/2"	5'-6"	5'-8 3/4"	5'-8 3/4"	5'-11 1/2"	3'-8"	4'-10 11/16"	5'-10 3/8"	7'-4"	9'-9 5/16"
23	5'-0 3/8"	5'-3 1/4"	5'-9"	5'-11 7/8"	5'-11 7/8"	6'-2 3/4"	3'-10"	5'-1 5/16"	6'-1 5/8"	7'-8"	10'-2 11/16"
24	5'-3"	5'-6"	6'-0"	6'-3"	6'-3"	6'-6"	4'-0"	5'-4"	6'-4 13/16"	8'-0"	10'-8"

CONCRETE BLOCK TYPES & SIZES

NOMINAL DIMENSIONS W × L × H (ACTUAL DIMENSIONS ARE ⅜" LESS)

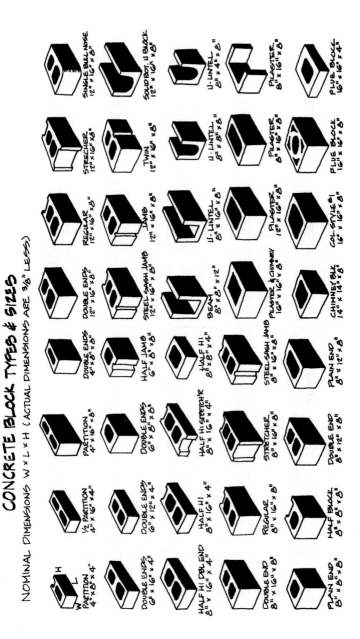

SINGLE BULL NOSE
12" × 16" × 8"

SOLID BOT. U BLOCK
12" × 16" × 8"

U- LINTEL
8" × 4" × 8"

PLASTER
8" × 16" × 8"

FLUE BLOCK
16" × 16" × 4"

STRECHER
12" × 16" × 8"

TWIN
12" × 16" × 8"

U- LINTEL
8" × 16" × 8"

PLASTER
8" × 16" × 8"

FLUE BLOCK
16" × 16" × 8"

REGULAR
12" × 16" × 8"

JAMB
12" × 16" × 8"

U- LINTEL
8" × 16" × 8"

PLASTER
12" × 16" × 8"

COL. STYLE #1
16" × 16" × 8"

DOUBLE ENDS
12" × 16" × 8"

STEEL SASH JAMB
12" × 16" × 8"

BEAM
8" × 8" × 12"

PLASTER & CHIMNEY
16" × 16" × 8"

CHIMNEY BLK.
14" × 14" × 8"

DOUBLE ENDS
4" × 16" × 8"

HALF JAMB
6" × 8" × 8"

HALF HI
8" × 8" × 4"

STEEL SASH JAMB
8" × 16" × 8"

PLAIN END
8" × 12" × 8"

PARTITION
4" × 16" × 8"

DOUBLE ENDS
6" × 8" × 8"

HALF HI STRETCH'R
8" × 16" × 4"

STRETCHER
8" × 16" × 8"

DOUBLE END
8" × 12" × 8"

½ PARTITION
4" × 16" × 4"

DOUBLE ENDS
6" × 12" × 4"

HALF HI
8" × 16" × 4"

REGULAR
8" × 16" × 8"

HALF BLOCK
8" × 8" × 8"

PARTITION
4" × 8" × 4"

DOUBLE ENDS
6" × 16" × 4"

HALF HI DBL END
8" × 16" × 4"

DOUBLE END
8" × 16" × 8"

PLAIN END
8" × 8" × 8"

CONCRETE BLOCK COURSING

CSC	4" HIGH BLK.	8" HIGH BLK.	CSC	4" HIGH BLK.	8" HIGH BLK.
1	4"	8"	38	12'-8"	25'-4"
2	8"	1'-4"	39	13'-0"	26'-0"
3	1'-0"	2'-0"	40	13'-4"	26'-8"
4	1'-4"	2'-8"	41	13'-8"	27'-4"
5	1'-8"	3'-4"	42	14'-0"	28'-0"
6	2'-0"	4'-0"	43	14'-4"	28'-8"
7	2'-4"	4'-8"	44	14'-8"	29'-4"
8	2'-8"	5'-4"	45	15'-0"	30'-0"
9	3'-0"	6'-0"	46	15'-4"	30'-8"
10	3'-4"	6'-8"	47	15'-8"	31'-4"
11	3'-8"	7'-4"	48	16'-0"	32'-0"
12	4'-0"	8'-0"	49	16'-4"	32'-8"
13	4'-4"	8'-8"	50	16'-8"	33'-4"
14	4'-8"	9'-4"	51	17'-0"	34'-0"
15	5'-0"	10'-0"	52	17'-4"	34'-8"
16	5'-4"	10'-8"	53	17'-8"	35'-4"
17	5'-8"	11'-4"	54	18'-0"	36'-0"
18	6'-0"	12'-0"	55	18'-4"	36'-8"
19	6'-4"	12'-8"	56	18'-8"	37'-4"
20	6'-8"	13'-4"	57	19'-0"	38'-0"
21	7'-0"	14'-0"	58	19'-4"	38'-8"
22	7'-4"	14'-8"	59	19'-8"	39'-4"
23	7'-8"	15'-4"	60	20'-0"	40'-0"
24	8'-0"	16'-0"	61	20'-4"	40'-8"
25	8'-4"	16'-8"	62	20'-8"	41'-4"
26	8'-8"	17'-4"	63	21'-0"	42'-0"
27	9'-0"	18'-0"	64	21'-4"	42'-8"
28	9'-4"	18'-8"	65	21'-8"	43'-4"
29	9'-8"	19'-4"	66	22'-0"	44'-0"
30	10'-0"	20'-0"	67	22'-4"	44'-8"
31	10'-4"	20'-8"	68	22'-8"	45'-4"
32	10'-8"	21'-4"	69	23'-0"	46'-0"
33	11'-0"	22'-0"	70	23'-4"	46'-8"
34	11'-4"	22'-8"	71	23'-8"	47'-4"
35	11'-8"	23'-4"	72	24'-0"	48'-0"
36	12'-0"	24'-0"	73	24'-4"	48'-8"
37	12'-4"	24'-8"	74	24'-8"	49'-4"

___ 6. Concrete Block (CMU)
    ___ *a.* Types: Plain (gray), colored, pavers, special shapes (such as "slump"), and special surfaces (split faced, scored, etc.).
    ___ *b.* Size: See p. 219.
    ___ *c.* Coursing: See p. 220.
    ___ *d.* **Costs: CMU (Regular weight, gray, running bond, typical reinforcing and grout)**

4″ walls:	**$5.00/SF**	**(Typical 25 to 30%M and 75 to**
6″ walls:	**$5.50/SF**	**70%L)**
8″ walls:	**$6.50/SF**	**(Variations for special block, such as**
12″ walls:	**$8.25/SF**	**glazed, decorative, screen, etc. + 15 to**
		150%)

Deduct 30 to 40% for residential work.

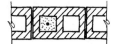

___ 7. Stone
    ___ *a.* *Type unit*
        ___ (1) *Ashlar:* Best for strength and stability; is square-cut on level beds. Joints of ½″ to ¾″.

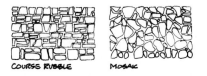

COURSED ASHLAR   RANDOM ASHLAR   3 HT. RANDOM ASHLAR

        ___ (2) *Squared stone* (course rubble): Next-best for strength and stability; is fitted less carefully than ashlar, but more carefully than rubble.

COURSE RUBBLE   MOSAIC

        ___ (3) *Rubble:* Built with a minimum of dressing, with joints unevenly coursed, or in a completely irregular pattern. Stones are lapped for bond and many stones extend through wall (when full-width wall) to bond it transversely. If built carefully, with all interstices completely filled with good cement mortar, has ample durability for ordinary structures.

___ *b.* <u>*Typical materials*</u>
    ___ (1) Limestone
    ___ (2) Sandstone
    ___ (3) Quartzite
    ___ (4) Granite

RANDOM RUBBLE

___ *c.* <u>*Wall types*</u>
    ___ (1) Full width
    ___ (2) Solid veneer (metal ties to structural wall)
    ___ (3) Thin veneer (set against mortar bed against structural wall)

___ *d.* **Costs: 4″ veneer (most common): $12.00 to $14.50/SF (40%M and 60%L) (Variation: + 50%)**
18″ rough stone wall (dry): $40/CF (40%M and 60%L)

___ 8. <u>Glass Block</u>
    ___ *a.* <u>*Thickness*</u> 3″ and 4″.
    ___ *b.* <u>*Size,*</u> 4½″, 6″, 7½″, 8″, 9½″, and 12″ square.
    ___ *c.* <u>*Reinforcing*</u> at 16″ oc.
    ___ *d.* <u>*Interior Panels:*</u> 25 LF max. and 250 SF max.
    ___ *e.* **Costs: 4″ thick, 6, 8, or 12″ sq = $25 to $30/SF (55% M and 45% L).**

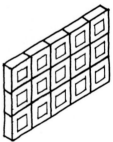

NOTES

NOTES

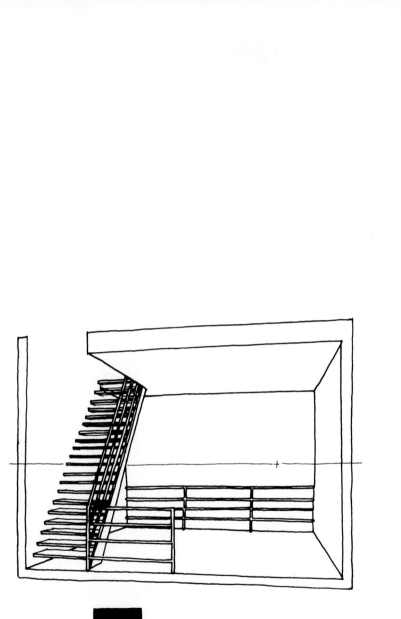

5 METALS

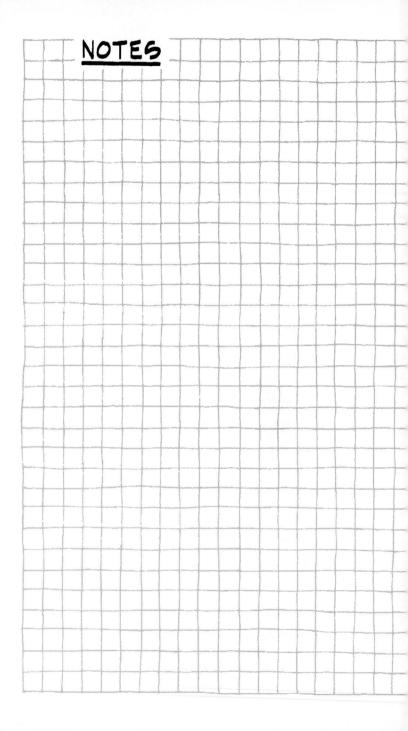

NOTES

___ A. METALS

(4) (25) (32) (49)

___ 1. General
    ___ *a.* *Ferrous metals* (contain iron)
        ___ (1) *Iron:* Soft, easily worked, oxidizes rapidly, susceptible to acid.
        ___ (2) *Cast-iron:* Brittle, corrosion-resistant, high compressive strength. Used for gratings, stairs, etc.
        ___ (3) *Malleable iron:* Same as cast-iron, but better workability.
        ___ (4) *Wrought iron:* Soft, corrosion- and fatigue-resistant, machinable. Used for railings, grilles, screws, and ornamental items.
        ___ (5) *Steel:* Iron with carbon. Strongest metal. Used for structural purposes.
        ___ (6) *Stainless steel:* An alloy for maximum corrosion resistance. Used for flashing, handrails, hardware, connections, and equipment.
    ___ *b.* *Nonferrous metals* (not containing iron)
        ___ (1) *Aluminum:* Soft, ductile, high corrosion resistance, low strength.
        ___ (2) *Lead:* Dense, workable, toxic, corrosion-resistant. Improved with alloys for hardness and strength. Used as waterproofing, sound isolation, and radiation shielding.
        ___ (3) *Zinc:* Corrosion-resistant, brittle, low-strength. Used in "galvanizing" of other metals for corrosion resistance for roofing, flashing, hardware, connections, etc.
        ___ (4) *Chromium and nickel:* Used as alloy for corrosion-resistant bright "plating."
        ___ (5) *Monel:* High corrosion resistance. Used for fasteners and anchors.
        ___ (6) *Copper:* Resistant to corrosion, impact, and fatigue. Ductile. Used for wiring, roofing, flashing, and piping.
        ___ (7) *Bronze:* An alloy for "plating."
        ___ (8) *Brass:* Copper with zinc. Used for hardware, handrails, grilles, etc.

___ 2. Metal Corrosion
    ___ *a.* Galvanic action, or corrosion, occurs between dissimilar metals or metals and other metals when sufficient moisture is present to carry an electric

current. The farther apart two metals are on the following list, the greater the corrosion of the more susceptible one:

Anodic (+): Most susceptible to corrosion
　　　　　　　Magnesium
　　　　　　　Zinc
　　　　　　　Aluminum
　　　　　　　Cadmium
　　　　　　　Iron/steel
　　　　　　　Stainless steel (active)
　　　　　　　Soft solders
　　　　　　　Tin
　　　　　　　Lead
　　　　　　　Nickel
　　　　　　　Brass
　　　　　　　Bronzes
　　　　　　　Nickel-copper alloys
　　　　　　　Copper
　　　　　　　Stainless steel (passive)
　　　　　　　Silver solder
Cathodic (−): Least susceptible to corrosion

___ *b.* Metals deteriorate also when in contact with chemically active materials, particularly when water is present. Examples include aluminum in contact with concrete or mortar, and steel in contact with treated wood.

___ 3. <u>Gauges:</u> See pp. 229.

___ 4. <u>Light Metal Framing</u>

    ___ *a.* <u>Joists</u>

        ___ (1) Makes an economical floor system for light loading and spans up to 32′

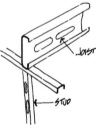

        ___ (2) Depths: 6″, 8″, 9″, 10″, 12″

        ___ (3) Spacings: 16″, 24″, 48″ oc

        ___ (4) Gauges: 12 through 18 (light = 20–25 GA; structural = 18–12 GA)

        ___ (5) Bridging, usually 5′ to 8′ oc

    ___ *b.* <u>Studs</u>

        ___ (1) Sizes

            ___ (*a*) Widths: ¾″, 1″, 1⅜″, 1⅝″, 2″

            ___ (*b*) Depths: 2½″, 3⅝″, 4″, 6″, 8″

METAL GAUGES

GAUGE NO.	GRAPHIC SIZES	U.S. STD. REVISED		GRAPHIC SIZES
		DECIMAL	FRACTION	
000		.3750"	3/8"	
00		.3437"	11/32"	
0		.3125"	5/16"	
1.		.2812"	9/32"	
2.		.2656"	17/64"	
3.		.2391"	15/64"	
4.		.2242"	7/32°	
5.		.2092"	13/64"	
6.		.1943"	3/18"	

7		.1793"	11/64" +	
8		.1644"	11/64" –	
9		.1495"	6/32" –	
10		.1345"	9/64" –	
11		.1196"	1/8" –	
12		.1046"	7/64" –	
13		.0897"	3/32" –	
14		.0747"	5/64" –	
15		.0673"	1/16" +	
16		.0598"	1/16" –	
17		.0538"	3/64" +	
18		.0478"	3/64" +	
19		.0418"	3/64" –	
20		.0359"	1/32" +	
21		.0329"	1/32" +	
22		.0299"	1/32" –	
23		.0269"	1/32" –	
24		.0239"	1/32" –	
25		.0209"	1/64" +	
26		.0179"	1/64" +	
27		.0164"	1/64" +	
28		.0149"	1/64" –	
29		.0135"	1/64" –	
30		.0120"	1/64" –	

   ___ (2) Gauges: 14, 15, 16, 18, 20

   ___ (3) Spacings: 12″, 16″, 24″ oc

___ 5. <u>Miscellaneous Metals</u>

   ___ *a. <u>Nails</u>*

      ___ (1) Size: Penny designated as d. A 2-penny nail
is 1″ long. Each additional "penny" adds ¼″
length, to:

         12-penny = 3¼″ long

         16-penny = 3½″

         20-penny = 4″

         30-penny = 4½″

         40-penny = 5″

         50-penny = 5½″

         60-penny = 6″

      Rule of thumb: Use nail with length 3×
thickness of board being secured.

      ___ (2) Types

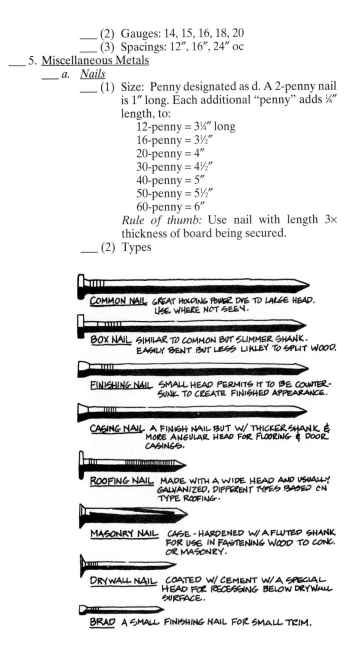

COMMON NAIL GREAT HOLDING POWER DUE TO LARGE HEAD. USE WHERE NOT SEEN.

BOX NAIL SIMILAR TO COMMON BUT SLIMMER SHANK. EASILY BENT BUT LESS LIKLEY TO SPLIT WOOD.

FINISHING NAIL SMALL HEAD PERMITS IT TO BE COUNTER-SUNK TO CREATE FINISHED APPEARANCE.

CASING NAIL A FINISH NAIL BUT W/ THICKER SHANK & MORE ANGULAR HEAD FOR FLOORING & DOOR CASINGS.

ROOFING NAIL MADE WITH A WIDE HEAD AND USUALLY GALVANIZED, DIFFERENT TYPES BASED ON TYPE ROOFING.

MASONRY NAIL CASE-HARDENED W/ A FLUTED SHANK FOR USE IN FASTENING WOOD TO CONC. OR MASONRY.

DRYWALL NAIL COATED W/ CEMENT W/ A SPECIAL HEAD FOR RECESSING BELOW DRYWALL SURFACE.

BRAD A SMALL FINISHING NAIL FOR SMALL TRIM.

___ *b.*   Screws and bolts

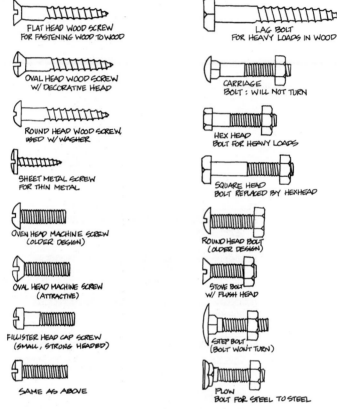

FLAT HEAD WOOD SCREW
FOR FASTENING WOOD TO WOOD

OVAL HEAD WOOD SCREW
W/ DECORATIVE HEAD

ROUND HEAD WOOD SCREW,
USED W/ WASHER

SHEET METAL SCREW
FOR THIN METAL

OVEN HEAD MACHINE SCREW
(OLDER DESIGN)

OVAL HEAD MACHINE SCREW
(ATTRACTIVE)

FILLISTER HEAD CAP SCREW
(SMALL, STRONG HEADED)

SAME AS ABOVE

LAG BOLT
FOR HEAVY LOADS IN WOOD

CARRIAGE
BOLT : WILL NOT TURN

HEX HEAD
BOLT FOR HEAVY LOADS

SQUARE HEAD
BOLT REPLACED BY HEXHEAD

ROUND HEAD BOLT
(OLDER DESIGN)

STONE BOLT
W/ FLUSH HEAD

STEP BOLT
(BOLT WON'T TURN)

PLOW
BOLT FOR STEEL TO STEEL

___ 6. <u>Stairs</u>
    ___ *a.* See p. 163 for code requirements.
    ___ *b.* **Costs: steel pan w/cement fill, 4′ wide w/landing, w/o railing: cost per flight (12 risers) = \$3900 (80% M & 20% L). Add \$185 for each additional riser.**

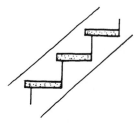 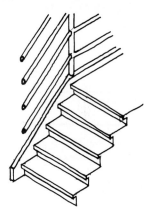

___ 7. <u>Railings</u>
    ___ *a.* Code requirements (97 UBC)
        ___ (1) Guardrails are required where walking surface ends and there is a drop of more than 30″. This includes landings at stairs.
            ___ (*a*) Heights required:
                36″ residential
                42″ other
            ___ (*b*) If open rails, openings between rails must be no more than 4″ at intermediates and no more than 6″ at bottom.
    ___ *b.* Requirements for handrails at stairs:
        ___ (1) No handrail required in private garages. Not required in private residences where stairway is less than 4 risers high.
        ___ (2) Handrail required on one side when stairway is less than 44″ wide, or in private residence.
        ___ (3) Handrail required on both sides when stairway is more than 44″ in width, and additional railings are required with each additional 88″ in width.

_____ (4) See below for additional requirements.

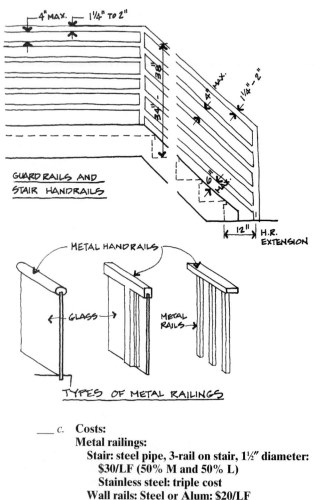

GUARD RAILS AND
STAIR HANDRAILS

TYPES OF METAL RAILINGS

_____ *c.* **Costs:**
Metal railings:
  Stair: steel pipe, 3-rail on stair, 1½″ diameter:
   $30/LF (50% M and 50% L)
   Stainless steel: triple cost
  Wall rails: Steel or Alum: $20/LF
   Stainless steel: double cost
  Freestanding, ornamental: $150 to $600/LF

NOTES

NOTES

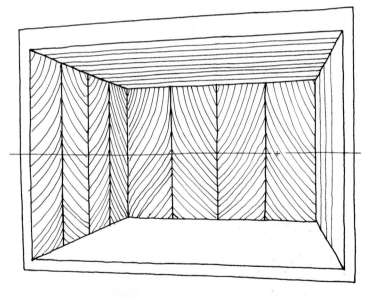

 WOOD

___ A. WOOD

$$\text{④ ⑪ ⑫ ㉛ ㊻ ㊾}$$

___ 1. <u>General</u> (*Note:* See p.250 for species table. See p. 294 for wood flooring.)

    ___ *a.* <u>*Two general types of wood*</u> are used in buildings:

        ___ (1) *Softwood* (from evergreen trees) for general construction

        ___ (2) *Hardwood* (from deciduous trees) for furnishings and finishes

    ___ *b.* <u>*Moisture and shrinkage:*</u> The amount of water in wood is expressed as a percentage of its oven-dry (dry as possible) weight. As wood dries, it first loses moisture from within the cells without shrinking; after reaching the fiber saturation point (dry cell), further drying results in shrinkage. Eventually wood comes to dynamic equilibrium with the relative humidity of the surrounding air. Interior wood typically shrinks in winter and swells in summer. Average equilibrium moisture content ranges from 6 to 11%, but wood is considered dry enough for use at 12 to 15%. The loss of moisture during seasoning causes wood to become harder, stronger, stiffer, and lighter in weight. Wood is most decay-resistant when moisture content is under 20%.

___ 2. <u>Lumber</u>

    ___ *a.* <u>*Sizes*</u>

        ___ (1) Sectional

Nominal sizes	To get actual sizes
2×'s up to 8×'s	deduct ½″
8×'s and larger	deduct ¾″

        ___ (2) Lengths

            ___ (*a*) Softwoods: cut to lengths of 6′ to 24′, in 2′ increments

            ___ (*b*) Hardwoods: cut to 1′-long increments

    ___ *b.* <u>*Economy:*</u> best achieved when layouts are within a 2′- or 4′-module, with subdivisions of 4″, 16″, 24″, and 48″

    ___ *c.* <u>*Defects:*</u> See diagram below and on following page.

DEFECT	END VIEW	LONG VIEW
BOW		

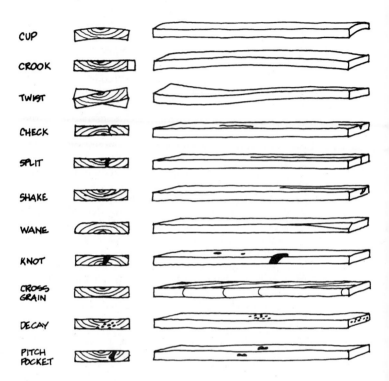

CUP

CROOK

TWIST

CHECK

SPLIT

SHAKE

WANE

KNOT

CROSS GRAIN

DECAY

PITCH POCKET

___ *d.* *Grades*
   ___ (1) *Factory or shop-type lumber:* used primarily for remanufacturing purposes (doors, windows, millwork, etc.).
   ___ (2) *Yard-type lumber*
      ___ (*a*) Boards:
         ___ 1″ to 1½″ thick, 2″ and wider
         ___ Graded for appearance only
         ___ Used as siding, subflooring, trim
      ___ (*b*) Dimensioned lumber:
         ___ 2″ to 4″ thick, 2″ and wider
         ___ Graded for strength (stress gr.)
         ___ Used for general construction
         ___ Light framing: 2″ to 4″ wide

    ___ Joists and planks: 6″ and wider
    ___ Decking: 4″ and wider (*select and commercial*).
  ___ (*c*) Timbers:
    ___ 5″ × 5″ and larger
    ___ Graded for strength and serviceability
    ___ May be classified as "structural."
___ (3) *Structural grades* (in descending order, according to stress grade):
  ___ (*a*) Light framing: *Construction, Standard,* and *Utility*
  ___ (*b*) Structural light framing (joists, planks): *Select Structural, No. 1, 2, or 3* (some species may also be appearance-graded for exposed work).
  ___ (*c*) Timber: *Select Structural No. 1.*
  Note: Working stress values can be assigned to each of the grades according to the species of wood.
___ (4) *Appearance grades*
  ___ (*a*) For natural finishes: *Select A or B.*
  ___ (*b*) For paint finishes: *Select C or D.*
  ___ (*c*) For general construction and utility: *Common, Nos. 1 thru 5.*

___ *e.* <u>Pressure-treated wood:</u> Softwood lumber treated by a process that forces preservative chemicals into the cells of the wood. The result is a material that is immune to decay. This should not generally be used for interiors. Where required:
___ (1) In direct contact with earth
___ (2) Floor joists less than 18″ (or girders less than 12″) from the ground
___ (3) Plates, sills, or sleepers in contact with concrete or masonry
___ (4) Posts exposed to weather or in basements
___ (5) Ends of beams entering concrete or masonry, without ½″ air space
___ (6) Wood located less than 6″ from earth
___ (7) Wood structural members supporting moisture-permeable floors or roofs, exposed to weather, unless separated by an impervious moisture barrier

___ (8) Wood retaining walls or crib walls
___ (9) For exterior construction such as stairs and railings, in geographic areas where experience has demonstrated the need

___ *f. Framing-estimating rules of thumb:* For 16-inch oc stud partitions, estimate one stud for every LF of wall, then add for top and bottom plates. For any type of framing, the quantity of basic framing members (in LF) can be determined based on spacing and surface area (SF):

12 inches oc	1.2 LF/SF
16 inches oc	1.0 LF/SF
24 inches oc	0.8 LF/SF

(Doubled-up members, bands, plates, framed openings, etc., must be added.) Framing accessories, nails, joist hangers, connectors, etc., may be roughly estimated by adding *0.5 to 1.5% of the cost of lumber.* Estimating lumber can be done in *board feet* where one BF is the amount of lumber in a rough-sawed board one foot long, one foot wide, and one inch thick (144 cubic inches) or the equivalent volume in any other shape. As an example, one hundred one-inch by 12-inch dressed boards, 16 feet long, contain:

$$100 \times 1 \times 12 \times 16/12 = 1600 \text{ BF}$$

Use the following table to help estimate board feet:

BF per SF of surface

	12-inch oc	16-inch oc	24-inch oc
2 × 4s	0.8	0.67	0.54
2 × 6s	1.2	1.0	0.8
2 × 8s	1.6	1.33	1.06
2 × 10s	2.0	1.67	1.34
2 × 12s	2.4	2.0	1.6

Costs: Rough lumber costs by board feet.

Studs	**$0.80 / BF**
Posts	**$0.90 / BF**
Joist	**$0.85 / BF**
Beams (Douglas fir)	**$1.00 / BF**

The above are materials only. Total in-place cost may be estimated by doubling the above numbers.

Stud walls: 2 × 4s @ 24″ oc: $0.93 (50% M and 50% L) with variation of ± 10%. Add 20% for each jump (i.e. 16″ and 12″ o.c.) 2 × 6s @ 24″ oc: $1.15/SF (M, L variation, and spacing the same as above)

___ 3. <u>Details</u>

WINDOW ROUGH OPENING

INSIDE WALL TO OUTSIDE WALL.

INSIDE WALL TO OUTSIDE WALL

WALL TO CL'G.

WALL TO CL'G.

OUTSIDE CORNER

OUTSIDE CORNER

OUTSIDE CORNER

___ 4. <u>Laminated Lumber</u>
   ___ *a.* <u>*Laminated timber*</u> (glu-lam beams): For large structural members, these are preferable to solid timber in terms of finished dressed appearance, weather resistance, controlled moisture content, and size availability.

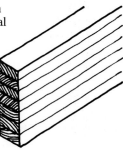

___ *b.*   <u>*Sheathing Panels*</u>
___ (1) *Composites:* Veneer faces bonded to recon-
            stituted wood cores
___ (2) *Nonveneered panels:*
    ___ (*a*) Oriented strand board (OSB)
    ___ (*b*) Particle board
___ (3) Plywood
    _ (*a*) Two main types

THICKNESS

ODD NUMBER OF PLIES.

GRAIN DIRECTION SAME.

FOR FACE & BACK

PLIES (LONGITUDINAL).

       ___ *Exterior grade*
       __ Made with waterproof adhe-
          sive
       __ C-grade face or better
       __ For permanent exterior use
       ___ *Interior grade*
       __ Made with water-resistant
          adhesives
       __ D-grade face or better
    ___ (*b*) Grading according to face veneers
       ___ N All heartwood or all sap-
            wood (for natural finish)
       ___ A Smooth paint grade
       ___ B Solid smooth surface
       ___ C Sheathing grade (lowest
            grade for exterior use)
       ___ D Lowest grade of interior
            plywood
    ___ (*c*) Engineered grades:
       ___ *Structural I and II, Standard,*
          and *C-C Exterior*
       ___ Span identification index

32/16   LEFT HAND NUMBER FOR ROOF SUPPORTS

          RIGHT HAND NUMBER FOR FLOOR SUPPORTS

    ___ (*d*) Thickness: 3 ply = ¼″, ⅜″
                        5 ply = ½″, ⅝″, ¾″
                        7 ply = ⅞″, 1″, 1⅛″,
                        and 1¼″
    ___ (*e*) Size sheets: 4′ (or 5′) × 8′ (or 12′)

___ 5. <u>Finish Wood</u> (Interior Hardwood Plywoods)
    ___ *a.* *Sizes*
        ___ (1) Thicknesses: ⅛″ to 1″ in ¹⁄₁₆″ and ⅛″ increments
        ___ (2) Widths: 18″, 24″, 32″, 36″, and 48″
        ___ (3) Lengths: 4′, 5′, 6′, 7′, 8′, and 10′
    ___ *b.* *Types*
        ___ (1) Technical: fully waterproof bond
        ___ (2) Type I (exterior): fully waterproof bond/ weather- and fungus-resistant
        ___ (3) Type II (interior): water-resistant bond
        ___ (4) Type III (interior): moisture-resistant bond
    ___ *c.* *Grades*
        ___ (1) Premium 1: very slight imperfections
        ___ (2) Good 1: suitable for natural finishes
        ___ (3) Sound 2: suitable for painted finishes
        ___ (4) Utility 3: may have open defects
        ___ (5) Backing 4: may have many flaws
    ___ *d.* *Grains and patterns*

ROTARY   FLAT SLICING   QUARTER SLICING   HALF ROUND   RIFT CUT   BACK
WOOD GRAIN FIGURES

 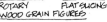

BOOK   SLIP   "V"   HERRINGBONE   CENTER   BALANCE

DIAMOND   REVERSE DIAMOND   BOX   REVERSE BOX   VERTICAL BUTT HORIZONTAL BOOK   RANDOM

VENEER MATCHING PATTERNS

Costs: Prefinished plywood paneling: $2.00 to $6.00/SF
        Trim: $2.50 to $5.30/LF
        Cabinetry: See p. 246

___ 6. <u>Cabinetry</u>
Grades are often a function of surface treatment.
___ *a.* *Economy* (lowest grade)
Usually not shop-built. Has no back. Usually has a lipped door. The underside of counter is not specifically treated, thus some warpage may occur. Divisions between sections are open frame. Shelves are usually adjustable with clips.
___ *b.* *Custom* (average grade)
Usually shop-built. Has a back. The edges of all exposed plywood or particle board are covered. The divisions between one area and another are solid. The drawers have hardwood guides for better wear. Adjustable shelves are usually attached with recessed standards. Finish is usually plastic laminate.
___ *c.* *Premium* (best grade)
Shop-built. Best construction procedures and materials. The corners are mitered. There are solid panels between drawers to prevent dust travel. Drawers are made completely of hardwood and use high-quality hardware. The countertops are attached with hidden clips or screwed, not nailed down. All joints are screwed or glued with blocks. Adjustable shelves are usually attached with recessed standards. Finishes are often high-gloss plastic laminates or laquered wood.
___ *d.* *Costs:*
For standard grade (custom):

Wall cabinet = $70/LF
Base cabinet = $130/LF
Countertop   = $30 to $65/LF
<u>   </u>
$230 to $265/LF (90%M and 10%L)

For premium grade add 65%.
For economy grade deduct 45%.

___ 7. <u>Plastic Laminates</u>
___ *a.* High-pressure laminates are a sandwich of 8 to 10 layers of resin-impregnated papers converted by heat and pressure into a plasticlike material.
___ *b.* Thickness: $\frac{1}{16}''$ general purpose; $\frac{1}{32}''$ for vert. surfaces.

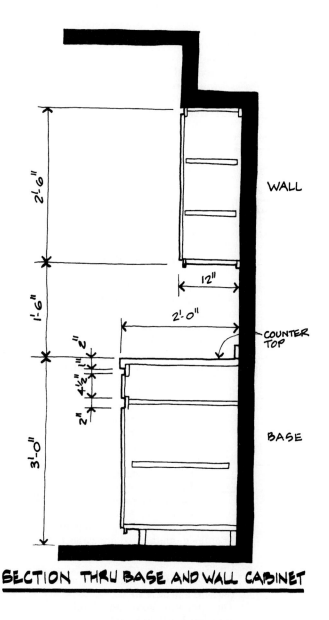

WALL

12"

2'-0"

COUNTER
TOP

2'-6"

1'-6"

2"

4½"

2"

BASE

3'-0"

SECTION THRU BASE AND WALL CABINET

___ *c.* Finishes:
    ___ gloss
    ___ satin
    ___ textured
    ___ low-glare
    ___ oil rub
___ *d.* Edge treatments

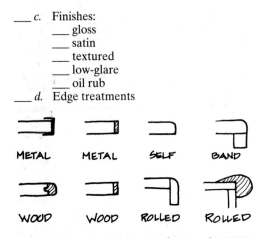

METAL   METAL   SELF   BAND

WOOD   WOOD   ROLLED   ROLLED

___ *e.* **Costs: materials only: $1.00 to $1.25/SF**

___ 8. <u>Solid Surfaces</u> (Solid Polymer Fabrications)
    ___ *a.* A modern synthetic with the appearance of marble or stone.
    ___ *b.* Leading manufacturer is "Corian," which is often used as a term for "solid surfaces."
    ___ *c.* Used for countertop vanities and work surfaces. Sometimes used for wall cladding and toilet partitions.
    ___ *d.* Size: ½″ typical for horizontal surface
        ¼″ for wall cladding
        Use on substrat (but some products can span up to 12′)

    ___ *e.* Made of
        ___ (1) Filler of minerals
        ___ (2) Binder of polymers (acrylic, polester, or plastic)
    ___ *f.* Colors and finishes vary from plain white and tans to grained, marbleized appearance. Surfaces come in matt, semigloss, and high gloss.
    ___ *g.* **Costs:**
        Average, ½″ thick, solid color, matt: $30 to $50/SF (50% M and 50% L)
        Top-end, with nonstandard color, semi- or high-gloss finish: $40 to $60/SF

NOTES

SPECIES

		TYP. FORMS				USES BLD'G.				USES PART'N	
● DENOTES COMMON USES AND PROPERTIES O POSSIBLE OR LIMITED USAGE □ TREATED WOOD ONLY * FLAME SPREAD RATING SCALE OF 1 TO 10 WHERE 1 IS LOWEST & 10 HIGHEST		VENEERS	BOARDS/PLANKS	DIMENSION	STRIPS/BLOCKS	POSTS	FRAMING	SHEATHING	SIDING	FRAMING	PANELING
SPECIES	COLOR										
SOFTWOODS											
1 CEDAR, WESTERN RED	RED BROWN TO WHITE SAPWOOD	O	●	●		●	●	●	●	●	●
2 CYPRESS, BALD	YELLOWISH BROWN					●	●	●	●	●	●
3 FIR, DOUGLAS (COAST)	REDDISH TAN		●	●	●	●	●	●	●	●	O
4 HEMLOCK, WESTERN	PALE BROWN		●	●		●	●	●	●	●	
5 LARCH, WESTERN	BROWN					●	●	●	●	●	
6 PINE - LODGEPOLE			●	●		O	●	O	O	O	
7 - PONDEROSA	WHITE TO PALE YELLOW		●	●		O	●	O	●	●	●
8 - RED	LIGHT BROWN		●	●		O	●	O	●	●	
9 - SOUTHERN	WHITE TO PALE YELLOW		●	●	●	O	●	●	●	●	●
10 - SUGAR	CREAMY WHITE		●	●		●	●	●	●	●	●
11 REDWOOD - OLD GROWTH	DEEP RED TO DARK BROWN	O	●	●		●	O	O	●	O	●
12 SPRUCE - BLACK						O	O	O	O	O	
13 - ENGLEMAN	CREAMY WHITE		●	●		O	O	O	O	O	
14 - RED						O	●	O	O	O	
15 - SITKA	LIGHT YELLOWISH TAN		●	●		O	●	O	O	O	
HARDWOODS											
1 ASH, WHITE	CREAMY WHITE TO LIGHT BROWN	●			O						O
2 BEECH	WHITE TO REDDISH BROWN	●			●						●
3 BIRCH, YELLOW	LIGHT BROWN	●			●						●
4 CHERRY	REDDISH BROWN	●			●						●
5 ELM, AMERICAN	BROWN	●									●
6 LOCUST, BLACK	GOLDEN BROWN					O					O
7 MAHOGANY	REDDISH BROWN	●			●						●
8 MAPLE (HARD) SUGAR	WHITE TO REDDISH BROWN	●			●						●
9 OAK, RED	REDDISH TAN TO BROWN	●			●						●
10 POPLAR, YELLOW	WHT. TO BROWN W/GREEN CAST	●							O		●
11 ROSEWOOD	MIXED REDS, BROWNS & BLACKS	●									●
12 TEAK	TAWNY YELLOW TO DARK BRN.	●			●						●
13 WALNUT, BLACK	DARK BROWN	●	O								●

JOISTS	ROUGH	FINISH	RAFTERS	DECKING	PILES	WD. FOUND.	RET. WALLS	POSTS	DECKS	FURNITURE	CABINETS	FURNITURE	SHRINKAGE	BENDG. STRENG.	COMPRESSION =	COMPRESSION ⊥	HARDNESS SIDE	IMPACT, BENDING	RESIST. TO DECAY	WEATHERING	PAINTABILITY	NOTES	
																						SOFTWOODS	
○			●	●				●	●	●	○	○	2	4	5	4	3	4	8	7	7	*70	1
○			●	●				●	●	●	○	○	5	6	6	6	6	6	8	7	7	*145-150	2
●	●	●	●	●	■	■	■	■	■				7	7	7	6	7	6	6	5	4	*70-100	3
●			●	●		■	■	■	■				7	6	6	5	6	7	5	5	5	*60-70	4
●			●	●	□				●				8	3	7	6	7	6	6	5	4		5
○			●						■				5	4	5	4	4	5	5	5	5	*93	6
○			●	●		■	■		■		○	○	4	3	4	5	4	5	5	5	6	*105-200	7
○			●	●		■			●		○	○	5	5	5	5	5	6	5	5	4	*142	8
○	●	●	●	●	■	■	■	■	■				7	7	7	6	7	6	5	5	5	*130-190	9
○			●	●					■		○	○	3	3	4	3	3	4	5	5	6		10
○			○	●				●	■	●	○	○	2	5	6	5	5	4	8	7	7	*70	11
○			○	○						□			5	4	5	3	5	5	5	5	5		12
○			○	○						□			5	3	3	3	3	4	5	5	5		13
○			○	○						□			6	5	5	5	5	4	5	5	5		14
○			●	●						□			6	5	5	5	5	5	5	5	5		15
																						HARDWOODS	
		○										●	5	6	6	6	6	6	4	5	5		1
											●	●	8	5	5	5	5	5	5	5	6		2
		○									●	●	7	5	4	4	5	6	5	5	6	*105-110	3
		○									●	●	3	4	5	3	4	3	6	5	5		4
												●	6	3	3	8	4	4	5	5	5		5
						○	○	○					2	8	8	8	8	5	8	5	5		6
		●									○	○											7
		●									○	●	6	6	6	6	6	5	5	5	6	*104	8
		●									○	○	7	3	3	5	5	3	5	5	5	*100	9
											○	○	4	3	3	2	3	3	5	5	7	*170-185	10
											●	●											11
		○							○		●	●											12
		○									●	●	4	6	6	4	6	4	7	6	5	*130-140	13

NOTES

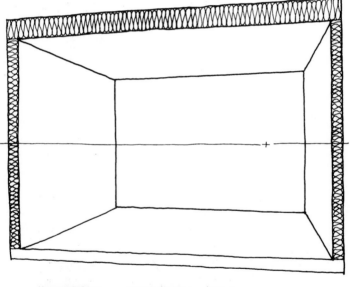

7

THERMAL
AND MOISTURE
PROTECTION

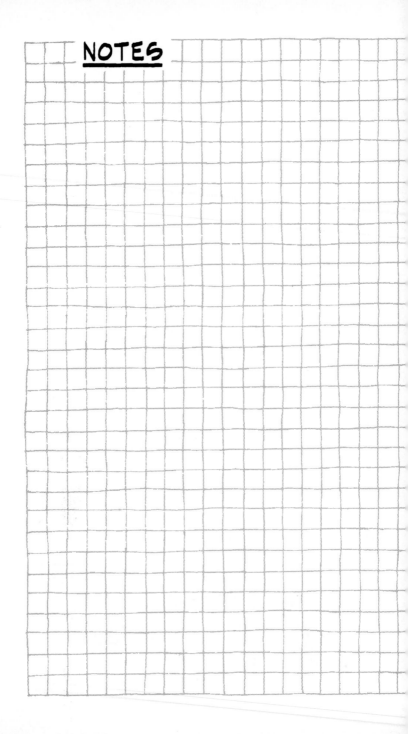

NOTES

___ A. WATER AND DAMPPROOFING

The interior designer may be involved with waterproofing where interior water is concerned. Examples might be showers and interior planters.

   ___ 1. <u>Waterproofing</u>

      Waterproofing is the prevention of water flow (usually under hydrostatic pressure such as saturated soil) into the building. This usually involves basement walls or decks, and can be achieved by:

      ___ *a.* Membranes: Layers of asphalt with plies of saturated felt or woven fabric

      ___ *b.* Hydrolithic: Coatings of asphalt or plastics (elastomeric)

      ___ *c.* Admixtures: To concrete

Typical costs:
Elastomeric, ½″ neoprene: $2.00/SF (50% M and 50% L)
Bit. membrane, 2-ply felt: $1.20/SF (35% M and 65% L)

   ___ 2. <u>Dampproofing</u>

      Dampproofing is preventing dampness (from earth or surface water without hydrostatic pressure) from penetrating into the building. This can be:

      ___ *a.* Below grade: 2 coats asphalt paint, dense cement plaster, silicons, and plastics.

      ___ *b.* Above grade: See paints and coatings, p. 300.

Typical costs:
Asphalt paint, per coat: $0.55/SF (50% M and 50% L)

___ B. VAPOR BARRIERS

This section will give the interior designer an idea of vapor mitigation, if involved with roofs and exterior walls.

    ___ 1. General

        ___ *a.* Vapor can penetrate walls and roof by:

            ___ (1) Diffusion—vapor passes through materials due to:

                ___ (*a*) Difference in vapor pressure between inside and outside.

                ___ (*b*) Permeability of construction materials.

            ___ (2) Air leakage by:

                ___ (*a*) Stack effect

                ___ (*b*) Wind pressure

                ___ (*c*) Building pressure

        ___ *b.* Vapor is not a problem until it reaches its *dew point* and condenses into moisture, causing deterioration in the building materials of wall, roof, and floor assemblies.

    ___ 2. Vapor Barriers

Vapor barriers should be placed on the warm or humid side of the assembly. For *cold* climates this will be toward the inside. For *warm, humid* climates, this will be toward the outside. Barriers are also often put under slabs-on-grade to protect flooring from ground moisture.

    Vapor barriers are measured by *perms* (grains/SF/hr/inch mercury vapor pressure difference). One grain equals about one drop of water. For a material to qualify as a vapor barrier, its perm rate must be *1.0* or less. A good perm rate for foil laminates, polyethylene sheets, etc. equals *0.1* or less (avoid aluminum foil against mortar). See p. 259 for perms of various materials. Care must be taken to avoid puncturing the barrier.

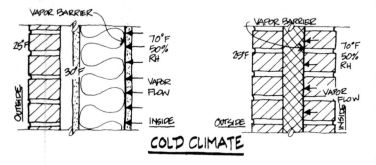

COLD CLIMATE

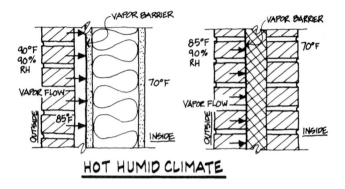

HOT HUMID CLIMATE

Other methods for sealing out moisture are elastomeric coatings on interior wall- board in cold climates and at exterior masonry or stucco walls in hot, wet climates. See p. 300 for coatings. Care must be taken to caulk all joints and cracks.

Typical costs: Polyethylene sheets, 2–10 mill. $.15 to $.20/SF

___ C. INSULATION ⑦

This section will give the interior designer typical insulation requirements and solutions for use if involved with roofs and exterior walls.

___ 1. <u>Insulation</u> is the entrapment of air within modern lightweight materials, to resist heat flow.

___ 2. In the design of a building, design the different elements (roof, wall, floor) to be at the minimum ΣR. Each piece of construction has some resistance to heat flow, with lightweight insulations contributing the bulk of the resistance.

$$\Sigma R = R1 + R2 + R3 + R4 + R5, \text{etc.} \qquad *(\text{air films})$$

See p. 259 for resistance (r) of elements to be added.

Another common term is U Value, the coefficient of heat transmission.

$$U = \text{Btuh/ft}^2/°F = \frac{1}{\Sigma R}$$

___ 3. Other factors in control of heat flow:

___ *a.* The *mass* (density or weight) of building elements (such as walls) will delay and store heat. Time lag in hours is related to thermal conductivity, heat capacity, and thickness. This increases as weight of construction goes up with about *½% per lb/CF.* Desirable time lags in temperate climates are: Roof—12 hrs; north and east walls—0 hrs; west and south walls—8 hrs. This effect can also be used to increase R values, at the approximate rate of *+0.4%* for every added lb/CF of weight.

___ *b.* *Light colors* will reflect and *dark colors* will absorb the sun's heat. Cold climates will favor dark surfaces, and the opposite for hot climates. For summer roofs, the overall effect can be 20% between light and dark.

___ 4. Typical Batts:

R = 11   3½″ thick
R = 19   6″
R = 22   6½″
R = 26   8¼″
R = 30   9″

Typical Costs:
    Ceiling batt, 6″ R = 19: $.80/SF (60% M and 40% L)
                9″ R = 30: $1.10/SF
    Wall batt,   4″ R = 11: $.50/SF (50% M and 50% L)
                6″ R = 19: $.60/SF
    Add $.05/SF for foil backs.
    Rigid: $.60/SF, ¾″, R = 2.8 to $1.15/SF, 2¼″, R = 8.3.

____ 5. Insulating Properties of Building Materials:

Material	lbs. weight	r value (per in)	Perm
Water	60		
Earth dry	75 to 95	0.33	
saturated		0.05	
Sand/gravel dry	100–120		
wet			
Concrete req.	150	0.11	
lt. wt.	120	0.59	
Masonry			
Mortar	130	0.2	
Brick, common	120	0.2	1 (4″)
8″ CMU, reg. wt.	85	1.11	0.4
lt. wt.	55	2	
Stone	±170	0.08	
Metals			
Aluminum	165	0.0007	0 (1 mil)
Steel	490	0.0032	
Copper	555	0.0004	
Wood			
Plywood	36	1.25	½″ = .4 to 1
Hardwood	40	0.91	
Softwood	30	1.25	2.9 (¾″)
Waterproofing			0.05
Vapor barrier			0.05
Insulations			
Min. wool batt	4	±3.2	>50
Fill		3.7	>50
Perlite	11	2.78	
Board polystyrene		4	1–6
fiber		2.94	
glass fiber		4.17	
urethane		8.5	

Material	lbs. weight	r value (per in)	Perm
Air			
Betwn. nonrefl.		1.34	
One side refl.		4.64	
Two sides refl.			
Inside film		0.77 (av)	
Outside film			
winter		0.17	
summer		0.25	
Doors			
Metal			
Fiber core		1.69	
Urethane core		5.56	
Wood, solid 1¾″		3.13	
HC 1⅜″		2.22	
Glass, single	160	0.90	
Plaster (stucco)	110	0.2	
Gypsum	48	0.6	
CT	145		
Terrazzo			
Acoustical CLGs			
Resilient flooring		0.05	
Carpet and pad		2.08	
Paint			0.3 to 1 (see p. 300)

NOTES

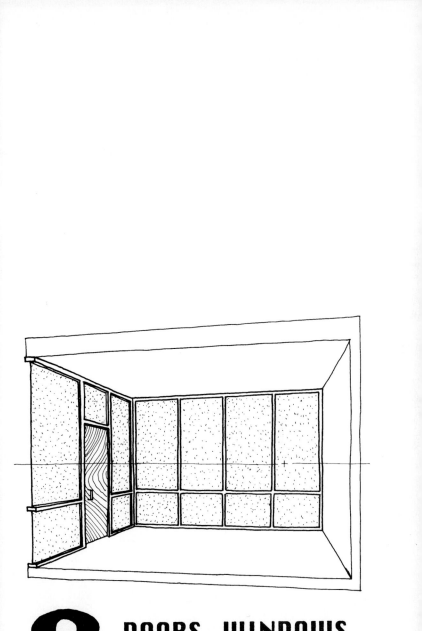

8 DOORS, WINDOWS, AND GLASS

NOTES

__ 1. <u>Accessible Door Approach</u> (ADA) ⑳

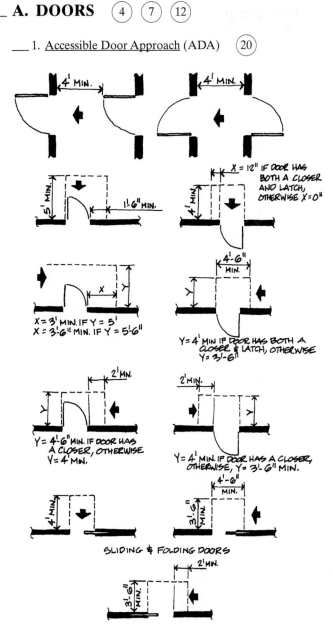

$X = 12"$ IF DOOR HAS BOTH A CLOSER AND LATCH, OTHERWISE $X = 0"$

$X = 3'$ MIN. IF $Y = 5'$
$X = 3'-6"$ MIN. IF $Y = 5'-6"$

$Y = 4'$ MIN IF DOOR HAS BOTH A CLOSER & LATCH, OTHERWISE $Y = 3'-6"$

$Y = 4'-6"$ MIN. IF DOOR HAS A CLOSER, OTHERWISE $Y = 4'$ MIN.

$Y = 4'$ MIN. IF DOOR HAS A CLOSER, OTHERWISE, $Y = 3'-6"$ MIN.

SLIDING & FOLDING DOORS

NOTE: ALL DOORS IN <u>ALCOVES</u> SHALL COMPLY W/ FRONT APPROACHES.

___ 2. <u>General</u>

    ___ *a.* Types by operation
        ___ (1) Swinging
        ___ (2) Bypass sliding
        ___ (3) Surface sliding
        ___ (4) Pocket sliding
        ___ (5) Folding
    ___ *b.* Physical types

(1) Flush   (2) Panelled   (3) French   (4) Glass

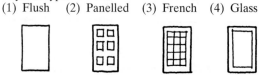

(5) Sash   (6) Jalousie   (7) Louver

(8) Shutter   (9) Screen   (10) Dutch

    ___ *c.* Rough openings (door dimensions +)

	Width	Height
In wood stud walls (r.o.)	+3½″	+3½″
In masonry walls (m.o)	+4″	+2″ to 4″

    ___ *d.* Fire door classifications

Fire door rating (in hours)	Opening class	Use of wall	Rating of wall (in hours)
3	A	Fire walls Fire separations	3 or 4
1½	B	Vertical shafts Exit stairs Fire separations	2

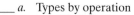

Fire door rating (in hours)	Opening class	Use of wall	Rating of wall (in hours)
1	B	Vertical shafts Exit stairs Fire separations	1
¾	C	Fire-resistive partitions Corridors Hazardous areas	1
½		Limited applic. corridors	1 or less
⅓		Corridors	
20 Min.		Smoke barriers	
1½	D	Severe exterior exposure	2 or more
¾	E	Exterior exposure	1 or less

____ *e.* Energy conservation: Specify exterior doors not to exceed:

    ____ (1) Residential: 0.5 CFM/SF infiltration

    ____ (2) Nonresidential: 11.0 CFM/LF crack infiltration

____ 3. <u>Hollow Metal Doors and Frames</u>

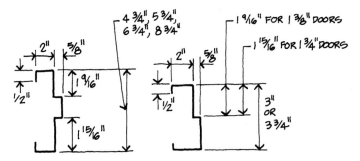

DOUBLE RABBET   SINGLE RABBET

____ *a.* Material (for gauges, see p. 229). Typical gauges of doors (16, 18, 20) and frames (12, 14, 16, 18)

Use	Frame	Door face
Heavy (entries, stairs, public toilets, mech. rms.)	12, 14	16
Medium to low (rooms, closets, etc.)	14, 16, 20	18

    ___ *b.*   Doors (total door construction of 16 to 22 GA)
             Thickness   1¾″ and 1⅜″
             Widths   2′ to 4′ in 2″ increments
             Heights   6′8″, 7′, 7′2″, 7′10″, 8′, 10′

Costs: Frames: 3′ × 7′, 18 GA $5.90/SF (of opening) or 16 GA at $6.65/SF (60% M and 40% L), can vary ±40%.

Doors: 3′ × 7′, 20 GA, 1¾″: $12.70/SF (85% M and 3′ × 6′8″, 20 GA, 1⅜″: $12.25/SF 15% L).

Add: lead lining: $660/ea., 8″ × 8″ glass, $120/ea., soundproofing $30/ea., 3-hour $120/ea., ¾-hour $25/ea.

___ 4. <u>Wood Doors</u>
    ___ *a.*   Types
        ___ (1) Flush
        ___ (2) Hollow core
        ___ (3) Solid core
        ___ (4) Panel (rail
                and stile)

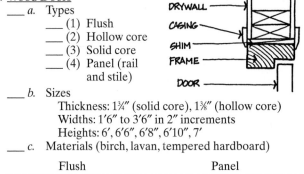

    ___ *b.*   Sizes
          Thickness: 1¾″ (solid core), 1⅜″ (hollow core)
          Widths: 1′6″ to 3′6″ in 2″ increments
          Heights: 6′, 6′6″, 6′8″, 6′10″, 7′
    ___ *c.*   Materials (birch, lavan, tempered hardboard)

Flush	Panel
Hardwood veneer	#1: hardwood or pine for transp. finish
Premium: for transp. finish	#2: Doug fir plywood for paint
Good #3: For paint.	
Sound: (for paint only)	

    ___ *d.*   Fire doors (with mineral composition cores) B and C labels available, see p. 266.

Typical costs:
       Wood frame: interior, pine: $3.50/SF (of opening)
                           exterior, pine: $6.80/SF
                           (triple costs for hardwoods)
       Door: H.C. 1⅜″, hardboard $4.60/SF
                 S.C. 1¾″, hardboard $9.50/SF (75% M and 25% L)
                 Hardwood veneers about same costs.
       For carved solid exterior doors, multiply costs by 4 to 6.

___ 5. <u>Other Doors</u>
    ___ *a.* Sliding glass doors

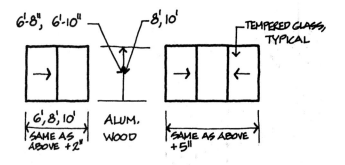

Typical costs (aluminum with ¼″ tempered glass):
    6′ wide: $770 to $870/ea. (85% M and 15% L)
    12′ wide: $1220 to $1690/ea.
    Add 10% for insulated glass.

    ___ *b.* Aluminum "storefront" (7′ height typical)

Typical cost with glass: $25/SF (85% M and 15% L). Variation of –25% to +55%.

    ___ *c.* Residential garage doors
            8′ min. width/car (9′ recommended)
            6′6″ min. height (7′2″ min. ceiling).

Costs: $25/SF (75% M and 25% L)

    ___ *d.* Folding doors
            2 panels: 1′6″, 2′0″, 2′6″, 3′0″ openings
            4 panels: 3′0″, 4′0″, 5′0″, 6′0″ openings
            6 panels: 7′6″ opening
            8 panels: 8′0″, 10′0″, 12′0″ openings

Costs: Accordion-folding closet doors with frame and trim: $20.00/SF

NOTES

For costs, see p. 322.
___ 1. General

   ___ *a.* In common with walls, windows are expected to keep out:
     (1) Winter wind
     (2) Rain in all seasons
     (3) Noise
     (4) Winter cold
     (5) Winter snow
     (6) Bugs and other flying objects
     (7) Summer heat

     They are expected, at the same time, to let in:

     (1) Outside views
     (2) Ventilating air
     (3) Natural light
     (4) Winter solar gain

   ___ *b.* Size designations: 3′ W × 6′ H = 3060
   ___ *c.* For types by operation, see p. 274.
   ___ *d.* For aid to selection of type, see p. 272.
   ___ *e.* Windows come in aluminum, steel, and wood. See pp. 276 and 277 for typical sizes.
   ___ *f.* Energy conservation: Specify windows to not exceed 0.34 CFM per LF of operable sash crack for infiltration.

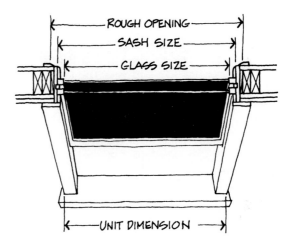

● INDICATES CHARACTERISTICS

WINDOW TYPES

DISADVANTAGES	DOUBLE HUNG	DOUBLE HUNG, REVERSED	CASEMENT, OUT	CASEMENT, IN	AWNING, CANOPY	PIVOTED, VERTICAL	PIVOTED, HORIZONTAL	TOP HINGED, OUT	BOTTOM HINGED, IN	FIXED SASH	JALOUSIE	MONITOR, CONTINUOUS	PROJECTED	HORIZONTAL SLIDING
ONLY 50% OF AREA OPENABLE	●	●												●
DOESN'T PROTECT FROM RAIN, WHEN OPEN	●	●	●			●								●
INCONVENIENT OPER. IF OVER OBSTRUCTION		●					●	●						●
HAZ'D. IF LOW VENT NEXT TO WALK			●			●	●	●				●	●	
REQUIRES WEATHER STRIPPING	●		●	●	●	●	●	●	●					●
HORZ. MEMBERS OBSTRUCT VIEW	●	●					●					●	●	
VERT. MEMBERS OBSTRUCT VIEW		●	●	●	●						●			●
WILL SAG IF NOT STRUCTURALLY STRONG			●	●										
GLASS QUICKLY SOILS WHEN VENT OPEN					●	●	●	●	●		●	●	●	
INFLOWING AIR CANNOT BE DIVERTED DOWN	●	●	●		●			●	●		●		●	●
EXCESSIVE AIR LEAKAGE											●			
HARD TO WASH											●			
INTERFERES WITH FURNITURE, DRAPES, ETC.				●		●	●		●					
SCREENS-STORM SASH DIFFICULT TO PROVIDE						●	●							●
SASH HAS TO BE REMOVED FOR WASHING	●							●		●		●		●

272

● INDICATES CHARACTERISTICS

WINDOW TYPES

ADVANTAGES	DOUBLE HUNG	DOUBLE HUNG, REVERSED	CASEMENT, OUT	CASEMENT, IN	AWNING, CANOPY	PIVOTED, VERTICAL	PIVOTED, HORIZONTAL	TOP HINGED OUT	BOTTOM HINGED, IN	FIXED SASH	JALOUSIE	MONITOR, CONTINUOUS	PROJECTED	HORIZONTAL SLIDING
NOT APT TO SAG	●	●			●	●	●	●	●	●		●		●
SCREEN & STORM SASH EASY TO INSTALL	●	●			●			●						●
PROVIDES 100% VENT OPENING			●	●	●	●	●	●	●		●	●		
EASY TO WASH W/ PROPER HARDWARE		●		●		●	●		●					
WILL DEFLECT DRAFTS			●	●		●	●		●					
OFFERS RAIN PROTECTION, PARTLY OPEN					●		●	●	●		●	●	●	
DIVERTS INFLOWING AIR UPWARD					●		●		●		●	●	●	
ODD SIZES ECONOMICALLY AVAILABLE										●	●	●		●
LARGE SIZES PRACTICAL														●

WINDOW TYPES BY OPERATION AND MATERIAL & COSTS

NOTE: GLASS EXCLUDED IN COSTS   * (90%M & 10%L)

TYPE		VENT	ALUMINUM	STEEL	WOOD
	FIXED	0%	$13.30/SF AVE. (70%M & 30%L) VARIATION ±7%	$18/SF AVE.	$25/SF AVE. * VARIATION -10% +20% PICTURE WINDOW
	CASEMENT	100%		$20 TO $26/SF AVE. (85%M & 15%L)	$35/SF AVE * VARIATION +70%, -40%
PROJECTED	AWNING	50 TO 100%	$24.25 TO $28.70/ SF AVE. (75%M & 25%L)	$26.25 TO $30.30/* SF AVE.	$40/SF AVE. (85%M & 15%L) VARIATION +60%, -40%
	HOPPER	50 TO 100%			
	SLIDING	50 TO 100%	$17 TO $19/SF AVE. (80%M & 20%L)		$26/SF AVE. VARIATION ±60%

				$30/SF AVE. (85%M $ 15%L) VARIATION +70%, -45%
DOUBLE-HUNG	50%	$18.50 TO $20.60/ SF AVE. *	$34/SF AVE *	
JALOUSIE	100%	$20/SF AVE. (80% M & 20%L)		
PIVOTING	100%		$20/SF AVE. (85% M $ 15%L)	

TYPICAL WOOD WINDOW SASH SIZES

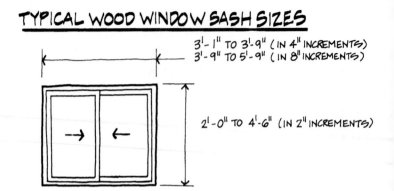

3'-1" TO 3'-9" (IN 4" INCREMENTS)
3'-9" TO 5'-9" (IN 8" INCREMENTS)

2'-0" TO 4'-6" (IN 2" INCREMENTS)

HORIZONTAL SLIDING WINDOWS

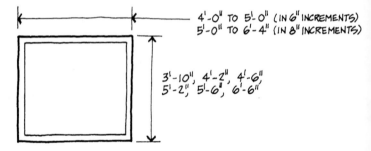

4'-0" TO 5'-0" (IN 6" INCREMENTS)
5'-0" TO 6'-4" (IN 8" INCREMENTS)

3'-10", 4'-2", 4'-6",
5'-2", 5'-6", 6'-6"

PICTURE WINDOWS

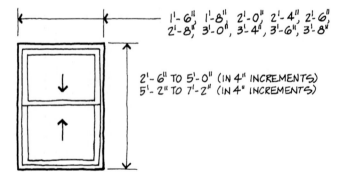

1'-6", 1'-8", 2'-0", 2'-4", 2'-6",
2'-8", 3'-0", 3'-4", 3'-6", 3'-8"

2'-6" TO 5'-0" (IN 4" INCREMENTS)
5'-2" TO 7'-2" (IN 4" INCREMENTS)

DOUBLE HUNG WINDOWS

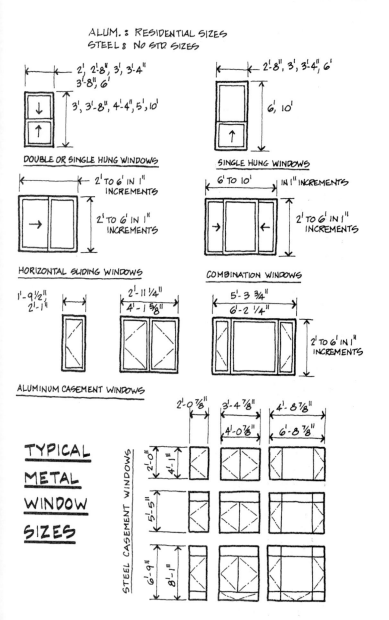

ALUM. : RESIDENTIAL SIZES
STEEL : NO STD SIZES

2', 2'-8", 3', 3'-4"
3'-8", 6'

3', 3'-8", 4'-4", 5', 10'

DOUBLE OR SINGLE HUNG WINDOWS

2'-8", 3', 3'-4", 6'

6', 10'

SINGLE HUNG WINDOWS

2' TO 6' IN 1" INCREMENTS

2' TO 6' IN 1" INCREMENTS

HORIZONTAL SLIDING WINDOWS

6' TO 10'   IN 1" INCREMENTS

2' TO 6' IN 1" INCREMENTS

COMBINATION WINDOWS

1'-9½"
2'-1"

2'-11¼"
4'-1⅝"

5'-3¾"
6'-2¼"

2' TO 6' IN 1" INCREMENTS

ALUMINUM CASEMENT WINDOWS

**TYPICAL
METAL
WINDOW
SIZES**

STEEL CASEMENT WINDOWS

2'-0⅞"   3'-4⅞"   4'-8⅞"
4'-0⅞"   6'-8⅞"

2'-0"
4'-1"

5'-5"

6'-9"
8'-1"

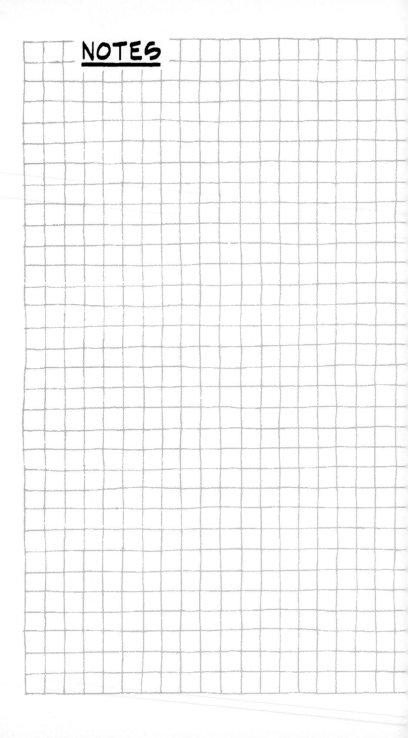

NOTES

___ C. HARDWARE ⑫ ⑳

___ 1. <u>General Considerations:</u> How to . . .
    ___ *a.* Hang the door
    ___ *b.* Lock the door
    ___ *c.* Close the door
    ___ *d.* Protect the door
    ___ *e.* Stop the door
    ___ *f.* Seal the door
    ___ *g.* Misc. the door
    ___ *h.* Electrify the door
___ 2. <u>Recommended Locations</u>   ___ 3. <u>Door Hand Conventions</u>

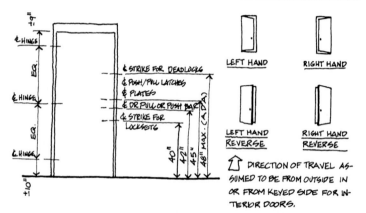

___ 4. <u>Specific Considerations</u>
    ___ *a.* Function and ease of operation
    ___ *b.* Durability in terms of:
        ___ (1) Frequency of use
           ___ (*a*) Heavy
           ___ (*b*) Medium
           ___ (*c*) Light
        ___ (2) Exposure to weather and climate (aluminum and stainless steel good for humid or coastal conditions)
    ___ *c.* Material, form, surface texture, finish, and color.
___ 5. <u>Typical Hardware</u>
    ___ *a.* Locksets (locks, latches, bolts)
    ___ *b.* Hinges
    ___ *c.* Closers
    ___ *d.* Panic hardware
    ___ *e.* Push/pull bars and plates

    ___ *f.* Kick plates
    ___ *g.* Stops and holders
    ___ *h.* Thresholds
    ___ *i.* Weatherstripping
    ___ *j.* Door tracks and hangers
___ 6. <u>Materials</u>
    ___ *a.* Aluminum
    ___ *b.* Brass
    ___ *c.* Bronze
    ___ *d.* Iron
    ___ *e.* Steel
    ___ *f.* Stainless steel
___ 7. <u>Finishes</u>

BHMA #	US #	Finish
___ 600	US P	Primed for painting
___ 605	US 3	Bright brass, clear coated
___ 606	US 4	Satin brass, clear coated
___ 612	US 10	Satin bronze, clear coated
___ 613	US 10B	Oxidized satin bronze, oil rubbed
___ 618	US 14	Bright nickel plated, clear coated
___ 619	US 15	Satin nickel plated, clear coated
___ 622	US 19	Flat black coated
___ 623	US 20	Light oxidized bright bronze clear C
___ 624	US 20D	Dark oxidized statuary bronze CC
___ 625	US 26	Bright chromium plated
___ 626	US 26D	Satin chromium plated
___ 628	US 28	Satin aluminum, clear anodized
___ 629	US 32	Bright stainless steel
___ 630	US 32D	Satin stainless steel

___ 8. <u>ADA-Accessible Hardware</u>

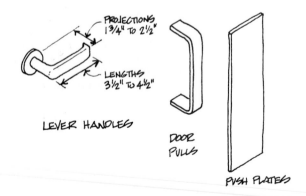

PROJECTIONS 1¾" TO 2½"

LENGTHS 3½" TO 4½"

LEVER HANDLES

DOOR PULLS

PUSH PLATES

___ 9. **Costs:**
    Residential: **\$90/door (80% M and 20% L)**
                              Variation −30%, +120%
    Commercial:
      Office:
        Interior: **\$180/door (75% M and 25% L)**
        Exterior: **\$350/door (add ≈ \$425 for exit devices)**
      Note: **Special doors, such as for hospitals, can cost up to \$570/door**

NOTES

___ D. GLASS

___ 1. <u>General</u>

Glass is one of the great modern building materials because it allows the inside of buildings to have a *visual relationship* with the outside. However, there are a number of *problems* associated with its use.

___ 2. <u>Legal Requirements</u>

The UBC requires *safety glazing* at locations hazardous to human impact. Safety glazing is *tempered glass, wired glass,* and *laminated glass.* Hazardous locations are:

___ *a.* Ingress and egress doors

___ *b.* Sliding glass doors

___ *c.* Storm doors

___ *d.* Swinging doors

___ *e.* Shower and bathtub doors and enclosures

___ *f.* Glass in railings

___ *g.* Overhead or angled glass and skylights (must be plastic, wired glass, laminated glass, or tempered glass w/screen below)

___ *h.* Glass adjacent to doors and other glass areas within 24″ and less than 60″ high, per below:

___ *i.* Glass within 5′ of swimming pool

___ *j.* Glass within 5′ of enclosed stairway

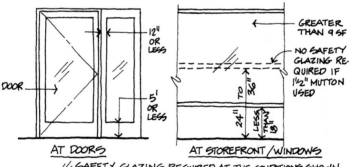

/// SAFETY GLAZING REQUIRED AT THE CONDITIONS SHOWN.

___ 3. **Costs:**
   ¼″ clear float glass: $7.00 to $9.00/SF (45% M and 55% L)
   Modifiers:
      Thickness:
         ⅛″ glass   **−40%**
         ⅜″ glass   **+50%**
         ½″ glass   **+150%**
      Structural:
         Tempered   **+20%**
         Laminated   **+45%**
      Thermal:
         Tinted or reflective   **+20%**
         Double-glazed and/or low E   **+100%**

NOTES

NOTES

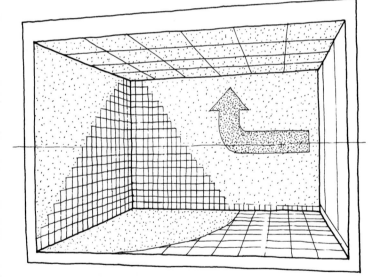

9 FINISHES

NOTES

__ A. PLASTER

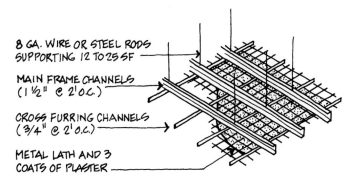

8 GA. WIRE OR STEEL RODS
SUPPORTING 12 TO 25 SF

MAIN FRAME CHANNELS
(1 ½" @ 2' O.C.)

CROSS FURRING CHANNELS
(3/4" @ 2' O.C.)

METAL LATH AND 3
COATS OF PLASTER

**TYPICAL
CEILING**

___ 1. Exterior (stucco) of cement plaster.
___ 2. Interior of gypsum plaster.
___ 3. Wall supports usually studs at between 12″ and 24″ oc. If wood, use 16″ oc min.
___ 4. Full plaster—3 coats (scratch, brown, and finish), but masonry walls can have 1 or 2 coats.
___ 5. Joints: Interior ceilings: 30′ oc max.
Exterior walls/soffits: 10′ to 20′ oc.
___ 6. Provide vents at dead air spaces (½″/SF).
___ 7. Curing: 48 hours moist curing, 7 days between coats.

Costs:

Ceilings with paint, plaster, and lath	**$1.50 to $6.50/SF (25% M and 75% L), can vary up to +60% for plaster**
Walls of stucco with paper-backed wire lath	**$2.00/SF for stucco + $.85/SF for lath (50% M and 50% L)**

__ B. GYPSUM WALLBOARD (DRYWALL)

(4) (12)

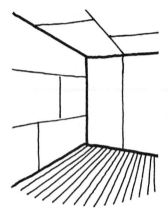

___ 1. Usually in $4' \times 8'$ (or $12'$) sheets from ¼″ to 1″ thick in about ⅛″ increments.

___ 2. Attach (nail or screw) against wood or metal framing—usually at 16″ (fire rating) to 24″ oc.

___ 3. Type "X", ⅝″ will give 1 hour fire rating. Roughly each additional ½″ layer will give 1 hour rating up to 4 hours, depending on backing and application.

___ 4. Water-resistant (green) available for wet areas or exterior.

___ 5. Can come in premanufactured panesl w/vinyl finishes.

Costs:

½″ gyp. bd.	$.60/SF ceilings
on wood	$1.00/SF columns and beams
frame	$.60/SF walls
(Approx. 50% M and 50% L)	

Increase 5% for metal frame. Varies about 15% in cost for ea. ⅛′ change in thickness. Add $.07/SF for fire resistance. Add $.12/SF for water resistance. Add $.35/SF for joint work and finish.

EXAMPLE:

FIND THE COST OF ⅝″ GYPB'D. WALL ON FRAME, READY FOR PAINT.

½″ = $0.60/SF (WALL) + 9¢ (15% FOR EXTRA ⅛″ THICKNESS) + $0.35 FOR FINISH.

∴ ⅝″ = $1.04/SF, SAY $1⁰⁵/SF

__ C. TILE ④ ⑫

__ 1. <u>Settings</u>
    __ *a.* Thick set (¾ to 1¼″ mortar bed) for slopes.
    __ *b.* Thin set (⅛″ mortar or adhesive) for faster and less expensive applications.

__ 2. <u>Joints</u>
⅛ to ¼″ (can be epoxy grouted for quarry tile floors).

__ 3. <u>Types</u>
    __ *a.* Ceramic glazed and unglazed for walls and floors of about ¼″ thick and 4 to 6″ square. Many trim shapes available.
    __ *b.* Ceramic mosaic for walls and floors of about ¼″ thick and 1 to 2″ square.
    __ *c.* Quarry tile of earth tones for strong and resistant flooring. Usually ½ to ¾″ thick by 4 to 9″ square.

Typical Costs:
> *Note:* **Costs can vary greatly, with special imports of great expense. Costs can go up with decorative designs.**

Glazed wall tile: $5.35/SF (50% M and 50% L), variation of −25%, +100%

Unglazed floor mosaic: $8.10/SF (65% M and 35% L), variation of +35%, −10%

Unglazed wall tile: $6.00/SF (40% M and 60% L), variation of +35%, −15%

Quarry tile: $8.80/SF (same as above), variation of ±10%

Bases: $8.80/LF (same as above), variation of ±10%

Additions: color variations: +10 to 20%
                  abrasive surface: +25 to 50%

___ D. TERRAZZO ④ ⑫

___ 1. A poured material (usually ½″ thick) of stone chips in a cement matrix, usually with a polished surface.

___ 2. Base of sand and concrete.

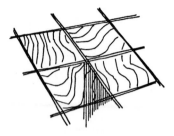

___ 3. To prevent cracking, exposed metal dividers are set approx. 3′ to 6′ oc each way.

___ 4. Newer, high-strength terrazzo (with chemical binders) is thin-set with far less jointing. Can also come in tile pavers of about 1″ thick × 9 to 24″ square.

Costs: $8.00 to $13.30/SF (45% M and 55% L)
Tiles: $17.00 to $26.00/SF

___ E. ACOUSTICAL TREATMENT

④ ⑫

Also, see p. 183.

___ 1. <u>Acoustical Ceilings:</u>
Can consist of small (¾″ thick × 1′ square) mineral fiber tiles attached to wallboard or concrete (usually glued). Also, acoustical mineral fibers with a binder can be shot on gypsum board or concrete.

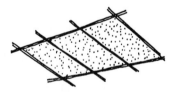

Costs: Small tiles $.85/SF (40% M and 60% L)

___ 2. <u>Suspended Acoustical Tile Ceilings:</u>
Can be used to create a plenum space to conceal mechanical and electrical functions. Typical applications are 2′ square or 2′ × 4′ tiles in exposed or concealed metal grids that are wire-suspended as in plaster ceilings. The finishes can vary widely.

Costs: Acoustical panels $1.00 to $2.00/SF (70% M and 30% L)
Suspension system $1.00 to $1.25/SF (80% M and 20% L)
When walls do *not* penetrate ceilings, can save $0.10 to $0.20/SF.

___ 3. <u>Other</u>

    ___ a. Other types of suspended ceilings can range from exposed metal to wood, to luminous baffles.

Costs: Special suspended ceilings and suspension system:
Metal w/ acoustic batts above: $7.70/SF (50% M and 50% L)
Luminous, plastic: $3.80/SF (75% M and 25% L)

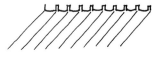

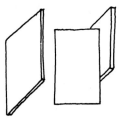

    ___ b. Ceiling baffles and banners for sound absorption.

    ___ c. Acoutical panels for special sound absorption (N.R.C. of 0.5 to 0.8) are available in various thicknesses and sizes up to 4′ × 12′

Costs: ¾″ fabric-covered panels, wall-mounted:
$7.50/SF (75% M and 25% L)

___ F. WOOD FLOORING ④ ⑫

___ 1. See part 6 for other woods.
___ 2. Finished flooring can be of hardwoods or softwoods, of which oak, southern pine, and Douglas fir are the most commonly used.
___ 3. All-heartwood grade of redwood is best for porch and exterior flooring.
___ 4. If substrate is concrete, often flooring is placed on small wood strips (sleepers); otherwise flooring is often nailed to wood substrates (plywood or wood decking).
___ 5. Because wood is very susceptible to moisture, allowance must be made for movement and ventilation. Allow for expansion at perimeters. Vapor barriers below concrete slabs are important.
___ 6. Use treated material in hot, humid climates.
___ 7. Three types of wood flooring:
   ___ *a.* Strip
   ___ *b.* Plank
   ___ *c.* Block (such as parque)

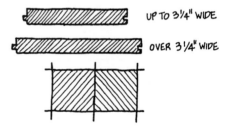

UP TO 3¼" WIDE

OVER 3¼" WIDE

Typical Costs:
      Wood strip fir $3.40/SF (70% M and 30% L)
      Oak +45% +10% finish
      Maple +45% clean and wax = $0.30/SF

___ G. MASONRY FLOORING ④ ⑫

See Part 4 on materials.

Typical Costs:
      ¾″ × 4″ × 8″ brick: $8.10/SF
      (65% M and 35% L)
      Add 15% for special patterns.

___ 1. <u>Resilient Flooring Consists of:</u>
    ___ *a.* *Sheet vinyl:* Most common of sheet flooring. Use sheet vinyl where it is desirable to have the fewest joints such as in high-maintenance wet areas. Can be located below, on, or above grade. Not the most resilient. Durability is good to moderate. Poor in quietness.
    ___ *b.* *Vinyl tiles:* Vinyl tiles are the most commonly used of resilient floorings. Can be of homogeneous or composition materials. Can be located below, on, or above grade. Moderately good to poor resilience. Best in durability. Poor in quietness. Also used for wall bases.

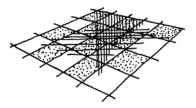

    ___ *c.* *Rubber tiles:* Can come in special studded designs for greater slip resistance. Can be located below, on, or below grade. Have good resilience, durability, and quietness. Also used for static resistance and wall base as well as stair treads.
    ___ *d.* *Cork tiles:* Most comfortable to walk on because of their high resilience. Also the quietest, but the worst for durability. Can be located on grade.
    ___ *e.* *Linoleum sheet or tiles:* Has mostly passed out of use, along with asphalt tiles. Can be used on slab on grade only. Poor for resilience and quietness. Has moderate durability.
___ 2. Is approx. ¹⁄₁₆″ to ⅛″ thick with tiles being 9 to 12″ square.
___ 3. Applied to substrate with mastic. Substrate may be plywood flooring, plywood or particleboard over wood deck, or concrete slabs.
___ 4. Vapor barriers are often required under slabs.
___ 5. Vinyl or rubber base is often applied at walls for this and other floor systems.
___ 6. Protect resilient flooring from furniture weights by using cups or casters.

A wide range of colors and patterns is available for flooring.

Typical Costs:

Solid vinyl tile ⅛″ × 12″ × 12″	$3.00/SF (75% M and 25% L), can go up 20% for various patterns and colors; double for "conductive" type.
Sheet vinyl	$2.75/SF (90% M and 10% L), variation of −70% and +100% for various patterns and colors.
Vinyl wall base	$1.75/LF (40% M and 60% L). Can vary +15%.
Stair treads	$8.00/LF (60% M and 40% L). Can vary from −10% to +40%.

___ 1. General

Most wall-to-wall carpeting is produced by looping yarns through a coarse-fiber backing, binding the backs of the loops with latex, then applying a second backing for strength and dimensional stability. Finally the loops may be left uncut for a rough, nubby surface or cut for a soft, plush surface.

___ 2. Quality

The quality of carpeting is often determined by its *face weight* (ounces of yarn or pile per square yard), not its total weight. Weights run:

___ *a.* Low traffic: 20–24 oz/SY
___ *b.* Medium traffic: 24–32 oz/SY
___ *c.* High-end carpet: 26–70 oz/SY

___ 3. A better measure of comparison:

$$weight\ density\ factor = \frac{face\ weight \times 36}{pile\ height} = oz/CY$$

Ideally, this should be as follows:

___ *a.* Residential: 3000 to 3600 oz/CY
___ *b.* Commercial: 4200 to 7000 oz/CY

___ 4. There are Two Basic Carpet Installation Methods:

___ *a.* *Padded and stitched* carpeting: Stretched over a separate pad and mechanically fastened at joints and the perimeter. Soft foam pads are inexpensive and give the carpet a soft, luxurious feel. The more expensive jute and felt pads give better support and dimensional stability. Padding adds to foot comfort, helps dampen noise, and some say, adds to the life of the carpet.

___ *b.* *Glued-down* carpets: Usually used in commercial areas subject to heavily loaded wheel traffic. They are usually glued down with carpet adhesive with a pad. This minimizes destructive flexing of the backing and prevents rippling.

___ 5. Maintenance Factors

___ *a.* *Color:* Carpets in the midvalue range show less soiling than very dark or very light colors. Consider the typical regional soil color. Consider patterned or multicolored carpets for heavy traffic areas in hotels, hospitals, theaters, and restaurants.

___ *b.* *Traffic:* The heavier the traffic, the heavier the density of carpet construction. If rolling traffic is a factor, carpet may be of maximum density for minimum resistance to rollers. Select only level-loop or dense, low-cut pile.

___ 6. <u>Carpet Materials:</u>

Fiber	Advantages	Disadvantages
Acrylic (rarely used)	Resembles wool	Not very tough; attracts oily dirt
Nylon (most used)	Very tough; resists dirt, resembles wool; low static buildup	None
Polyester deep pilings	Soft and luxurious	Less resilient; attracts oily dirt
Polypropylene indoor-outdoor	Waterproof; resists fading and stains; easy to clean	Crushes easily
Wool	Durable; easy to clean; feels good; easily dyed	Most expensive

___ 7. **Costs: (90% M and 10% L) (Variation ±100%) Figure 10% waste.**
Repair/level floors: $1.65 to $6.10/SY (45% M and 55% L)
Padding
  Sponge: $5.60/SY (70% M and 30% L) Variation ±10%
  Jute: −10%
  Urethane: −25%
Carpet
  Acrylic, 24 oz, medium traffic: $20.50/SY
  **   28 oz, medium/heavy traffic: $25.50/SY**
Residential
  Nylon, 15 oz, light traffic: $15.25/SY
  **   28 oz, medium traffic: $18.00/SY**
Commercial
  Nylon, 28 oz, medium traffic: $19.00/SY
  **   35 oz, heavy traffic: $22.35/SY**
  Wool, 30 oz, medium traffic: $30.00/SY
  **   42 oz, heavy traffic: $41.00/SY**
Carpet tile: $2.50 to $5.00/SY

CARPET TYPES

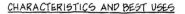

TYPE OF WEAVE   CHARACTERISTICS AND BEST USES

LEVEL LOOP : EVEN HEIGHT, TIGHTLY SPACED UN-CUT LOOPS. TEXTURE IS HARD AND PEBBLY. HARD WEARING AND EASY TO CLEAN. IDEAL FOR OFFICES AND HIGH TRAFFIC AREAS.

MULTI-LEVEL LOOP : UNEVEN HEIGHT IN PATTERNS, TIGHTLY SPACED UNCUT LOOPS. TEXTURE IS HARD & PEBBLY. HARD-WEARING & EASY TO CLEAN. IDEAL FOR OFFICES AND HIGH TRAFFIC AREAS.

PLUSH 'CUT' PILE : EVENLY CUT YARNS WITH MINIMAL TWIST. EXTREMELY SOFT, VELVETY TEXTURE. VACUUMING AND FOOTPRINTS APPEAR AS DIFFERENT COLORS, DEPENDING ON LIGHT CONDITIONS. IDEAL FOR FORMAL ROOMS W/ LIGHT TRAFFIC.

FRIEZE 'CUT' PILE : EVENLY CUT YARNS WITH TIGHT TWIST. EXTREMELY SOFT, VELVETY TEXTURE. VACUUMING AND FOOTPRINTS AP-PEAR AS DIFFERENT COLORS, DEPENDING ON LIGHT CONDITIONS. IDEAL FOR FORMAL RM'S WITH LIGHT TRAFFIC.

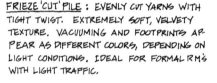

CUT AND LOOP : COMBINATION OF BOTH PLUSH AND LEVEL-LOOP. HIDES DIRT FAIRLY WELL. IDEAL FOR RESIDENTIAL APPLICATIONS.

INDOOR-OUTDOOR : CUT, TIGHTLY TWISTED YARNS THAT TWIST UPON THEMSELVES. TEXT-URE IS ROUGH. HIDES DIRT EXTREMELY WELL AND IS NEARLY AS TOUGH AS LEVEL-LOOP. IDEAL FOR RESIDENTIAL APPLICATIONS.

___ J. PAINT AND COATINGS ⑫ ㊺

___ 1. General
    ___ a. *Paints and coatings* are liquids (the "vehicle") with pigments in suspension, that are applied to building surfaces to protect and decorate them.
    ___ b. *Applications:* brushed, rolled, sprayed
    ___ c. *Failures:* 90% are due to either moisture problems or inadequate preparation of surface.
    ___ d. *Surface preparation:*
        ___ (1) Wood: Sand if required; paint immediately.
        ___ (2) Drywall: Let dry (0 to 7 days). If textured surface is required, prime prior to texturing.
        ___ (3) Masonry and stucco: Wait for cure (28 days).
    ___ e. *Qualities:*
        ___ (1) Thickness
            ___ (a) Primers (and "undercoats"): ½ to 1 dry mills/coat.
            ___ (b) Finish coats: 1 to 1½ dry mills/coat.
        ___ (2) Breathability: Allowing vapor passage to avoid deterioration of substrate and coating. Required at (see p. 256):
            ___ (a) Masonry and stucco: 25 perms
            ___ (b) Wood: 15 perms
            ___ (c) Metals: 0 perms
    ___ f. *Paint surfaces:*
        ___ (1) Flat: Softens and distributes illumination evenly. Reduces visibility of substrate defects. Not easily cleaned. Usually used on ceilings.
        ___ (2) Eggshell: Provides most of the advantages of gloss without its glare.
        ___ (3) Semigloss
        ___ (4) Gloss: Reflects and can cause glare, but also provides smooth, easily cleanable, nonabsorbtive surface. Increases visibility of substrate defects.
    ___ g. *Legal restrictions:*
        ___ (1) Check state regulations on paints for use of volatile organic compounds (VOC), use of solvents, and hazardous waste problems.
        ___ (2) Check fire department restrictions on spraying interiors after occupancy or during remodelling.

___ 2. <u>Material Types</u>

   ___ *a.* Water-repellent preservatives: For wood.

   ___ *b.* Stains: Solid (opaque), semitransparent, or clear.

   ___ *c.* Wood coatings: Varnish, shellac, lacquers.

   ___ *d.* Wood primer-sealer: Designed to prevent bleeding through of wood resin contained in knots and pitch pockets, and to seal surface for other coatings. Usually apply 2 coats to knots. Since primer-sealer is white, cannot be used on clear finishes.

   ___ *e.* Latex primer: Best first coat over wallboard, plaster, and concrete. Adheres well to any surface except untreated wood.

   ___ *f.* Alkyd primer: Used on raw wood. Latex "undercoats" can also be used.

   ___ *g.* CMU filler: A special latex primer for reducing voids and to smooth surface on masonry. Does not waterproof.

   ___ *h.* Latex paint: A synthetic, water-based coating, this is the most popular paint because it complies with most environmental requirements, is breathable, and cleans up with water. Use for almost all surfaces including primed (or undercoated) wood. Adheres to latex and flat oils. Avoid gloss oils and alkyds other than primers. Subdivided, as follows:

      ___ (1) Polyvinyl acetate (PVA): Most commonly used. Provides 25+ perms.

      ___ (2) Acrylic: Smoother, more elastic, more durable, often used as a primer. Provides less than 5 perms.

   ___ *i.* Alkyd paint: A synthetic semisolvent-based coating, replacing the old oils. This seems to be going out of use due to environmental laws. Used for exterior metal surfaces. Not breathable.

___ 3. <u>Paint Systems</u> and **Costs (30% M and 70% L):**

Material	Finish	Prime	Top coats	**Costs**
Preparation (sanding, etc., if required)				**$0.10/SF up to $5/SF**
		Exterior		
Wood				
General	gloss	alkyd *	ext. alkyd enamel	**$0.60/SF**
	flat	(same)	ext. alkyd or latex	
	stain		semitrans. or solid	
Floors				
Clear	gloss		alkyd enamel or latex acrylic	**$0.60/SF**
Redw'd.	stain		semitrans. alkyd	
Doors				**$1.00 to**
Windows				**2.00/SF**
Masonry, concrete, and stucco				
	clear	prime sealer or CMU filler	water-repellent	**$0.70/SF**
	flat	(same)	exterior latex	
Metals	gloss	galv. iron: zinc oxide steel: zinc chromate	ext. alkyd enamel	**$0.40/SF**
	flat	(same)	ext. latex acrylic	**(same)**
		Interiors		
Wood				
General	gloss	enamel undercoat	alkyd enamel or latex enamel	**$0.25 to $0.70/SF**
	flat	(same)	(same)	
Floors	gloss	stain, if req'd.	alkyd floor enamel	**(same)**
	clear	(same)	alkyd base varnish	**(same)**
Plaster/drywall				
	gloss	latex	latex	
	flat	latex	latex	
Brick		latex	latex	**(same)**
CMU		CMU filler	latex	**(same)**
Metals	gloss	see exterior	epoxy or alkyd enamel	**(same)**
	flat		alkyd or latex	

*or latex "undercoat"

__ K. WALL COVERINGS

__ 1. <u>Wallpaper</u>
    __ a. *General*
        Comes in many different patterns and colors at usually moderate cost, but is often subject to soiling, abrasion, and fading.
    __ b. *Types:*
        __ (1) Prepasted or unpasted
        __ (2) Trimmed or untrimmed
        __ (3) Washable and scrubbable
        __ (4) Lining (used for foils)
        __ (5) Strippable (paste stays on wall when paper is stripped off wall).
    __ c. *Patterns*
        __ (1) Repeat (one pattern per roll)
        __ (2) Random patterns
        __ (3) Straight match (i.e., plaids)
        __ (4) Drop-match (repeat every other roll)
    __ d. Allow a 20% margin for waste.
    __ e. Other finishes include vinyl, foils, fabrics, felts, and wood veneers.
__ 2. **Costs: Regular wallpaper: $0.75 to $1.00/SF (50% M and 50% L)**
    Grass cloths: $1.35 to $2.85/SF
    Flexible wood veneer: $4.75 to $5.75/SF
    Vinyl: $1.00 to $2.00/SF
    Aluminum Foil: $2.00/SF

NOTES

10 SPECIALTIES

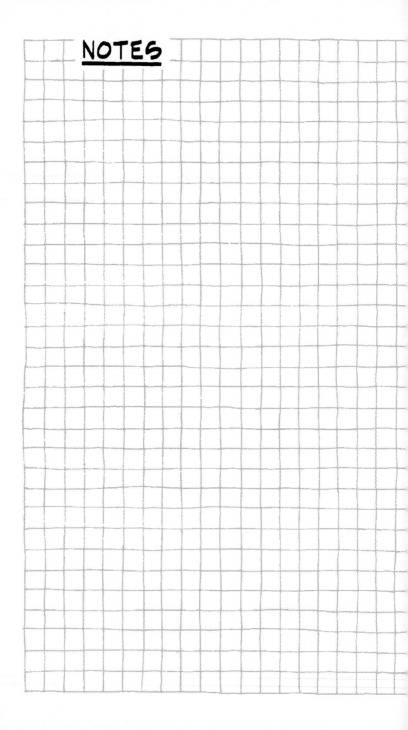

NOTES

__ A. VISUAL DISPLAY BOARDS (4) (40)

___ 1. Chalkboards
   ___ *a.* *Type*
      Porcelain enamel standard, painted on composition or natural slate of different core construction (except slate).
   ___ *b.* *Sizes*
      Thickness: $\frac{1}{32}$ to $\frac{3}{8}''$. $4' \times 12'$ typical dimensions.
      Costs: Wall hung, aluminum frame w/ chalk trough, $4' \times 12'$: $500 (95% M and 5% L).
___ 2. Bulletin or Tackboards
   ___ *a.* *Type*
      Cork or fiberboard (vinyl- or burlap-covered)
   ___ *b.* *Sizes*
      Thickness: $\frac{1}{8}$ to $\frac{1}{2}''$. Height: 4'. Lengths: 8', 12', 14', 16'+
      Costs: Cork, unframed, $\frac{1}{2}''$ thick: $5.60/SF (65% M and 35% L).

__ B. TOILET PARTITIONS ④

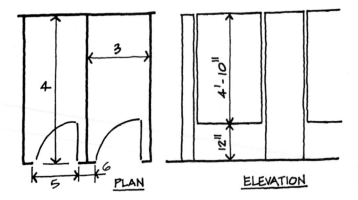

PLAN   ELEVATION

___ 1. <u>Types:</u>
    ___ *a.* Floor mounted (with pilasters, as shown).
    ___ *b.* Wall-hung (must provide supports in wall).
    ___ *c.* Ceiling-hung (must provide supports above ceiling).

___ 2. <u>Finishes:</u>
    Baked enamel, porcelain enamel, plastic laminate, stainless steel, marble (not wall-hung).

___ 3. <u>Typical Widths:</u> 2′6″, 2′8″, 2′10″ (most-used), and 3′0″

___ 4. <u>Typical Depths:</u>
    ___ *a.* Open front: 2′6″ to 4′0″
    ___ *b.* Closed front (door): 4′6″ to 4′9″

___ 5. <u>Typical Doors:</u> 1′8″, 1′10″, 2′0″, 2′4″, and 2′6″

___ 6. <u>Typical Pilasters:</u> 3, 4, 5, 6, 8, or 10 inches

___ 7. For HC-accessible, see pp. 87–89.

Costs:	**Painted metal**	**(75 to 85% M)**
		(plastic lam.: +25 to 35%)
		(stainless steel: +100 to 160%)
		(marble: +130 to 190%)
Floor-mounted:		$480/stall
Wall-hung:		$580/stall
Ceiling-hung:		$585/stall
For HC stall w/ grab bars:		add +$270/stall
For urinal screen:		$275/screen

___ C. CORNER GUARDS (4)

___ 1. Range from 3″ or 4″ angles cast into concrete or masonry (usually for exteriors) to ½″ clear plastic on interior wood finishes. A typical interior application in a utilitarian space with high traffic (such as a commercial kitchen) might be a surface applied 3″ × 3″ × 3′ high stainless steel angle.

___ 2. **Costs:**
Stainless steel, 16 ga., 3½″ angle: $25/LF
Clear plastic, 2½″ angle: $10/LF

___ 1. Used in offices, hospitals, laboratories, open area schools, computer rooms, telecommunications centers, and so forth. They provide mechanical and electrical accessibility and flexibility in placing desks, computers, telephone services, machines, and general office equipment.

___ 2. Types are steel, aluminum, steel or aluminum encasing wood or cementous fill or lightweight concrete. Top surface is usually carpet or vinyl.

___ 3. Sizes are usually 2' × 2' with 1½" thickness. Clearance below is usually 4 to 12".

___ 4. Be sure to check for added ceiling height required and floor-mounted equipment weight.

___ 5. **Costs: 24" square steel panels w/carpet: $13.50 (80% M and 20% L)**

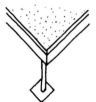

__ E. FIREPLACES (4)

___ 1. Typical Opening Sizes (see drawings below):

W	H	D	S
2′	1.5′ to 1.75′	1.33′ to 1.5′	
3′	2′	1.67′	6½″
4′	2.12′	1.75′	6″
5′	2.5′ to 2.75′	2′ to 2.17′	9″
6′	2.75′ to 3′	2.17′ to 2.33′	9″

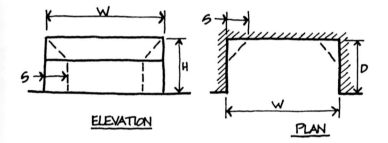

ELEVATION   PLAN

___ 2. For energy conservation, provide:
  ___ *a.* Outside combustion air ducted to firebox
  ___ *b.* Glass doors
  ___ *c.* Blower
___ 3. Per UBC:
  ___ *a.* Hearth extension to front must be 16″ (or 20″ if opening greater than 6 SF).
  ___ *b.* Hearth extension to side must be 8″ (or 12″ if opening greater than 6 SF).
  ___ *c.* Thickness of wall of firebox must be 10″ brick (or 8″ firebrick).
  ___ *d.* Top of chimney must be 2′ above any roof element within 10′.

Costs: Fabricated metal: $500 to $1500 (75% M and 25% L)
Masonry: $3000 to $6000

__ F. GRAPHICS (4)

__ 1. <u>General:</u>
Visual identification and direction by signage is very important for "wayfinding" to, between, around, in, and through buildings. Signage is enhanced by:

 __ *a.* Size
 __ *b.* Contrast
 __ *c.* Design of letter character and graphics.

__ 2. <u>Building Signage</u>
 __ *a.* Site directional/warning signs should be:
  __ (1) 6' from curb
  __ (2) 7' from grade to bottom
  __ (3) 100'–200' from intersections
  __ (4) 1 to 2.5 FT SQ
 __ *b.* Effective pedestrian viewing distance 20 to 155'
 __ *c.* Effective sign size: ≈10'/inch height (10' max. viewing distance per inch of height of sign).
 __ *d.* Effective letter size: ≈50'/inch of height.
 __ *e.* As a rule, letters should constitute about 40% of sign and should not exceed 30 letters in width.
 __ *f.* Materials
  __ (1) Exterior
   __ (*a*) Building: fabricated aluminum, illuminated plastic face, back-lighted, cast aluminum, applied letter, die-raised, engraved, and hot-stamped.
   __ (*b*) Plaque and sign: cast bronze or aluminum, plastic/acrylic, stone, masonry, and wood.
  __ (2) Interior
   __ (*a*) Permanent mounting: vinyl tape/adhesive backing, silastic adhesive, or mechanical attachment.
   __ (*b*) Semipermanent: vinyl tape square on inserts.
   __ (*c*) Changeable: dual-lock mating fasteners, magnets, magnetic tape or tracks.

___ *g.* Mounting heights

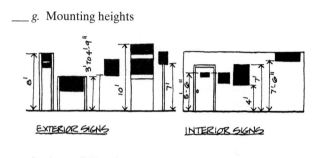

EXTERIOR SIGNS   INTERIOR SIGNS

___ *h.* Accessibility signage per ADA required at:
    ___ (1) Accessible parking.
    ___ (2) Building entries (when accessible, not required when all are).
    ___ (3) Accessible facilities, such as at rest rooms (when accessible, not required when all are).

Costs:

___ **Exterior building, I.D., backlighted, with ind. letters**	**$5000 to $9000 (same)**
___ **Plaques, cast alum. or bronze**	**$300 to $600 (85% M and 15% L)**
___ **Plastic, Bakelite**	**$50 to $150/SF (40% M and 60% L)**
___ **Neon, small size**	**$2000 to $4000 (same as above)**
___ **Exit, electrical**	**$200 (45% M and 55% L)**
___ **Metal letters**	**$40 to $75/ea. (60% M and 40% L)**
___ **Plexiglass**	**$85 to $100/SF (95% M and 5% L)**
___ **Vinyl**	**$20 to $30/SF (75% M and 25% L)**

___ 1. <u>Types:</u> Steel, plastic laminate, wood.
___ 2. <u>Sizes:</u>
    ___ a. Heights: 60 to 72″
    ___ b. Depths: 12″, 15″, 18″, and 21″
    ___ c. Widths: 9″, 12″, 15″, 18″ and 24″
___ 3. **Costs: Steel box locker, 12″ × 15″ × 72″: $165/ea. (80% M and 20% L)**

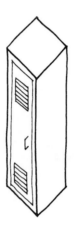

__ 1. <u>Class of Fire</u>
  __ a. Class A: Fires of wood, paper, textile, or rubbish. Locate extinguisher within 75′ travel distance.
  __ b. Class B: Fires of gasoline, oil, grease, or fat. Locate extinguisher within 30 to 50′ travel distance.
  __ c. Class C: Fires of an electrical nature.
__ 2. <u>Occupancy Class Requirements</u>
  __ a. *Light hazard:*
      __ (1) Occupancy: Schools, offices, and public buildings
      __ (2) Number: One class A extinguisher per 3000 SF
  __ b. *Ordinary hazard:*
      __ (1) Occupancy: Dry goods shop, warehouse.
      __ (2) Number: One class A extinguisher per 1500 SF.
  __ c. *Extra hazard:*
      __ (1) Occupancy: Paint shops, etc.
      __ (2) Number: One class A extinguisher per 1000 SF.
__ 3. See local fire dept. for exact requirements.
__ 4. Also see page 383 for cabinets.
  Costs: ABC all-purpose portable:
  2½ lbs: $30/ea
  20 lbs: $95/ea
  Cabinets: $150 to $200/ea.

___ 1. <u>Types</u>

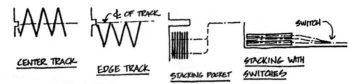

___ 2. <u>Data</u>
 ___ (1) Stack widths:
  ___ (*a*) Accordion: 5 to 12″
  ___ (*b*) Panels: 15 to 17″
 ___ (2) Stack depths: Usually ⅙ to ⅛ of opened width.
 ___ (3) Panels usually 48″ wide.
 ___ (4) Acoustic: STC 43 to 54 available.
 ___ (5) Flame spread: Class I available.

Costs:

**Folding, acoustical, vinyl, wood-framed: $55 to $75/SF
(70% M and 30% L) Variation: −35 to +50%.
Accordion, vinyl-faced: $15 to $40/SF. Variation: ±20%**

__ J. BATHROOM ACCESSORIES

Costs given are for average quality. For better finishes (i.e., brass), add 75 to 100%:

Mirrors: $30/SF (90% M and 10% L). Variation of ±25%.

Misc. small items (holders, hooks, etc.): $15 to $30/ea. (double, if recessed).

Bars

Grab: $30 to $35/ea.

Towel: $15 to $25/ea.

Medicine cabinets: $60 to $300/ea.

Tissue dispensers: $30 to $60/ea.

Towel dispensers: $120/ea. (increase by 2½ times if waste receptacle included).

___ 1. Solid metal (industrial), typical.
    ___ a. Widths: 24″ to 48″ in 6″ increments.
    ___ b. Depths: 9″ to 18″ in 3″ increments. 24″ to 36″ in 6″ increments.
    ___ c. Heights: 3′–3″, 6′–3″, 7′–3″, 8′–3″, and 10′–3″.
    ___ d. Shelves can be adjusted in 1″ increments.
___ 2. Shelving comes in other sizes than those above. Other types include wire, wood, etc. (prefabricated or built in).

Costs: Metal industrial shelving, 4′W × 12″D: $8.50/SF shelf.

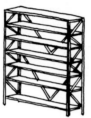

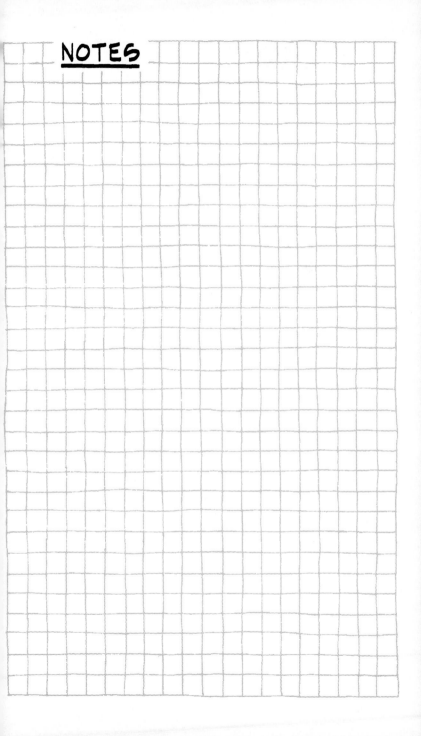

NOTES

NOTES

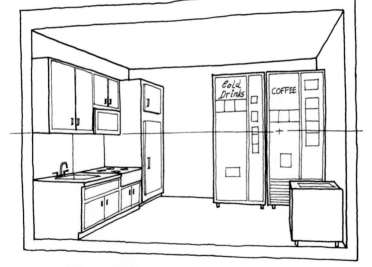

 **EQUIPMENT**

NOTES

__ A. CENTRAL VACUUM CLEANING

Costs: $1000 for first 1200 SF installed and $0.15 for each SF added.

__ B. SAFES

Costs: Office, 4-hour, 1.5′ × 1.5′ × 1.5′ = $3500
Jeweler's, 36″ × 25″ × 18″ = $20,900

__ C. CHURCH (TYPICAL SIZES)

__ 1. <u>Pews</u>
Allow minimum of 18″ per person, with each pew no longer than 21′.
Costs: $70 to $110/LF
__ 2. <u>Pulpits</u>
2′ square, movable
5′ square, fixed
Costs: $1000 to $7500
__ 3. <u>Altar</u>
Costs: $1500 to $9000
__ 4. <u>Communion Table</u>
3′ × 7′
__ 5. <u>Baptismal Font</u>
2′ × 2′
Costs: $2500 to $4500

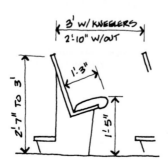

___ D. LIBRARY

___ 1. Stacks
For general sizing of stack area, plan on 16 books per SF. Allow 3′ to 4.5′ aisles between stacks. Shelves are 12 to 14″ vertically. Shelving units can be steel or wood. Typical depths are 8″, 10″, and 12″. Double for 2 sides. Typical heights of units are 42″, 60″, 82″, and 90″. Typical widths are 3′. Track shelving can save up to 45% space.
Costs: Metal, double-face, 10″ shelf × 90″ high: $125/LF

___ 2. Study Carrels
Plan on 2′ D × 3′ W × 4′ H for each carrel seating space.
Costs: Carrel, hardwood: $650 to $850
Add for wood chair: $100

___ E. THEATER STAGE EQUIPMENT

Costs: Total stage equipment: $85 to $450/SF of stage
Audience Seating: $125 to $285/seat

___ F. BARBER EQUIPMENT

Costs: $2500 to $5250/chair

___ G. CASH REGISTER/CHECKOUT STATIONS

Costs: Supermarket, single conveyor: $2200
Restaurant or store register: $550 to $2500

__ H. LAUNDRY ROOM EQUIPMENT

___ 1. <u>Residential</u>

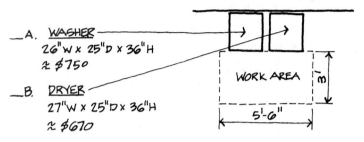

___ A. WASHER
26"W x 25"D x 36"H
≈ $750

___ B. DRYER
27"W x 25"D x 36"H
≈ $670

WORK AREA

3'

5'-6"

___ 2. <u>Commercial</u>

    ___ *a.* For general planning a coin-operated laundry of about 700 SF will have 14 washers and 9 tumblers (dryers) with folding tables, seating, and vending machines.

    ___ b. Coin-operated washers' sizes vary from 20 lb = 28″ W and 30″ D to 50–60 lb = 40″ W and 40″ D. Typical height 44″. Allow 18″ clearance at sides, 24″ behind, and 48″ in front.

    ___ c. Coin-operated dryers' sizes vary from 30 lb = 31″ W and 44″ D to 200 lb = 72″ W and 54″ D. Allow 24″ behind & 48″ in front.

    ___ d. Both washers and dryers need 2′ behind for drainage trough and venting.

    ___ e. Commercial laundries must be accessible per ADA by using a front-loaded machine.

    Costs: Commercial dryer, coin-operated dryer: $2550/ea.

    Washer: $1125/ea.

___ I. PROJECTION SCREENS

Costs:
Wall or ceiling hung: $7.50 to $11.50/SF

___ J. FOOD SERVICE EQUIPMENT

Costs:
Restaurants: $76.50 to $125/SF kitchen area
Office buildings: $61.50 to $100/SF kitchen area
Hospitals: $80 to $135/SF kitchen area

___ K. RESIDENTIAL KITCHEN EQUIPMENT

Costs:
Refrigerator, 33″ W × 32″ D × 66″ H: $700 to $2000
Dishwasher, 23″ W × 24″ D × 33″ H: $500 to $750
Sink: $400 to $600
Range/Oven, 36″ W × 27″ D × 36″ H: $1000 to $2500
Wall oven (microwave), 25″ W × 22″ D × 18″ H: $320 to $620

___ L. VENDING MACHINES

___ 1. <u>Typical Types and Sizes</u> (in inches)

Type	W	D	H
Money	12	18	38
Candy	34	28	72
Cold Drinks	37	26	72
Hot Drinks	38	33	72
Refer Food	41	36	72
Microwave	22	13	12

___ 2. A.D.A. prefers (does not require) the reach heights shown above for accessibility.

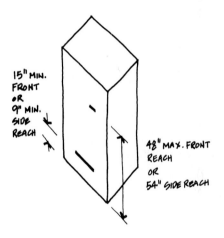

15" MIN.
FRONT
OR
9" MIN.
SIDE
REACH

48" MAX. FRONT
REACH
OR
54" SIDE REACH

NOTES

12 INTERIOR
FURNISHINGS

NOTES

__ A. GENERAL COSTS (4) (20)

Costs for furniture and interior objects will vary more than any other item for buildings. These can vary as much as −75% to +500% (or more). Costs given in this part are a reasonable middle value and are "list" prices. See p. 5 for discounting.

__ B. FABRICS

___1. <u>Association of Contract Textiles (ACT) Recommendations</u>
Check for following:

___ *a.* Flammability
Upholstery must pass CAL 117.
Drapery must pass NFPA 701.
Wall covering must pass ASTM
E-84.

___ *b.* Abrasion resistance

a	A	Test
15,000 double rubs	30,000 double rubs 40,000	Wyzenbeek Martindale

___ *c.* Colorfastness to light
Must pass Class 4 (40 to 60 hours
exposure for UV).

___ *d.* Colorfastness to wet and dry
crocking (Pigment colorfastness
in fabric).

   ___ *e.* Miscellaneous other physical properties
       ___ (1) Brush pill test: measures
               tendency for ends of a
               fiber to mat into fuzz balls.
       ___ (2) Yard/seam slippage test:
               establishes fabric's likeliness
               to pull apart at seams. Must pass 25 lbs for
               upholstery and 15 lbs on drapery.
       ___ (3) Breaking/tensile strength test: evaluates
               fabric's breaking or tearing. Must pass:

Upholstery	50 lbs
Panel fabrics	35 lbs
Drapery over 6 oz	25 lbs
under 6 oz	15 lbs

___ 2. **Costs:**
    Upholstery Fabrics

Blends:	**$15 to $75/SY**
Nylons:	**$20 to $50/SY**
Polyester:	**$35 to $45/SY**
Silk:	**$45 to $75/SY**
Wool:	**$30 to $80/SY**
Vinyl:	**$15 to $25/SY**

Add $5/SY for flameproofing.

___ C. ARTWORK AND ACCESSORIES

___ 1. <u>Artwork</u> (photos, reproductions, etc.)
    Costs: $45 to $750/ea.
___ 2. <u>Ash Urns and Trash Receptacles</u>
    Costs: $90 to $290/ea.

___ D. MANUFACTURED CASE WORK

See p. 246.

___ E. WINDOW TREATMENTS

___ 1. Draperies
- ___ *a.* Any fabric hung at windows in straight, loose folds. Usually of heavy fabric. Drawn from one or two sides.
- ___ *b.* Should be hung 2″ to 4″ from glass and slightly off floor.
- ___ *c.* Fullness is the amount of material for folds:
  100% = 2 times window width
  200% = 3 times window width
- ___ *d.* Linings are used behind, for black out and to lessen heat flow at window.
- ___ *e.* **Costs: $20 to $105/SY**

___ 2. Shades
- ___ a. Operate from top down in rolling mechanism. Shade material may be translucent or opaque. Shades reduce light while providing privacy. May be of fabric, vinyl, bamboo, or woven wood.
- ___ b. **Costs: $2 to $20/SF**

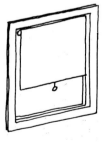

___ 3. <u>Blinds</u>
  ___ *a.* Are of slats that are stacked when gathered. Materials can be metal, vinyl, or fabric on vinyl.
  ___ *b.* Horizontal are usually 1″ to 2″ wide and curved for better light reflectance.
  ___ *c.* Vertical are usually 3″ up to 7″ wide and are straight.
  ___ *d.* **Costs: $4.20 to $6.70/SF**

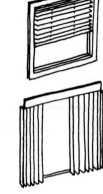

___ 4. <u>Curtains</u>
  ___ *a.* Are usually of a sheer fabric to let light in but keep privacy.

___ 5. <u>Shutters</u>
  ___ *a.* Are usually thin louvered wood doors with adjustable slats.

___ F. FURNITURE

See p. 331 for advice on furnishings costs. Costs given in this section are list price (retail), rounded, and approximate range depending on fabric options.

See p. 43 for space planning.

This section advises on different types of furnishings and their costs. This includes both residential and commercial furnishings. As shown in the Table of Contents, this section has 10 categories of furniture examples.

___ 1. <u>Site Furnishings</u>
See p. 201.
___ 2. <u>Lounge/Lobby/Living Room</u>

___ a. **General Average Costs**	**Residential**	**Commercial**
Lounge chair, 36″ × 36″:	$800	$900
Sofa, 36″ × 84″:	$2000–$3500	$3500
Coffee table, 30″ × 60″:	$500–$800	$450–$600

UPHOSTERED SOFA # 836-72
BY BAKER FURNITURE
COST: $4050 - $6460

UPHOSTERED CHAIR # 836-38 BY BAKER FURNITURE
COST: $2240 - $3580

UPHOSTERED CHAIR # 6453
BY BAKER FURNITURE
COST: $1940 - $2410

UPHOSTERED CHAIR # 6453
BY BAKER FURNITURE
COST: $1940 - $2410

LOUNGE CHAIR #2021
GREGSON DESIGN GROUP
COST: $1540

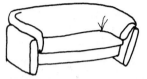

THREE SEAT SOFA #2023
GREGSON DESIGN GROUP
COST: $1890

CHAIR #260
"BLOOM" SERIES
BY BRAYTON
COST: $1560 - $2640

CHAIR #235
"BRAVO/OPEN"
BY BRAYTON
COST: $915 - $2190

TWO SEAT SOFA W/WOOD
ARMS, "STUDIO" #190·2
BY BRAYTON
COST: $2140 - $4375

BARCELONA CHAIR & STOOL
BY BRULTON
COST: $6800

STACK CHAIR #1230
KIRO SERIES BY
ARCADIA
COST: $325 - $400

STACK CHAIR W/ ARMS
KIRO SERIES BY
ARCADIA
COST: $340 - $425

ARM CHAIR #5171,
5100 SERIES BY HON
COST: $525 - $640

LOVESEAT #5172
5100 SERIES BY HON
COST: $700 - $850

COUCH #5173
5100 SERIES BY HON
COST: $930 - $1135

LOUNGE CHAIR # 6923
'KARRA' SERIES BY A.G.I.
COST: $1000 - $1980

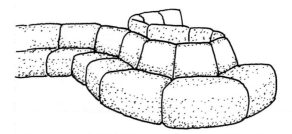

UPHOLSTERED CURVED RECEPTION SEATING
'LINN' SERIES BY ARGUST INC.   COST:
INSIDE SEGMENT   STRAIGHT SEGMENT
3051-20 FF : $945 - $1430   # 3001-FF : $ 775 -
                                                          $ 1180

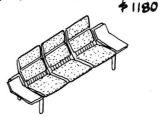

FREE STANDING UPHOLSTERED SEATING BY WILKHAHN
        2 SEAT UNIT   3 SEAT UNIT
762/62 : $4100 - $5110   # 763-62 : $5275 - $6725

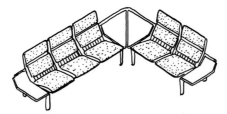

FREE STANDING UPHOLSTERED SEATING BY WILKHAHN
3 SEAT UNIT # 763/73 AND 2 SEAT UNIT # 762-95
COST : $ 11000 TO $14000

___ 3. <u>General Use</u>

PLASTIC STACK CHAIR
#7500 BY VIRCO
COST: $45 - $60

METAL FOLDING CHAIR
#162 BY VIRCO
COST: $15 - $20

ADJUSTABLE HEIGHT FOLDING
TABLE W/ P.L. TOP, 6000
SERIES BY VIRCO, 30"× 72"
COST: $160 - $205

PERFORATED STEEL SIDE
CHAIR, "ROMO" SERIES BY
FIXTURE FURNITURE
COST: $225

LIGHT WEIGHT BANQUET
TABLE, 60" DIA., METAL,
BY FIXTURE FURNITURE
COST: $495

UPHOLSTERED CHAIR W/ARMS,
"ROMO" SERIES BY FIXTURE
FURNITURE
COST: $250 - $410

___ 4. <u>Benches, Side Tables, Low Tables, Stools, Bookcases</u>

2 SEAT WOOD BENCH
"CHECKER" SERIES #10462
BY INTREX CORP.
COST: $1225

2 SEAT WOOD BENCH W/
CUSHION, "INTERJOIN" SERIES
BY INTREX CORP.
COST: $1850 - $2120

LAMINATE DRUM TABLE
"MONOFORMS" BY INTREX
COST: 15"D x 15"H = $300
         24"D x 24"H = $535

LAMINATE CUBE TABLE
"MONOFORMS" BY INTREX
COST: 18"x 18"x 15" = $375
         30"x 30"x 24" = $775

COCKTAIL TABLE #4353
BY BAKER FURNITURE
44"W 30"D 16"H
COST: $4545

COCKTAIL TABLE #4353
BY BAKER FURNITURE
45"W 28"D   16"H
COST: $1835

BARSTOOL #BS269
BY SHAFER (CHROME
OR BRASS)
COST: $190 - $215

BARSTOOL #BS287
BY SHAFER
COST: $190 - $220

WOOD BOOKSHELVES
BY NUCRAFT, RADIUS
#R-8412 & R-8412-A
COST: $3650 - $4015

WOOD BOOKSHELVES
BY NUCRAFT, SELF-EDGE
#SE-8424, SE 7224, SE 4224-A
COST: $6340 - $6970

___ 5. <u>Office</u>

TASK CHAIR, # 679
VAIL SERIES BY ARCADIA
COST : $600 - $825

LOW BACK, # 721
ELITE SERIES BY ARCADIA
COST : $875 - $1050

EXECUTIVE HIGH - BACK
UPHOLSTERED CHAIR
#6520, WOOD BY HON
COST: $830 - $1015

DESK, TRANSITIONAL WOOD,
97000 SERIES BY HON
COST : 60" x 30" = $1460
       72" x 36" = $1650
4' x 2' SIDE TABLE = $ 800

DESK, LAMINATE WOOD,
94000 SERIES BY HON
COST : $1160
SIDE TABLE : 4'x 2' = $680

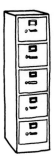

METAL VERTICAL FILE
5 DRAWER, 210 SERIES,
BY HON, 60" H
COST: LETTER W/LOCK 15"× 28"= $510
LEGAL   16"× = $610

METAL LATERAL FILE,
5 DRAWER, 67" H, 800
SERIES BY HON
COST: 30" W = $830
42" W = $1080

LAMINATE BOOKCASE, 6 SHELF
36" W × 11½" D × 84" H,
1890 SERIES BY HON
COST: $280

METAL STORAGE CABINET,
5 ADJUSTABLE SHELVES
BY HON, 36" W × 72" H
COST: 24" D $450
18" D $390

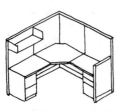

WORK STATION FOR
SECRETARY / WORD PROCESS-
ING, 6' × 6' × 64" HIGH
COST: $3225

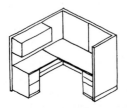

WORK STATION FOR SECRE-
TARY / CLERK.
6' × 6' × 64" HIGH
COST: $2930

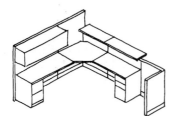

WORK STATION FOR
EXECUTIVE SECRETARY
8' × 9.5' × 64" HIGH
COST: $4175

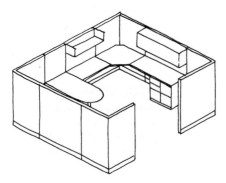

WORK STATION FOR
MANAGER
11.5' × 12.5' × 64" HIGH
COST: $6975

___ 6. <u>Dining/Conference</u>

ROUND, ANELLO TABLE
BY BRUETON
COST : 42" DIA. = $4500 - $6400
      60" DIA. = $7280 - $10940

SQUARE ANELLO TABLE
BY BRUETON
COST = 42" DIA = $4500 - $6440
      60" DIA = $7470 - $11130

RECTANGULAR ANELLO TABLE
BY BRUETON
COST : 36" x 72" = $6200 - $8830

BOAT SHAPED LAMINATE
CONFERENCE TABLE,
144" L x 48" W, 80000 SERIES
BY HON
COST : $880

BANQUET TABLE, # 421-312
TOWN & COUNTRY COLLECTIONS
45" W x 120" L
COST : $4520

GAMING TABLE, 421-311,
TOWN & COUNTRY COLLECTIONS
48" DIA.
COST : $1890

___ 7. <u>School Desks and Chairs</u>

FOLDING TABLET ARM
CHAIR, GROUP 2, BY
VERCO
COST: $50 - $65

FOLDING STOOL TABLES
W/ P.L. TOPS BY VERCO,
12 STOOLS. 27"OR 29"W × 12'L
COST: $1470 - $2016

ARM **ARMLESS** **TABLET**

UPHOLSTERD AND PERFORATED STEEL
STACK CHAIRS, "ROMO", BY FIXTURE FURN-
ITURE.
COST: ARM = $250 - $410/EA.
        ARMLESS = $200 - $435/EA.
        TABLET = $275 - $440/EA.

___ 8. <u>Bedroom</u>

___ **General Average Costs**	**Residential**	**Commercial**
Bed:	$500 to $1500	
Side table, 24″ × 30″:	$175–$350	$125
Writing table, 24″ × 48″:	$650	$400
Chest of drawers, 24″ × 72″:	$1500	$1000

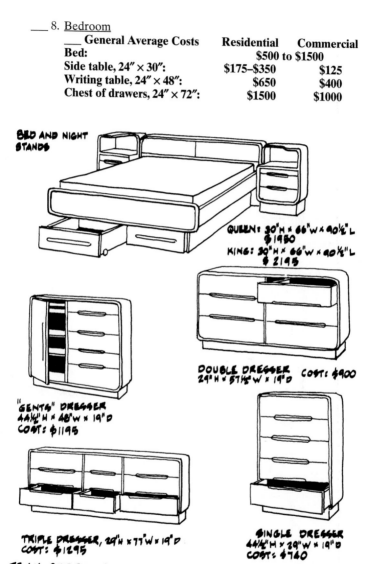

BED AND NIGHT STANDS

QUEEN: 30"H × 66"W × 90½"L
$1950

KING: 30"H × 66"W × 90½"L
$2195

"GENTS" DRESSER
44½"H × 48"W × 19"D
COST: $1195

DOUBLE DRESSER
29"H × 57½"W × 19"D   COST: $900

TRIPLE DRESSER, 29"H × 77"W × 19"D
COST: $1295

SINGLE DRESSER
44½"H × 29"W × 19"D
COST: $740

TEAK BEDROOM FURNITURE, 81 SERIES, BY SUN CABINETS

___ 9. <u>Lamps</u>
See p. 411 for Lighting.
Typical costs: Table lamp $250
Floor lamp $300

CIAO TABLE LAMP # T6
BY KOCH + LOWY
COST: $275 - $300

CYLINDER TABLE LAMP,
BRASS OR CHROME, #T245CI,
BY KOCH + LOWY
COST: $315 - $335

"DYNASTY" TORCH # F4026B
BY KOCH + LOWY
COST: $390 TO $490

"PHARMACY" FLOOR LAMP,
#F6040 BY KOCH + LOWY
COST: $145 - $160

RUSTED IRON DESK LAMP,
#2384-499, BY THE MONT-
CLAIR COLLECTION
COST: $275

HANDPAINTED PORCELAIN
TABLE LAMP, #2363-241 BY
THE MONTCLAIR COLLECTION
COST: $655

___ 10. <u>Other Average Costs</u>
     ___ a. Theater seating
         $120 to $225/seat
     ___ b. Church pews
         $70 to $110/LF
     ___ c. Dormitory furnishings
         $1900 to $3600/student
     ___ d. Hospital beds
         $825 to $1340/bed
     ___ e. Hotel furnishings
         $1500 to $7850/room
     ___ f. Multiple seating
         ___ (1) Classroom
             $65 to $120/seat
         ___ (2) Lecture hall
             $130 to $370/seat
         ___ (3) Auditorium
             $100 to $200/seat
     ___ g. Restaurants
         ___ (1) Tabletop and base (4 top)
             $150
         ___ (2) Tabletop and base (2 top)
             −25%
         ___ (3) Tabletop and base (6 top)
             +25%
         ___ (4) Chairs
             $150
         ___ (5) Booth
             $25/LF depth (table and base excluded)
         ___ (6) Banquette
             $13/LF length (table and chairs excluded)

NOTES

___ G. RUGS AND MATS

Also see p. 297 for carpet.

___ 1. <u>Oriental Rugs</u>

    ___ a. <u>*Age*</u>

        ___ (1) Antique: over 75 years old

        ___ (2) Semiantique: less than 75 years old

        ___ (3) New: 10 to 15 years old

    ___ b. <u>*Construction*</u>

        ___ (1) Kelims: Smooth on both sides

        ___ (2) Sumak: Woven into herringbone effect.

        ___ (3) Knotted: Pile on top and smooth on back.

    ___ c. <u>*Type*</u>

        ___ (1) Persian

            ___ (a) Motifs: curvilinear floral designs, vases, birds, etc. Medallion in center.

            ___ (b) Sizes: 10′ × 15′, 13′ × 24′

        ___ (2) Turkish

            ___ (a) Motifs: Prayer rugs, altar designs, tulips. Reds and greens.

            ___ (b) Sizes: 3′ × 5′, 5′ × 7′, 6′ × 10′

        ___ (3) Caucasian

            ___ (a) Motifs: geometric figures of men, birds, and animals. Dark reds.

            ___ (b) Sizes: 5′ × 7′, 6′ × 10′

        ___ (4) Turkoman

            ___ (a) Motifs: Rows of rectilinear octagons. Dark reddish browns.

            ___ (b) Sizes: 6′ × 10′, 15′ × 24′

        ___ (5) Chinese

            ___ (a) Motifs: Chinese symbols, cloud bands, flowers, birds.

            ___ (b) Sizes: 5′ × 8′, 9′ × 12′

        ___ (6) Other: Moroccan, Afghan, Pakistani, etc.

      ___ d. **Costs: New: $1000+**
               Antique: $100,000+
___ 2. <u>Entry Mats</u>
        Costs: Recessed, rubber, ⅜″ thick: $22.50/SF

___ **B. INTERIOR PLANTS**

___ 1. <u>Profiles of Common Interior Plants</u>

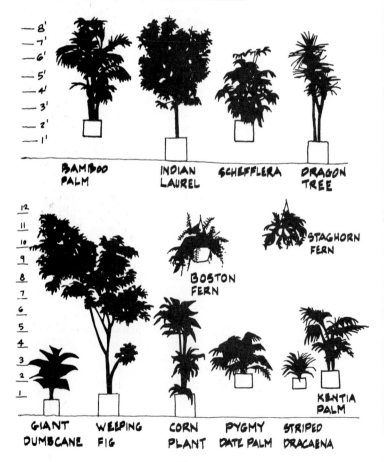

BAMBOO PALM   INDIAN LAUREL   SCHEFFLERA   DRAGON TREE

STAGHORN FERN

BOSTON FERN

KENTIA PALM

GIANT DUMBCANE   WEEPING FIG   CORN PLANT   PYGMY DATE PALM   STRIPED DRACAENA

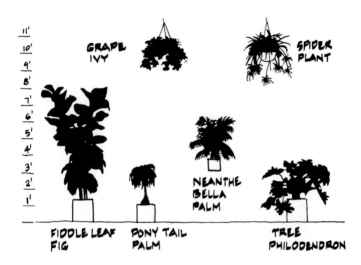

GRAPE IVY

SPIDER PLANT

NEANTHE BELLA PALM

FIDDLE LEAF FIG

PONY TAIL PALM

TREE PHILODENDRON

11'
10'
9'
8'
7'
6'
5'
4'
3'
2'
1'

___ 2. <u>Some Plants Requiring Low Light Levels:</u>

Common Name	Botanical Name
Cleveland Peace Lily	*Spathiphyllumx "Clevelandii"*
Corn Plant Dracaena	*Dracaena Fragrans "Massageana"*
Franscher Evergreen	*Aglaomema X Fransher*
Golden Evergreen	*Aglaomema "Pseudobracteatum"*
Janet Craig Dracaena	*D. Deremensis "Janet Craig"*
Malay Beauty Aglaomena	*A. "Malay Beauty"*
Mauna Loa Peace Lily	*Spathiphyllum X "Mauna Loa"*
Neanthe Bella Palm	*Chamaedorea Elegans "Bella"*
Parrot Jungle Evergreen	*Aglaonema "Parrot Jungle"*
Pewter Aglaonema	*A. "Malay Beauty"*
Silver King Evergreen	*Aglaonema X "Silver King"*
Silver Queen Evergreen	*A. X "Silver Queen"*
Snow Queen Evergreen	*A. X "Snow Queen"*
Striped Dracaena	*D. Deremensis "Warneckei"*
Variegated Chinese Evergreen	*Aglaonema Commutatum*
Warneck Dracaena	*D. Deremensis "Warneckei"*
White Rajah	*Aglaonema "Pseudobracteatum"*

___ 3. <u>Interior Plants Information</u>
    ___ a.   *Types:*
        ___ (1) Multistem tree
        ___ (2) Standard tree
        ___ (3) Plant clump
        ___ (4) Hanging plants
    ___ b.   *Needs:*
        ___ (1) Light: (Also see p. 411 on lighting)
            ___ (a) Need 10–12 hours on a regular daily basis, but some plants can survive on 2 hours per day.
            ___ (b) Should have 50 fc min. on ground plane or 75 fc min. on desk height.
            ___ (c) Light needs to be full-spectrum. Specify "U.V. full-spectrum" lighting.
        ___ (2) Water:
            ___ (a) Provide for regular watering by hand, hose, or drip. Provide water w/low concentrations of floride and chlorine, and PH value of 5 to 6.
            ___ (b) Provide proper drainage, even if it is necessary to connect into building's plumbing system with sump pumps or syphon tubes.
        ___ (3) Soil:
            Needs to be porous with 50% solids, 25% moisture, and 25% air.

___ 4. Costs:
    Live:
    5′ tree without pot = $50/ea.
    Bush: $25 to $50/ea.
    Table Top Plants: $10/ea.
    Hanging Plants: $10 to $25/ea.
    Artificial Silk: Double above costs.
    Pots: $5 to $25/ea.

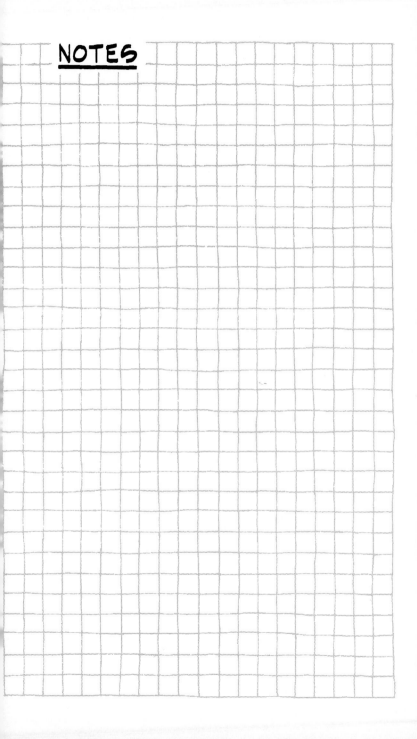

NOTES

NOTES

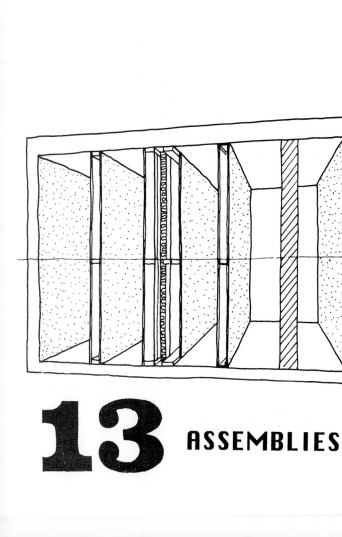

13 ASSEMBLIES

NOTES

A. INTERIOR WALL ASSEMBLIES

The following wall assemblies give:
___ Width
___ Sound transmission rating (STC). Also see p. 188.
___ Fire rating in hours resistance. Also see p. 152.
___ Costs
___ Finishes are *not* included

___ 1. Drywall Partitions
    ___ a. Wood frame:

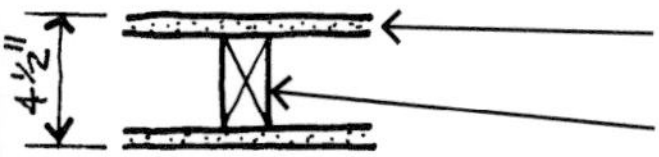

½″ gypsum board, each side 2 × 4 studs at 24″ OC	STC = 30 to 34 Fire rating = 0 hour **Cost: $2.75/SF**
⅝″ gypsum board, type X, each side 2 × 4 studs at 16″ OC	STC = 30 to 34 Fire rating = 1 hour **Cost: $3.00/SF**
⅝″ gypsum board, type X, each side ½″ wood fiber board, each side 2 × 4 studs at 16″ OC	STC = 45 to 49 Fire rating = 1 hour **Cost: $4.20/SF**
⅝″ gypsum board, type X, each side Resilient channel at 24″ OC, each side 2 × 4 studs at 16″ OC	STC = 45 to 49 Fire rating = 1 hour **Cost: $4.00/SF**
⅝″ gypsum board, both sides Resilient channel 1½″ sound insulation 2 × 4 studs at 16″ OC	STC = 50 to 54 Fire rating = 1 hour **Cost = $4.60/SF**
2 layers, ⅝″ type X gypsum board Resilient channel 2 × 4 studs at 16″ OC ⅝″ gypsum board ½″ gypsum board ⅜″ gypsum board	STC = 60 to 64 Fire rating = 1 hour **Cost = $5.70/SF**

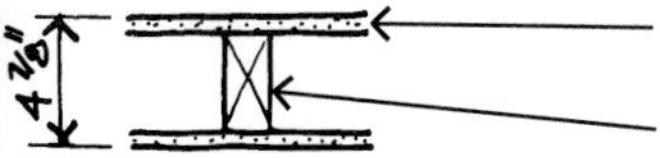

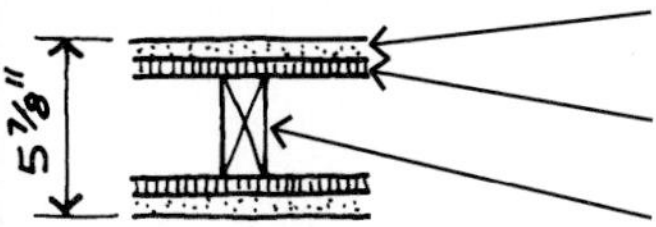

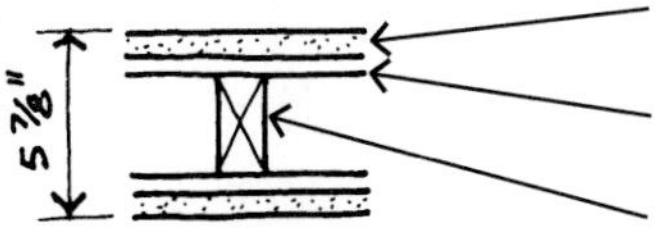

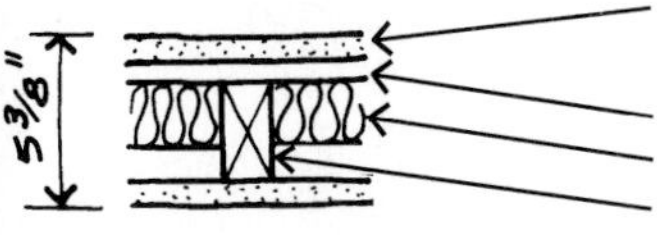

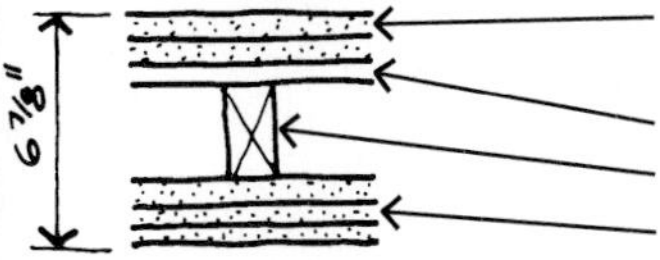

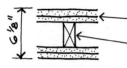

2 layers, ⅝″ gypsum
board, type X, each side
2 × 4 studs at 16″ OC

STC = 40 to 44
Fire rating = 2 hour
Cost = $4.20/SF

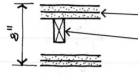

2 layers, ⅝″ gypsum
board, each side
2 × 4 studs at 16″ OC,
staggered

STC = 50 to 54
Fire rating = 2 hour
Cost = $4.50/SF

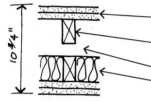

2 layers ⅝″ gypsum
board, each side
2 × 4 studs at 16″ OC,
each side
1″ air gap
3½″ sound insulation

STC = 55 to 59
Fire rating = 2 hour
Cost = $6.00/SF

___ b. <u>Metal frame:</u>

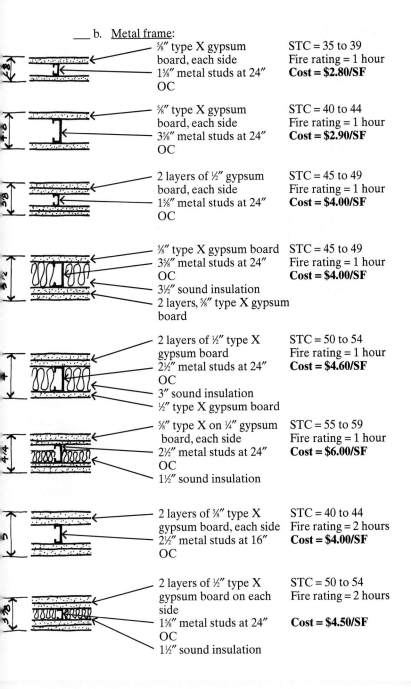

⅝″ type X gypsum
board, each side
1⅝″ metal studs at 24″
OC

STC = 35 to 39
Fire rating = 1 hour
Cost = $2.80/SF

⅝″ type X gypsum
board, each side
3⅝″ metal studs at 24″
OC

STC = 40 to 44
Fire rating = 1 hour
Cost = $2.90/SF

2 layers of ½″ gypsum
board, each side
1⅝″ metal studs at 24″
OC

STC = 45 to 49
Fire rating = 1 hour
Cost = $4.00/SF

⅝″ type X gypsum board
3⅝″ metal studs at 24″
OC
3½″ sound insulation
2 layers, ⅝″ type X gypsum
board

STC = 45 to 49
Fire rating = 1 hour
Cost = $4.00/SF

2 layers of ½″ type X
gypsum board
2½″ metal studs at 24″
OC
3″ sound insulation
½″ type X gypsum board

STC = 50 to 54
Fire rating = 1 hour
Cost = $4.60/SF

⅝″ type X on ¼″ gypsum
board, each side
2½″ metal studs at 24″
OC
1½″ sound insulation

STC = 55 to 59
Fire rating = 1 hour
Cost = $6.00/SF

2 layers of ⅝″ type X
gypsum board, each side
2½″ metal studs at 16″
OC

STC = 40 to 44
Fire rating = 2 hours
Cost = $4.00/SF

2 layers of ½″ type X
gypsum board on each
side
1⅝″ metal studs at 24″
OC
1½″ sound insulation

STC = 50 to 54
Fire rating = 2 hours

Cost = $4.50/SF

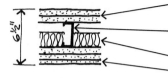

2 layers, type X gypsum board on each side
3⅝" metal studs at 24" OC
2" sound insulation
⅜" gypsum board

STC = 55 to 59
Fire rating = 2 hours
Cost = $5.20/SF

___ 2. <u>Masonry Walls</u>
    ___ *a.* Hollow concrete block (unfinished):

Width	STC	Fire rating	**Costs**
4"	37	1 hour	**$4.60/SF**
6"	42	1½ hour	**$5.00/SF**
8"	47	2 hours*	**$5.80/SF**

*3 to 4 hours if grouted solid

    ___ b. Common brick

Wythe	Width	STC	Fire rating	**Costs**
1	4"	41	1 hour	**$9.75/SF**
2	8"	49	3-4 hours	**$18.00/SF**

___ 3. <u>Glazed Wall</u> (¼" tempered glass)

	Costs
Anodized aluminum frame	**$30-$35/SF**
Wood oak frame	**$20-$25/SF**

CEILING SELECTION TABLE

ASSEMBLY	COST COMPARISON	WEIGHT (LBS/SF)	SOUND ABSORB.	SOUND TRANSM.	LATERAL LOAD	IMPACT	UPLIFT	DEFLECTION	HUMIDITY	FINISH PRE-	FINISH IN PLACE TEXT.	FINISH IN PLACE PAINT	NOTES
SUSP. ACOUSTIC TILE W/ EXPOSED GRID	1 TO 2	2 TO 3	G	F TO P	E TO P	P TO F	P TO G	G	P TO F	●			
SUSP. ACOUSTIC TILE W/ CONCEALED GRID	4 TO 5	→	→	→	F	P	G	→	P	●			
SUSP. PLASTER	3 TO 5	4 TO 5	P	G	P	→	→	F TO P	F TO P		●	●	
SUSP. GYPBOARD	2 TO 3	3 TO 4	→	→	G	→	→	→	G TO P		●	●	
ACOUSTIC TILE ATTACHED	4 TO 5	2 TO 3	G	G	N/A	→	N/A	N/A	P TO F			●*	* "NON-BRIDGING" PAINT
SPRAY ON	1 TO 2	.2 TO .3	→	→	→	→	→	→	P		●		

● DENOTES COMMON USAGE
P = POOR
F = FAIR
G = GOOD

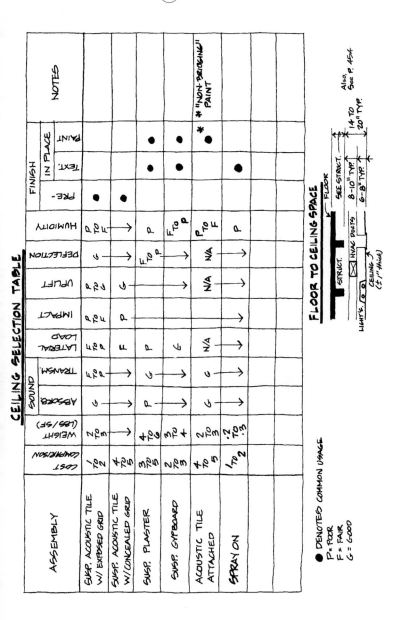

FLOOR TO CEILING SPACE

FLOOR
SEE STRUCT.
STRUCT.
HVAC DUCTS
14 TO 20" TYP.
8-10" TYP.
6-8" TYP.
LIGHT'G.
CEILING (± 1" thick)
Also, See P. 454

FLOORING SELECTION TABLE

TYPE	COST COMPARISON	WEIGHT (PSF)	COMFORT	MOISTURE DRY	MOISTURE OCC. WET	MOISTURE FREQ. WET	FOOT LOW	FOOT MOD	FOOT HIGH	WHEEL RUB.	WHEEL STEEL	IMPACT	CLEANING MILD	CLEANING HEAVY	LOCATION OUTSIDE	LOCATION BELOW GR.	LOCATION ON GRADE	LOCATION ABOVE GR.	SUBSTRATE WOOD	SUBSTRATE CONC.	SLIP RESIST.*	CONDUCTIVE	OTHER
STONE	.9 TO 3	15 TO 40	P	●	●	●	○	●	●	○		●	●	○	●	●	●	●		●	○		
BRICK	4 TO 9	20 TO 40	P	●	●	●	●	●	●	●		●	●	●	●	●	●	●	●	●	○		
CONCRETE	1.2 - 2.5	10 TO 75	P	●	●	●	●	●	●	●	○	●	●	●	●	●	●	●		●	●	○	
C.T.	2 - 4	4 - 6	P	●	●	●	●	●	●	○			●	●	●	●	●	●	●	●	●		
Q.T.	4 - 5.5	4 - 6	P	●	●	●	●	●	●	○		●	●	●	●	●	●	●	●	●	●	●	
RESILIENT	.6 - 2	1 - 2	G	●	●		●	●	●	●		●	●				●	●	●	●	●	●	
WOOD	3 - 5	1 - 10	F	●	●		●	●	●	●		○	●					●	●	●	●	○	
CARPET	1.5 - 5	.5 - 1	G	●			●	●	●			●	●				●	●	●	●	●	○	
EPOXY	3 - 5	3 - 7	F	●	●	●	●	●	●	●	●	●	●	●	●	●	●	●	●	●	●	●	

● DENOTES COMMON USAGE OR SUITABILITY

○ DENOTES POSSIBLE OR LIMITED USAGE OR SUITABILITY

* SLIP RESISTANCE

RECOMMENDATIONS FOR STATIC COEFFICIENT OF FRICTION :
NORMAL = 0.5 MIN. H.C. (ADA) = 0.6 MIN. RAMP = 0.8 MIN.

0.2 OR LESS IS VERY SLICK. 0.3 TO 0.4 IS SMOOTH. BROOM FINISH CONCRETE IS USUALLY 0.5 TO 0.7. GRIT STRIPES FOR STAIRS OR RAMPS ARE 0.8 OR ABOVE.

THE COEFFICIENT OF FRICTION IS THE RATIO OF HORIZONTAL FORCE TO VERTICAL FORCE. WAYES SHOULD MEET ASTM D-2047.

NOTES

NOTES

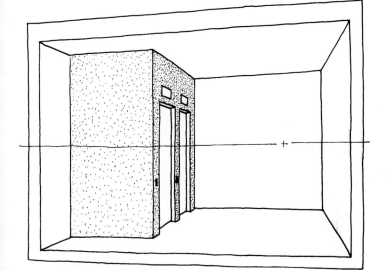

14 CONVEYING SYSTEMS

NOTES

A. ELEVATORS (10)

The interior designer is not likely to be involved in the design of elevators or escalators. Nevertheless, this section is included for background information.

___ 1. <u>Hydraulic Elevators</u>

Hydraulic elevators are the least expensive and slower type. They are moved up and down by a piston. This type is generally used in low-rise buildings (2 to 4 stories) in which it is not necessary to move large numbers of people quickly.

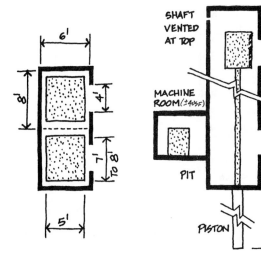

PLAN   SECTION

Costs:

Passenger elevators	**$46,300 (50 fpm, 2000 lbs) to $64,000 (150 fpm, 3000 lbs) per shaft. 3 stops, 3 openings. Add: stop = +$5300; 50 fpm/stop = +$3500; 500 lb/stop = +$3500; custom interior = +$5000.**
Hydraulic freight elevators	**$56,750 (50 fpm, 3000 lbs) to $86,100 (150 fpm, 6000 lbs).**

___ 2. <u>Traction Elevators</u>

Traction elevators hang on a counter-weighted cable and are driven by a traction machine that pulls the cable up and down. They operate smoothly at fast speeds and have no limits.

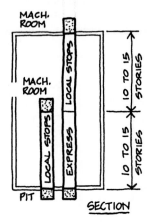

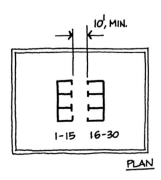

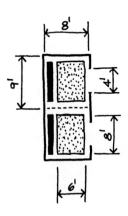

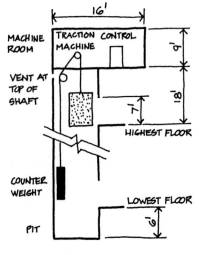

Costs:

Passenger elevators/shaft	**$64,280 (50 fpm, 2000 lbs) to $103,740 (300 fpm, 4000 lbs) for 6 stops, 6 openings. Add: stop = +$4000; 50 fpm/stop = +$2000; 500 lb/stop = +$2000; opening per stop = +$4500; custom interior = +$4800.**
Freight elevators (2 stops)/shaft	**$132,000 (50 fpm, 3500 lbs) to $139,400 (200 fpm, 5000 lbs).**

___ 3. <u>Elevator Rules of Thumb</u>

   ___ *a.* <u>*Commercial*</u>

      ___ (1) One passenger elevator for each 30,000 SF of net floor area.

      ___ (2) One service elevator for each 300,000 SF of net floor area.

      ___ (3) Lobby width of 10′ minimum.

      ___ (4) Banks of elevators should consist of 4 or fewer cars so that people can respond easily to the arrival of an elevator.

      ___ (5) In high buildings, the elevator system is broken down into zones serving groups of floors, typically 10 to 15 floors. Elevators that serve the upper zones express from the lobby to the beginning of the upper zone. The elevators that serve the lower zones terminate with a machine room above the highest floor served.

      ___ (6) Very tall buildings have sky lobbies served by express elevators. People arriving in the lobby take an express elevator to the appropriate sky lobby where they get off the express elevator and wait for the local elevator system.

      ___ (7) Lay out so that maximum walk to an elevator does not exceed 200′.

      ___ (8) Per ADA, accessible elevators *are required at shopping centers and offices of health care providers.* Elevators are *not* required in facilities that are less than 3 stories or less than 3000 SF per floor. But, if elevators are provided, at least one will be accessible (see p. 372).

   ___ b. *Residential*

      ___ (1) In hotels and large apartment buildings, plan on one elevator for every 70 to 100 units.

      ___ (2) In a 3- to 4-story building, it is possible to walk up if the elevator is broken, so one hydraulic elevator may be acceptable.

      ___ (3) In the 5- to 6-story range, two elevators are necessary. These will be either hydraulic (slow) or traction (better).

      ___ (4) In the 7- to 12-story range, two traction elevators are needed.

      ___ (5) Above 12 stories, two to three traction elevators are needed.

      ___ (6) Very tall buildings will require commercial-type applications.

      ___ (7) Plan adequate space and seating at lobby and hallways.

   ___ c. *ADA-accessible elevators* (see item 8, p. 371):

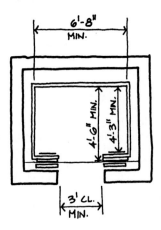
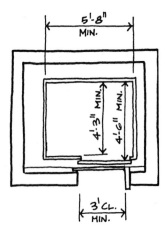

B. ESCALATORS

When the building design requires moving large numbers of people up and down a few floors, escalators are a good choice.

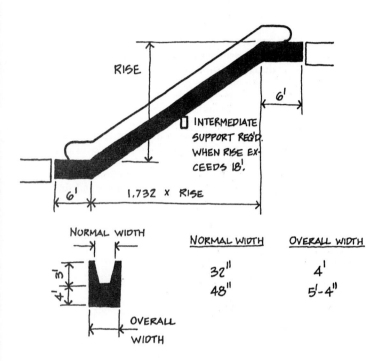

NORMAL WIDTH	OVERALL WIDTH
32"	4'
48"	5'-4"

Costs:
Escalator costs range from $88,800 for 12′ rise, 32″ width, to $139,500 for 25′ rise, 48″ width. For glass side enclosures add $11,500 to $13,500.

___ 1. <u>Escalator Rules of Thumb</u>
    ___ *a.* All escalators rise at a 30-degree angle.
    ___ *b.* There needs to be a minimum of 10′ clear at top and bottom landings.
    ___ *c.* Provide beams at top and bottom for the escalator's internal truss structure to sit on.
    ___ *d.* The escalator will require lighting that does not produce any distorting shadows that could cause safety problems.
    ___ *e.* Escalators need to be laid out with a crowded flow of people in mind. Crossover points where people will run into each other must be avoided.
    ___ *f.* Current trends in the design of retail space use the escalators as a dramatic and dynamic focal feature of open atrium spaces.
    ___ *g.* Because escalators create open holes through building floor assemblies, special smoke and fire protection provisions are necessary.

NOTES

NOTES

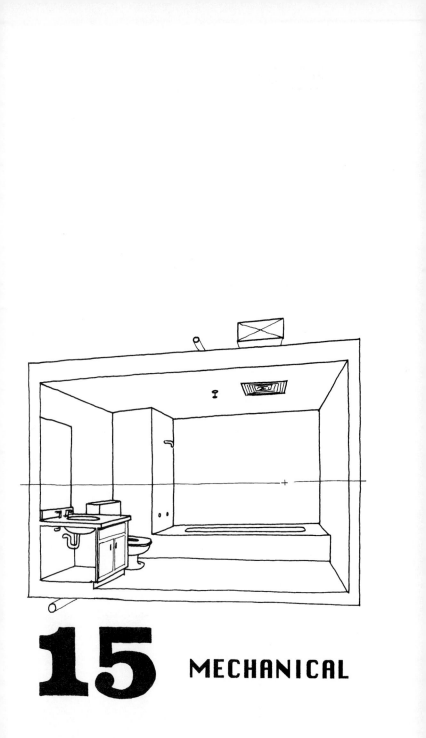

15 MECHANICAL

NOTES

___ A. THE PLUMBING SYSTEM

(1) (10) (25) (26)

The interior designer is not likely to be involved in plumbing design, except for fixture selection or maybe toilet room layout. Nevertheless, this section is included for background information.

Costs: **As a rough rule of thumb, estimate $800 to $1200/fixture (50% M and 50% L) for all plumbing within the building. Assume 30% for fixtures and 70% for lines. Also, of the lines, assume 40% for waste and 60% for supply. For more specifics on fixtures, only:**

| Fixture | Residential | | | Commercial |
	Low	Medium	High	
WC	$150	$500	$850	$100 to $300
Lavatories	$100	$150	$250	same
Tub/shower	$100	$400	$800	
Urinals				$250 to $600
Kitchen sinks	$150	$300	$450	

___ 1. <u>Water Supply</u>

    ___ *a.* The water supply is under pressure, so there is flexibility in layout of the water main to the building. In warm climates the *water meter* can be outside, but in cold climates it must be in a heated space. For small buildings allow a space of *20″ W × 12″ D × 10″ H.* After entering the building the water divides into a hot- and cold-water distribution system at the hot water heater. For small buildings allow for a *gas heater* a space *36″ dia. × 60″ H* and for *electric heaters, 24″ dia. × 53″ H.* Where bathrooms are spread far apart, consideration should be given to multiple hot water heaters or circulated hot water.

        Costs: **Water heaters (residential) = $500 to $1500/ea.**
                Water heaters (commercial) = $1500 to $3000/ea (80% M and 20% L).
                Electric is cheaper for small buildings but high for large buildings.

    ___ *b.* If the water is "hard" (heavy concentration of calcium ions), a *water softener* may be needed. Provide *18″ dia. × 42″ H* space.

        Costs: **Water softener = $2000 to $10,000**

___ *c.* If water is obtained from a private *well,* a *pump* is needed. If the well is *deep,* the pump is usually at the bottom of the well. For this case provide space for a *pressure tank* that is *20" dia. × 64"H.* If the well is *shallow* (20' to 25' deep) the pump may be provided inside the building. Space for pump and tank should be *36"W × 20"D × 64"H.*

Costs: Well = $140 to $200 per LF of shaft

___ *d.* Water supply *pipes* are usually copper or plastic and range from ½" to 2" for small buildings, but 2½" to 6" for larger buildings or higher-water-use buildings. Hot and cold pipes are usually laid out parallel. Piping should be kept out of exterior walls in cold climates to prevent winter freeze-ups.

___ *e.* The city water pressure will push water up 2 or 3 stories. Buildings taller than this will need a *surge tank* and *water pressure pumps.* This equipment takes approximately *100 to 200 SF* of space.

Costs: Surge tank and pumps = $5000 to $20,000

___ 2. <u>Plumbing Fixtures</u>

___ *a.* The men's and women's *restrooms* need to be laid out to determine their size and located in the building. Economical solutions are shared plumbing walls (toilet rooms back to back) and for multistory buildings, stacked layouts.

___ *b.* See UBC Table A-29-A (p. 386) or UPC Table 4-1 (p. 390) for *toilet requirements* (WC, lavatories, urinals, and drinking fountains) based on occupancy type. The number of fixtures calculated is the minimum required, not the suggested quantity for good design. Check the site jurisdiction as to which of the two tables applies. A check of the local ordinance should be made to be sure there are not further restrictions. Typical toilet room layouts, including requirements for the handicapped, are shown on p. 79.

___ *c.* In *cold* climates, chases for plumbing lines should not be on exterior walls, or if so, should be built in from exterior wall insulation.

Costs: See p. 379.

___ 3. <u>Sanitary Sewer</u>

___ *a.* Horizontal runs of drainage piping are difficult to achieve inside the building. The best arrangement is to bring the plumbing straight down (often along a column) and make connections horizontally under the building.

___ b. The *sanitary drainage system* collects waste water from the plumbing fixtures, which flows by gravity down through the building and out into the city sewer. Because of the slope requirement, long horizontal runs of drainage pipe will run out of ceiling space to fit in. Ideally, sanitary drainage pipes (called plumbing stacks) should 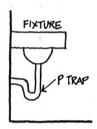 run vertically down through the building collecting short branch lines from stacked bathrooms. A *4″* stack can serve approx. *50* WCs and accompanying lavatories. A *6″* stack can serve approximately *150* WCs and lavatories. Pipes are typically of cast-iron or plastic (ABS). Each fixture is drained through a "P" trap with a water seal. This, and venting the system to the roof, keeps sewer gases from entering the building.

___ c. The *building drain* runs horizontally under the building collecting waste water from multiple vertical stacks. A *4″ to 6″* pipe requires a minimum slope of *1%*, and an *8″* pipe requires a minimum slope of ½%. The lowest (or basement) *floor elevation* needs to be set higher than the rim elevation of the next upsteam manhole of the sewer main. If the building drain is below the sewer main, an automatic underground *ejector pump* is needed.

___ 4. Fire Protection

   ___ a. A *sprinkler system* is the most effective way to provide fire safety.

      ___ (1) The UBC requires sprinklers at certain occupancies (see p. 156).

      ___ (2) Sprinkler *spacing* (maximum coverage per sprinkler):

         ___ (*a*) Light hazard

            ___ 200 SF for smooth ceiling and beam-and-girder construction

            ___ 225 SF if hydraulically calculated for smooth ceiling, as above

___ 130 SF for open wood joists

___ 168 SF for all other types of construction

___ (*b*) Ordinary hazard

___ 130 SF for all types of construction, except:

___ 100 SF for high-pile storage (12′ or more).

___ (*c*) Extra hazard

___ 90 SF for all types of construction

___ 100 SF if hydraulically calculated.

___ (3) Notes

___ (*a*) Most buildings will be the *225 SF* spacing.

___ (*b*) Maximum spacing for light and ordinary hazard = 15′
High-pile and extra hazard = 12′

___ (*c*) Small rooms of light hazard, not exceeding *800 SF:* locate sprinklers max. of *9′* from walls.

___ (*d*) Maximum distance from walls to last sprinkler is ½ *spacing* (except at small rooms). Minimum is *4″*.

___ (*e*) City ordinances should be checked to verify that local rules are not more stringent than UBC requirements.

___ (*f*) The sprinkler riser for small buildings usually takes a space about *2′6″ square.* Pumps and valves for larger buildings take up to about *100 to 500 SF.*

**Costs: Wet pipe systems: $1.00 to $3.50/SF
For dry pipe systems, add $.05/SF.**

___ *b.* Large buildings often also require a *stand-pipe,* which is a large-diameter water pipe extending vertically through the building with fire-hose connections at every floor.

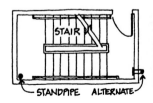

STANDPIPE   ALTERNATE

The system is either wet or dry. The UBC defines three classes (see p. 384):

___ (1) *Class I* is dry with 2½″ outlets. There is a connection point on every landing of every required stairway above or below grade, and on both sides of a horizontal exit door. This type of standpipe is for the fire department to connect their large hoses to.

___ (2) *Class II* is wet with 1½″ outlets and a hose. This type is located so that every part of the building is within 30′ of a nozzle attached to 100′ of hose. This type is for use by building occupants or the fire department.

___ (3) *Class III* is wet with 2½″ outlets and 1½″ hose connections. These are located according to the rules for both Class I and II.

SIAMESE FITTING

Often, two *Siamese* fittings are required in readily accessible locations on the outside of the building to allow the fire department to attach hoses from pumper trucks to the dry standpipe and to the sprinkler riser.

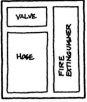

HOSE CABINET

Also, when required, *fire hose cabinets* will be located in such a way that every point on a floor lies within reach of a *30′* stream from the end of a *100′* hose. A typical recessed wall cabinet for a wet standpipe hose and fire extinguisher is *2′9″W × 9″D × 2′9″H*. See UBC Table 9-A on p. 384 for standpipe requirements. See p. 315 for fire extinguishers.

TABLE 9-A—STANDPIPE REQUIREMENTS

OCCUPANCY	NONSPRINKLERED BUILDING[1]		SPRINKLERED BUILDING[2,3]	
× 304.8 for mm × 0.0929 for m²	Standpipe Class	Hose Requirement	Standpipe Class	Hose Requirement
1. Occupancies exceeding 150 feet in height and more than one story	III	Yes	I	No
2. Occupancies four stories or more but less than 150 feet in height, except Group R, Division 3[6]	[I and II[4]] (or III)	[5] Yes	I	No
3. Group A Occupancies with occupant load exceeding 1,000[7]	II	Yes	No requirement	No
4. Group A, Division 2.1 Occupancies over 5,000 square feet in area used for exhibition	II	Yes	II	Yes
5. Groups I; H; B; S; M; F, Division 1 Occupancies less than four stories in height but greater than 20,000 square feet per floor[6]	II[4]	Yes	No requirement	No
6. Stages more than 1,000 square feet in area	II	No	III	No

[1]Except as otherwise specified in Item 4 of this table, Class II standpipes need not be provided in basements having an automatic fire-extinguishing system throughout.

[2]The standpipe system may be combined with the automatic sprinkler system.

[3]Portions of otherwise sprinklered buildings that are not protected by automatic sprinklers shall have Class II standpipes installed as required for the unsprinklered portions.

[4]In open structures where Class II standpipes may be damaged by freezing, the building official may authorize the use of Class I standpipes that are located as required for Class II standpipes.

[5]Hose is required for Class II standpipes only.

[6]For the purposes of this table, occupied roofs of parking structures shall be considered an additional story. In parking structures, a tier is a story.

[7]Class II standpipes need not be provided in assembly areas used solely for worship.

___ 5. <u>Gas</u>
   To allow for the gas meter and piping, provide a space *1'6"W × 1'D × 2'H.*

___ 6. <u>Solar Hot Water Systems</u>
   ___ *a.* In the U.S. the average person uses *20 gallons* of HW/day.
   ___ *b.* Mount collectors at tilt equal to about the site latitude.
   ___ *c.* Typical collectors are 4' × 8' and 4' × 10'.
   ___ *d.* Typical relationship between collector area and storage volume is *1:3* to *1:7* gallons per SF of collector.
   ___ *e.* Types of systems
      ___ (1) *Open loop, recirculation:* The most widely used system in climates where freezing is of little concern.
      ___ (2) *Open loop, drain down:* Includes valving arrangement from collectors and piping when water temperature approaches freezing.
      ___ (3) *Closed loop, drain back:* Use of separate fluid (such as water) circulated through collectors where it is heated and transferred to HW storage through heat exchanger.
      ___ (4) *Closed loop, antifreeze:* Most widely used with heat exchanger.
   ___ *f.* Auxiliary heat: Typically an electric element in HW tank top.
   ___ *g.* For rough estimates:
      ___ (1) Northeast U.S.: 60 SF collector and 80 gallon tank will provide 50 to 75% of HW needs for a family of four.
      ___ (2) Southwest U.S.: 40 SF of collector will do same.

Costs: $3300 to $6300 per system

TABLE A-29-A—MINIMUM PLUMBING FIXTURES[1,2,3]

Each building shall be provided with sanitary facilities, including provisions for accessibility in accordance with Chapter 11. Plumbing fixtures shall be provided for the type of building occupancy with the minimum numbers as shown in Table A-29-A. The number of fixtures are the minimum required as shown in Table A-29-A and are assumed to be based on 50 percent male and 50 percent female. The occupant load factors shall be as shown in Table A-29-A.

EXCEPTION: Where circumstances dictate that a different ratio is needed, the adjustment shall be approved by the building official.

TYPE OF BUILDING OR OCCUPANCY[4]	WATER CLOSETS[5] (fixtures per person)		LAVATORIES[6] (fixtures per person)		BATHTUB OR SHOWER (fixtures per person)
	MALE	FEMALE	MALE	FEMALE	
For the occupancies listed below, use 30 square feet (2.78 m²) per occupant for the minimum number of plumbing fixtures.					
Group A Conference rooms, dining rooms, drinking establishments, exhibit rooms, gymnasiums, lounges, stages and similar uses including restaurants classified as Group B Occupancies	1:1-25 2:26-75 3:76-125 4:126-200 5:201-300 6:301-400 Over 400, add one fixture for each additional 200 males or 150 females.	1:1-25 2:26-75 3:76-125 4:126-200 5:201-300 6:301-400	one for each water closet up to four; then one for each two additional water closets		
For the assembly occupancies listed below, use the number of fixed seating or, where no fixed seating is provided, use 15 square feet (1.39 m²) per occupant for the minimum number of plumbing fixtures.					
Assembly places— Auditoriums, convention halls, dance floors, lodge rooms, stadiums and casinos	1:1-50 2:51-100 3:101-150 4:151-300 Over 300 males, add one fixture for each additional 200, and over 400 females add one for each 125.	3:1-50 4:51-100 6:101-200 8:201-400	1:1-200 2:201-400 3:401-750 Over 750, add one fixture for each additional 500 persons.	1:1-200 2:201-400 3:401-750	

(Continued)

97 UBC FIXTURE COUNT

For the assembly occupancies listed below, use the number of fixed seating or, where no fixed seating is provided, use 30 square feet (2.29 m²) per occupant for the minimum number of plumbing fixtures.

Occupancy			
Worship places Principal assembly area	one per 150	one per 75	one per two water closets
Worship places Educational and activity unit	one per 125	one per 75	one per two water closets

For the occupancies listed below, use 200 square feet (18.58 m²) per occupant for the minimum number of plumbing fixtures.

Occupancy			
Group B Offices or public buildings	1:1-15 2:16-35 3:36-55 Over 55, add one for each 50 persons.		one per two water closets

For the occupancies listed below, use 50 square feet (4.65 m²) per occupant for the minimum number of plumbing fixtures.

Occupancy			
Group E Schools—for staff use All schools	1:1-15 2:16-35 3:36-55 Over 55, add one fixture for each additional 40 persons.	1:1-15 2:16-35 3:36-55	one per 40
Schools—for student use Day care	1:1-20 2:21-50 Over 50, add one fixture for each additional 50 persons.	1:1-25 2:26-50 Over 50, add one fixture for each additional 50 persons.	1:1-25 2:26-50
Elementary	one per 30	one per 25	one per 35
Secondary	one per 40	one per 30	one per 40

For the occupancies listed below, use 50 square feet (4.65 m²) per occupant for the minimum number of plumbing fixtures.

Occupancy			
Education Facilities other than Group E Others (colleges, universities, adult centers, etc.)	one per 40	one per 30	one per 40

(Continued)

TABLE A-29-A—MINIMUM PLUMBING FIXTURES^{1,2,3}—(Continued)

TYPE OF BUILDING OR OCCUPANCY^4	WATER CLOSETS^5 (fixtures per person)		LAVATORIES^6 (fixtures per person)		BATHTUB OR SHOWER (fixtures per person)
	MALE	FEMALE	MALE	FEMALE	
For the occupancies listed below, use 2,000 square feet (185.8 m^2) per occupant for the minimum number of plumbing fixtures.					
Group F Workshop, foundries and similar establishments, and Group H Occupancies	1:1-10 2:11-25 3:26-50 4:51-75 5:76-100 Over 100, add one fixture for each additional 300 persons.	1:1-10 2:11-25 3:26-50 4:51-75 5:76-100	one for each two water closets		one shower for each 15 persons exposed to excessive heat or to skin contamination with irritating materials
For the occupancies listed below, use the designated application and 200 square feet (18.58 m^2) per occupant of the general use area for the minimum number of plumbing fixtures.					
Group I Hospital waiting rooms	one per room (usable by either sex)		one per room		
Hospital general use areas	1:1-15 2:16-35 3:36-55 Over 55, add one fixture for each additional 40 persons.	1:1-15 3:16-35 4:36-55	one per each two water closets		
Hospitals Patient room Ward room	one per room one per eight patients		one per room one per 10 patients		one per room one per 20 patients
Jails and reformatories Cell Exercise room	one per cell one per exercise room		one per cell one per exercise room		
Other institutions (on each occupied floor)	one per 25	one per 25	one per 10	one per 10	one per eight

(Continued)

388

	Water Closets	Urinals	Lavatories	Bathtubs or Showers
For the occupancies listed below, use 200 square feet (18.58 m²) per occupant for the minimum number of plumbing fixtures.				
Group M Retail or wholesale stores	1:1-50 2:51-100 3:101-400 Over 400, add one fixture for each additional 500 males and one for each 150 females.		one for each two water closets	
For Group R Occupancies, dwelling units and hotel guest rooms, use the chart. For congregate residences, use 200 square feet (18.58 m²) for Group R, Division 1 Occupancies and 300 square feet (27.87 m²) for Group R, Division 3 Occupancies for the minimum plumbing fixtures.				
Group R Dwelling units Hotel guest rooms	one per dwelling unit one per guest room		one per dwelling unit one per guest room	one per dwelling unit one per guest room
Congregate residences	one per 10 Add one fixture for each additional 25 males and one for each additional 20 females.	one per 8	one per 12 Over 12, add one fixture for each additional 20 males and one for each additional 15 females	one per eight For females, add one bathtub per 30. Over 150, add one per 20.
For the occupancies listed below, use 5,000 square feet (464.5 m²) per occupant for the minimum number of plumbing fixtures.				
Group S Warehouses	1:1-10 2:11-25 3:26-50 4:51-75 5:76-100 Over 100, add one for each 300 males and females.	one per 40 occupants of each sex	1:1-10 2:11-25 3:26-50 4:51-75 5:76-100 Over 100, add one for each 300 males and females.	one shower for each 15 persons exposed to excessive heat or to skin contamination with poisonous, infectious or irritating materials

NOTE: Occupant loads over 30 shall have one drinking fountain for each 150 occupants.

[1] The figures shown are based on one fixture being the minimum required for the number of persons indicated or any fraction thereof.

[2] Drinking fountains shall not be installed in toilet rooms.

[3] When the design occupant load is less than 10 persons, a facility usable by either sex may be approved by the building official.

[4] Any category not mentioned specifically or about which there are any questions shall be classified by the building official and included in the category which it most nearly resembles, based on the expected use of the plumbing facilities.

[5] Where urinals are provided, one water closet less than the number specified may be provided for each urinal installed, except the number of water closets in such cases shall not be reduced to less than one half of the minimum specified.

[6] Twenty-four inches (610 mm) of wash sink or 18 inches (457 mm) of a circular basin, when provided with water outlets for such space, shall be considered equivalent to one lavatory.

Minimum Plumbing Facilities¹

Each building shall be provided with sanitary facilities, including provisions for the physically handicapped as prescribed by the Department having jurisdiction. For requirements for the handicapped, ANSI A117.1-1992, Accessible and Usable Buildings and Facilities, may be used.

The total occupant load shall be determined by minimum exiting requirements. The minimum number of fixtures shall be calculated at fifty (50) percent male and fifty (50) percent female based on the total occupant load.

Type of Building or Occupancy²	Water Closets¹⁴ (Fixtures per Person)		Urinals⁵,¹⁰ (Fixtures per Person)	Lavatories (Fixtures per Person)		Bathtubs or Showers (Fixtures per Person)	Drinking Fountains³,¹³ (Fixtures per Person)
Assembly Places – Theatres, Auditoriums, Convention Halls, etc. – for permanent employee use	Male 1: 1-15 2: 16-35 3: 36-55 Over 55, add 1 fixture for each additional 40 persons.	Female 1: 1-15 3: 16-35 4: 36-55	Male 0: 1-9 1: 10-50 Add one fixture for each additional 50 males.	Male 1 per 40	Female 1 per 40		
Assembly Places – Theatres, Auditoriums, Convention Halls, etc. – for public use	Male 1: 1-100 2: 101-200 3: 201-400 Over 400, add one fixture for each additional 500 males and 1 for each additional 125 females.	Female 3: 1-50 4: 51-100 8: 101-200 11: 201-400	Male 1: 1-100 2: 101-200 3: 201-400 4: 401-600 Over 600 add 1 fixture for each additional 300 males.	Male 1: 1-200 2: 201-400 3: 401-750 Over 750, add one fixture for each additional 500 persons.	Female 1: 1-200 2: 201-400 3: 401-750		1: 1-150 2: 151-400 3: 401-750 Over 750, add one fixture for each additional 500 persons.
Dormitories⁹ School or Labor	Male 1 per 10 Add 1 fixture for each additional 25 males (over 10) and 1 for each additional 20 females (over 8).	Female 1 per 8	Male 1 per 25 Over 150, add 1 fixture for each additional 50 males.	Male 1 per 12 Over 12 add one fixture for each additional 20 males and 1 for each 15 additional females.	Female 1 per 12	1 per 8 For females, add 1 bathtub per 30. Over 150, add 1 per 20.	1 per 150¹²
Dormitories – for staff use	Male 1: 1-15 2: 16-35 3: 36-55 Over 55, add 1 fixture for each additional 40 persons.	Female 1: 1-15 3: 16-35 4: 36-55	Male 1 per 50	Male 1 per 40	Female 1 per 40	1 per 8	

97 UPC FIXTURE COUNT

Type of Building or Occupancy	Water Closets	Urinals	Lavatories	Bathtubs or Showers	Drinking Fountains
Dwellings [4] Single Dwelling Multiple Dwelling or Apartment House	1 per dwelling		1 per dwelling or apartment unit	1 per dwelling or apartment unit	
Hospital Waiting rooms	1 per room		1 per room		1 per 150 [12]
Hospitals – for employee use	Male: 1: 1-15, 2: 16-35, 3: 36-55 Female: 1: 1-15, 2: 16-35, 3: 36-55 Over 55, add 1 fixture for each additional 40 persons.	Male: 0: 1-9, 1: 10-50 Add one fixture for each additional 50 males.	Male: 1 per 40 Female: 1 per 40		
Hospitals Individual Room Ward Room	1 per room 1 per 8 patients		1 per room 1 per 10 patients	1 per room 1 per 20 patients	1 per 150 [12]
Industrial [6] Warehouses, Workshops, Foundries and similar establishments – for employee use	Male: 1: 1-10, 2: 11-25, 3: 26-50, 4: 51-75, 5: 76-100 Female: 1: 1-10, 2: 11-25, 3: 26-50, 4: 51-75, 5: 76-100 Over 100, add 1 fixture for each additional 30 persons		Up to 100, 1 per 10 persons Over 100, 1 per 15 persons [7,8]	1 shower for each 15 persons exposed to excessive heat or to skin contamination with poisonous, infectious, or irritating material	1 per 150 [12]
Institutional – Other than Hospitals or Penal Institutions (on each occupied floor)	Male: 1 per 25 Female: 1 per 20	Male: 0: 1-9, 1: 10-50 Add one fixture for each additional 50 males.	Male: 1 per 10 Female: 1 per 10	1 per 8	1 per 150 [12]

(Continued)

Minimum Plumbing Facilities[1] (Continued)

Type of Building or Occupancy[2]	Water Closets[14] (Fixtures per Person)		Urinals[5,10] (Fixtures per Person)	Lavatories (Fixtures per Person)		Bathtubs or Showers (Fixtures per Person)	Drinking Fountains[3,13] (Fixtures per Person)
Institutional – Other than Hospitals or Penal Institutions (on each occupied floor) – for employee use	Male 1: 1-15 2: 16-35 3: 36-55 Over 55, add 1 fixture for each additional 40 persons.	Female 1: 1-15 3: 16-35 4: 36-55	Male 0: 1-9 1: 10-50 Add one fixture for each additional 50 males.	Male 1 per 40	Female 1 per 40	1 per 8	1 per 150[12]
Office or Public Buildings	Male 1: 1-100 2: 101-200 3: 201-400 Over 400, add one fixture for each additional 500 males and 1 for each additional 150 females.	Female 3: 1-50 4: 51-100 8: 101-200 11: 201-400	Male 1: 1-100 2: 101-200 3: 201-400 4: 401-600 Over 600 add 1 fixture for each additional 300 males.	Male 1: 1-200 2: 201-400 3: 401-750 Over 750, add one fixture for each additional 500 persons	Female 1: 1-200 2: 201-400 3: 401-750		1 per 150[12]
Office or Public Buildings – for employee use	Male 1: 1-15 2: 16-35 3: 36-55 Over 55, add 1 fixture for each additional 40 persons.	Female 1: 1-15 3: 16-35 4: 36-55	Male 0: 1-9 1: 10-50 Add one fixture for each additional 50 males.	Male 1 per 40	Female 1 per 40		
Penal Institutions – for employee use	Male 1: 1-15 2: 16-35 3: 36-55 Over 55, add 1 fixture for each additional 40 persons.	Female 1: 1-15 3: 16-35 4: 36-55	Male 0: 1-9 1: 10-50 Add one fixture for each additional 50 males.	Male 1 per 40	Female 1 per 40		1 per 150[12]

(Continued)

Type of Building or Occupancy	Water Closets — Male	Water Closets — Female	Urinals — Male	Lavatories — Male	Lavatories — Female	Drinking Fountains
Penal Institutions – for prison use						
Cell	1 per cell			1 per cell		1 per cell block floor
Exercise Room	1 per exercise room		1 per exercise room	1 per exercise room		1 per exercise room
Restaurants, Pubs and Lounges[11]	1: 1-50 2: 51-150 3: 151-300 Over 300, add 1 fixture for each additional 200 persons	1: 1-50 2: 51-150 4: 151-300 Over 300, add 1 fixture for each additional 200 persons	1: 1-150 Over 150, add 1 fixture for each additional 150 males	1: 1-150 2: 151-200 3: 201-400 Over 400, add 1 fixture for each additional 400 persons	1: 1-150 2: 151-200 3: 201-400 Over 400, add 1 fixture for each additional 400 persons	
Schools – for staff use						
All schools	1: 1-15 2: 16-35 3: 36-55 Over 55, add 1 fixture for each additional 40 persons	1: 1-15 2: 16-35 3: 36-55 Over 55, add 1 fixture for each additional 40 persons	1 per 50	1 per 40	1 per 40	
Schools – for student use						
Nursery	1: 1-20 2: 21-50 Over 50, add 1 fixture for each additional 50 persons	1: 1-20 2: 21-50 Over 50, add 1 fixture for each additional 50 persons		1: 1-25 2: 26-50 Over 50, add 1 fixture for each additional 50 persons	1: 1-25 2: 26-50 Over 50, add 1 fixture for each additional 50 persons	1 per 150[12]
Elementary	1 per 30	1 per 25	1 per 75	1 per 35	1 per 35	1 per 150[12]
Secondary	1 per 40	1 per 30	1 per 35	1 per 40	1 per 40	1 per 150[12]
Others (Colleges, Universities, Adult Centers, etc.)	1 per 40	1 per 30	1 per 35	1 per 40	1 per 40	1 per 150[12]
Worship Places Educational and Activities Unit	1 per 150	1 per 75	1 per 150	1 per 2 water closets		1 per 150[12]
Worship Places Principal Assembly Place	1 per 150	1 per 75	1 per 150	1 per 2 water closets		1 per 150[12]

(Continued)

1. The figures shown are based upon one (1) fixture being the minimum required for the number of persons indicated or any fraction thereof.

2. Building categories not shown on this table shall be considered separately by the Administrative Authority.

3. Drinking fountains shall not be installed in toilet rooms.

4. Laundry trays. One (1) laundry tray or one (1) automatic washer standpipe for each dwelling unit or one (1) laundry tray or one (1) automatic washer standpipe, or combination thereof, for each twelve (12) apartments. Kitchen sinks, one (1) for each dwelling or apartment unit.

5. For each urinal added in excess of the minimum required, one water closet may be deducted. The number of water closets shall not be reduced to less than two-thirds (2/3) of the minimum requirement.

6. As required by ANSI Z4.1-1968, Sanitation in Places of Employment.

7. Where there is exposure to skin contamination with poisonous, infectious, or irritating materials, provide one (1) lavatory for each five (5) persons.

8. Twenty-four (24) lineal inches (610 mm) of wash sink or eighteen (18) inches (457 mm) of a circular basin, when provided with water outlets for such space, shall be considered equivalent to one (1) lavatory.

9. Laundry trays, one (1) for each fifty (50) persons. Slop sinks, one (1) for each hundred (100) persons.

10. General. In applying this schedule of facilities, consideration must be given to the accessibility of the fixtures. Conformity purely on a numerical basis may not result in an installation suited to the need of the individual establishment. For example, schools should be provided with toilet facilities on each floor having classrooms.

   a. Surrounding materials, wall and floor space to a point two (2) feet (610 mm) in front of urinal lip and four (4) feet (1219 mm) above the floor, and at least two (2) feet (610 mm) to each side of the urinal shall be lined with non-absorbent materials.

   b. Trough urinals are prohibited.

11. A restaurant is defined as a business which sells food to be consumed on the premises.

   a. The number of occupants for a drive-in restaurant shall be considered as equal to the number of parking stalls.

   b. Employee toilet facilities are not to be included in the above restaurant requirements. Hand washing facilities must be available in the kitchen for employees.

12. Where food is consumed indoors, water stations may be substituted for drinking fountains. Offices, or public buildings for use by more than six (6) persons shall have one (1) drinking fountain for the first one hundred fifty (150) persons and one (1) additional fountain for each three hundred (300) persons thereafter.

13. There shall be a minimum of one (1) drinking fountain per occupied floor in schools, theatres, auditoriums, dormitories, offices or public building.

14. The total number of water closets for females shall be at least equal to the total number of water closets and urinals required for males.

EXAMPLE:

PROBLEM: FIGURE THE REQUIRED PLUMBING FIX-
TURES FOR A 10000 SF OFFICE SPACE.
FIGURE FOR BOTH THE UBC AND THE U.P.C.

SOLUTION:

A. <u>BY U.B.C.</u> (TABLE A-29-A OF UBC, SEE P. 387)

1. GROUP B: 10000 SF ÷ 200 SF/OCC = 50 OCC
   ÷ 2 = 25/SEX

2. FIXTURES

	M (25)	W (25)
WC	~~2~~ 1	2
LAV	2	2
UR	1	

ALSO: 1 DF REQ'D.

B. <u>BY U.P.C.</u> (TABLE 4-1 OF U.P.C., SEE P. 392)

1. FIGURE OCC. LOAD FOR EXITING (SEE TABLE 10-A
   OF U.B.C. ON PP. 169-170).

   10000 SF ÷ 100 SF/OCC = 100 OCC ÷ 2 = 50/SEX

2. FIXTURES

	M (50	W (50)
WC	~~3~~ 2	
LAV	2	2
UR	~~1~~ 2	

NOTES

__ B. HEATING, VENTILATION, AND AIR-CONDITIONING (HVAC) ① ⑩

The interior designer may be involved with HVAC when doing a tenant improvement or remodel. This will probably involve working with an architect or engineer. This section is included to give the interior designer a basic understanding of HVAC functions.

See p. 399 for selection and **cost** table.

Costs: Equipment 20 to 30%; distribution system 80 to 70%; see p. 399 for costs of different systems.

During programming it is useful to do a functional partitioning of the building into major zones for:

___ 1. Similar schedule of use
___ 2. Similar temperature requirements
___ 3. Similar ventilation and air quality
___ 4. Similar internal heat generation
___ 5. Similar HVAC needs

During design, if possible, locate spaces with similar needs together. See p. 179 for energy conservation and equipment efficiency.

___ 1. General
HVAC systems can be divided into four major elements:
___ a. The *boiler and chiller* to create heat and cold for the system to use. (In small package systems this is an internal electric coil, gas furnace, or refrigeration compressor).
___ b. *Cooling tower* (or air-cooled condenser) located outside to exhaust heat.
___ c. *Air handlers* to transfer heat and cold to air (or at least fresh air) to be blown into the building zones. In large buildings this is in a fan room. (In small package systems this is an internal fan).
___ d. The *delivery system* of ducts, control boxes, and diffusers to deliver conditioned air to the spaces.
___ 2. Systems for Small Buildings
___ a. *Roof-mounted "package systems"* are typically used for residential and small to medium commercial buildings. They are AC units that house the first three parts in one piece of equipment that usually ends up on the roof. Used usually in warm or temperate climates. Typical sizes:

Size	Area served	Dimensions	System
2 to 5 tons	600 to 1500 SF	6' L × 4' W × 4' H	Single-zone constant
5 to 10 tons	1500 to 4500 SF	10' L × 7' W × 5' H	vol. delivery system; can serve more than
15 to 75 tons	4500 to 22,500 SF	25' L × 9' W × 6' H	one zone with variable air vol. delivery system

Notes:
    1. Units should have *3' to 4'* of clearance on all sides.
    2. A *ton is 12,000 Btu* of refrigeration.
    3. Each *ton is equal to 400 CFM.*

Roof Mounted
"Package" Unit

HVAC SYSTEMS AND COSTS

TYPE	HEATING	COOLING	BUILDING SMALL	BUILDING LARGE	FUEL ELECT.	FUEL GAS	FUEL OTHER	DELIVERY AIR	DELIVERY PIPES	MIN. OPERATING COST IN COLD CLIMATE	MIN. OPERATING COST IN MODERATE CLIMATE	MAX. CONTROL OF AIR VELOCITY & QUALITY	MAX. INDIVIDUAL CONTROL OF TEMP.	MINIMUM NOISE	MINIMUM VISUAL OBTRUSIVENESS	MIN. SPACE FOR EQUIP.	MIN. MAINTENANCE	MIN. FL. TO FL. HT.	MAX. FLEXIBILITY OF RENTAL SPACE	$ PER SF (50% H, 50% L) ±10%	$ TON OF A/C ±10%
1 ROOF MT'D "PACKAGE" UNITS	●	●	●		●	●		●						●		●	●			5	1400
2 CENTRAL FORCED AIR (& "SPLIT" SYSTEMS)	●	●	●		●	●		●		●		●		●	●	●				6.25	1200
3 FORCED HOT WATER	●		●		●	●			●	●				●	●	●				6.25	1600
4 EVAPORATIVE COOLING		●	●		●			●			●									5	2000
5 THROUGH WALL UNITS	●	●	●		●			●					●			●				2	600
6 ELECTRIC BASE BOARD	●		●		●								●	●		●				1.50	600
7 ELECT. FAN UNIT HEATERS	●		●		●										●	●				1.25	
8 RADIANT	●		●						●			●		●	●	●				2.50	
9 WALL FURNACE	●		●			●									●	●				1.50	
10 PASSIVE SOLAR	●		●							●	●									2.50	
11 ACTIVE SOLAR	●		●						●	●	●			●							
12 STOVES	●		●								●										
13 SINGLE ZONE CONSTANT VOL.	●	●		●	●	●	●	●				●		●	●	●	●			6.25	2200
14 MULTI ZONE CONSTANT VOL.	●	●		●	●	●	●	●				●								8.75	2500
15 VARIABLE AIR VOLUME	●	●		●	●	●	●	●			●	●	●	●	●	●			●	10	2700
16 DOUBLE DUCT	●	●		●	●	●	●	●				●	●			●		●	●	12.50	3000
17 INDUCTION	●	●		●	●	●	●	●	●	●	●	●	●		●			●	●	10	2700
18 FAN COIL WITH AIR	●	●		●	●	●	●	●	●	●	●	●	●		●			●	●	10	2500
19 FAN COIL UNITS	●	●		●	●	●	●		●	●	●	●	●	●	●			●	●	8.75	2200
20 HOT WATER BASE BOARDS	●			●	●	●	●		●	●	●			●		●				5	

CHARACTERISTICS and COSTS columns as labeled.

___ *b.* *Forced-air central heating* is typically used for residential and light commercial buildings. It heats air with gas, oil flame, or electrical resistance at a furnace. A fan blows air through a duct system. The furnace can be upflow (for basements), sideflow, or downflow (for attic). The furnace must be vented. Furnace sizes range between $2'W \times 2.5'D \times 7'H$ to $4'W \times 7'D \times 7'H$. Main ducts are typically $1' \times 2'$ horizontal and $1' \times .33'$ vertical.

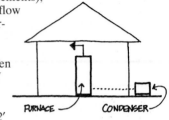

Can add cooling with a "*split system*" by adding evaporator coils in the duct and an exterior condenser. Typical condensers range from $2'W \times 2'D \times 2'H$ to $3.5'W \times 4'D \times 3'H$.

___ *c.* *Forced hot water heating* is typically used for residential buildings and commercial offices. A burner or electric resistance heats water to fin tube convectors (or fan coil unit with blowers). The fueled boiler must be vented and provided with combustible air. Boiler sizes range from $2'W \times 2'D \times 7'H$ to $3'W \times 5'D \times 7'H$. Fin tube convectors are typically $3''D \times 8''H$. Fan coils are $2'W \times 2.5'H$. There is *no cooling*.

___ *d.* *Evaporative cooling* is typically used for residential buildings. It works only in hot, dry climates. A fan draws exterior air across wet pads and into the duct 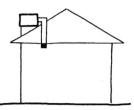 system. There is *no heating.* Cooler size typically is *3′W × 3′D × 3′H.* Main duct is typically *1.5′W × 1.5′D.*

___ *e.* *Through-wall units and package terminal units* are typically used for motels/ hotels as well as small offices. They are self-contained at an exterior wall and are intended for small spaces. These are usually electric (or *heat* 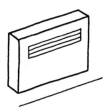 *pump* in mild climates), which are used for *both heating and cooling.* Interior air is recirculated and outside air is added. Typical sizes:

    Package terminal units *3.5′W × 1.5′D × 1.3′H*
    Through-wall units *2′W × 2′D × 1.5′H*

___ *f.* *Electric baseboard convectors* are typically used for residential buildings and commercial offices. They heat by electrical resistance in *3″D × 8″H* baseboards around the perimeter of the room. There is *no cooling.*

___ *g.* *Electric fan-forced unit heaters* are much like item *f* above, but are larger because of internal fans recirculating the air. There is *no cooling.* Typical sizes range from *1.5′W × 8″D × 8″H* to *2′W × 1′D × 1.8′H.*

___ *h.* *Radiant heating:* Electrical resistance wires are embedded in floor or ceiling. There is *no cooling.* An alternative is to have recessed radiant panels, typically *2′ × 2′* or *2′ × 4′.* For alternative cooling and heating use water piping. These are typically residential applications.

    ____ *i.* *Wall furnaces* are small furnaces for small spaces (usually residential). They must be vented. There is *no cooling.* They may be either gas or electric. The typical size is *14″W × 12″D × 84″H.*

    ____ *j.* Other miscellaneous small systems (typically residential):

      ____ (1) Passive solar heating (see p. 179)

      ____ (2) Active solar heating

      ____ (3) Heating stoves (must be properly vented!)

____ 3. <u>Custom Systems for Large Buildings</u>

These are where the first three parts (see p. 397) must have areas allocated for them in the floor plan. In tall buildings due to distance, mechanical floors are created so that air handlers can move air up and down *10 to 15* floors. Thus mechanical floors are spaced *20 to 30* floors apart.

A decentralized chiller and boiler can be at every other mechanical floor, or they can be centralized at the top or base of the building, with one or more air handlers at each floor. See p. 403 for equipment rooms.

    ____ *a.* *Delivery systems*

      ____ (1) *Air delivery systems:*

Because of their size, <u>ducts</u> are a great concern in the preliminary design of the floor-to-ceiling space. See p. 363. The main supply and return ducts are often run above main hallways because ceilings can be lower and because this provides a natural path of easy access to the majority of spaces served.

Air rates for buildings vary from *1 CFM/SF to 2 CFM/SF* based on usage and climate. Low-velocity ducts require *1 to 2 SF of cross-sectional area per 1000 SF* of building area served. High-velocity ducts require *0.5 to 1.0 SF of cross-sectional area.* Air returns are required and are about the same size, or slightly larger, than the main duct supply. (The above-noted dimensions are interior. Typically, ducts are externally lined with 1″ or 2″ of insulation.)

24″ x 10″ duct in plan
↑ width ↑ height

<u>DUCTS</u>

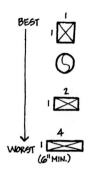

BEST

1

2

4

WORST 1

(6″ MIN.)

LARGE SYSTEMS

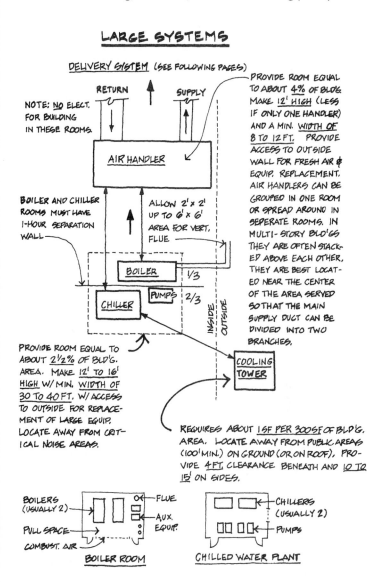

DELIVERY SYSTEM (SEE FOLLOWING PAGES)

NOTE: NO ELECT. FOR BUILDING IN THESE ROOMS.

RETURN   SUPPLY

AIR HANDLER

PROVIDE ROOM EQUAL TO ABOUT 4% OF BLD'G. MAKE 12' HIGH (LESS IF ONLY ONE HANDLER) AND A MIN. WIDTH OF 8 TO 12 FT. PROVIDE ACCESS TO OUTSIDE WALL FOR FRESH AIR & EQUIP. REPLACEMENT. AIR HANDLERS CAN BE GROUPED IN ONE ROOM OR SPREAD AROUND IN SEPERATE ROOMS. IN MULTI-STORY BLD'GS THEY ARE OFTEN STACKED ABOVE EACH OTHER. THEY ARE BEST LOCATED NEAR THE CENTER OF THE AREA SERVED SO THAT THE MAIN SUPPLY DUCT CAN BE DIVIDED INTO TWO BRANCHES.

BOILER AND CHILLER ROOMS MUST HAVE 1-HOUR SEPARATION WALL

ALLOW 2' x 2' UP TO 6' x 6' AREA FOR VERT. FLUE

BOILER   1/3

PUMPS   2/3

CHILLER

INSIDE   OUTSIDE

COOLING TOWER

PROVIDE ROOM EQUAL TO ABOUT 2½% OF BLD'G. AREA. MAKE 12' TO 16' HIGH W/ MIN. WIDTH OF 30 TO 40 FT. W/ ACCESS TO OUTSIDE FOR REPLACEMENT OF LARGE EQUIP. LOCATE AWAY FROM CRITICAL NOISE AREAS.

REQUIRES ABOUT 1 SF PER 300 SF OF BLD'G. AREA. LOCATE AWAY FROM PUBLIC AREAS (100' MIN.) ON GROUND (OR ON ROOF), PROVIDE 4 FT. CLEARANCE BENEATH AND 10 TO 15' ON SIDES.

BOILERS (USUALLY 2)

FLUE
AUX. EQUIP.

PULL SPACE

COMBUST. AIR

BOILER ROOM

CHILLERS (USUALLY 2)

PUMPS

CHILLED WATER PLANT

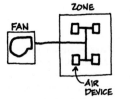

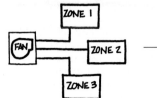

___ (a) _Single-zone constant-volume systems_ serve only one zone and are used for large, open-space rooms without diverse exterior exposure. This is a low-velocity system.

___ (b) _Multizone constant-volume systems_ can serve up to eight separate zones. They are used in modest-sized buildings where there is a diversity of exterior exposure and/or diversity of interior loads. This is a low-velocity system.

___ (c) _Subzone box systems_ often modify single-zone systems for appended spaces. They use boxes that branch off the main supply duct to create separate zones. The size of the boxes can be related to the area served:

Box	Area served
$4'L \times 3'W \times 1.5'H$	500 to 1500 SF
$5'L \times 4'W \times 1.5'H$	1500 to 5000 SF

The main ducts can be high-velocity, but the ducts after the boxes at each zone (as well as the return air) are low-velocity.

___ (d) _Variable-air-volume single-duct systems (V.O.V.)_ can serve as many subzones as required. It is the dominant choice in many commercial buildings because of its flexibility and energy savings. It is most effectively used for interior zones. At exterior zones hot water or electrical reheat coils are added to the boxes. Each zone's temperature is controlled by the volume of air flowing through its box. Typical above-ceiling boxes are:

8″ to 11″H for up to 1500 SF
served (lengths up to 5′)
up to 18″H for up to 7000 SF

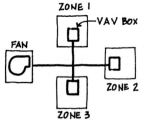

___ (*e*) <u>*Double-duct systems*</u> can serve as a good choice where *air quality control* is important. The air handler supplies hot air for one duct and cold air for the other. The mixing box controls the mix of these two air ducts. This system is not commonly used except in retrofits. It is a "caddie" but also a "gas guzzler."

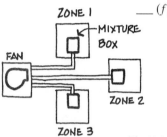

___ (*f*) <u>*Variable-air-volume dual-duct systems*</u> are high-end first cost and most likely used in a retrofit. One duct conveys cool air, one other hot air. This system is most common where a dual-duct constant-volume system is converted to VAV. The box is generally controlled to provide either heat or cool air in varying quantities, as required.

___ (2) <u>*Air/water delivery systems*</u>

These types of systems *reduce the ductwork* by tempering air near its point of use. Hot and cold water are piped to remote induction or fan coil units. Since the air ducts carry only fresh air, they can be sized at *0.2 to 0.4 SF per 1000 SF* of area served. The main hot and cold water lines will be *2" to 4"* in diameter, including insulation, for medium size buildings.

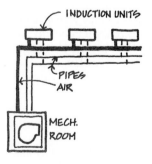

___ (*a*) <u>*Induction*</u> is often used for the *perimeter of high-rise office buildings* and is *expensive*. Air from a central air handler is delivered through high-velocity ducts to each induction unit. Hot and cold lines run to each unit. Each unit is located along the outside wall, at the base of the windows. They are *6" to 12" deep* and *1' to 3' high*.

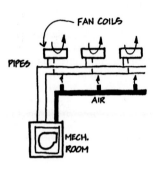

___ (b) *Fan coils with supplementary air* are used where there are *many small rooms needing separate control*. Hot and cold water lines are run through the coils. A fan draws room air through the coil for heating and cooling. A separate duct system supplies fresh air from a remote air handler.

The fan coils are *6″ to 12″ deep and 1′ to 3′ high.* They can also be a vertical shape (*2′ × 2′ × 6′ high*) to fit in a closet. They are often stacked vertically in a tall building to reduce piping. Fan coil units can be located in ceiling space.

___ (3) *Water delivery systems* use hot and cold water lines only. No air is delivered to the areas served.

___ (a) *Fan coil units* can have hot and/or cold water lines with fresh air from operable windows or an outdoor air intake at the unit.

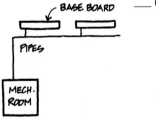

___ (b) *Hot water baseboards* supply only heat. Often used in conjunction with a cooling-only VAV system for perimeter zones. Baseboards are *6″ high by 5″ deep* and as long as necessary.

___ 4. <u>Diffusers, Terminal Devices, and Grilles</u>
These interface the HVAC system with the building interiors for visual impact and thermal comfort. Grilles are side-

wall devices. The opposite wall should be no greater than about *16′ to 18′* away (can throw up to 30′ in high rooms with special diffusers). Diffusers are down-facing and must be coordinated with the lighting as well as uniformly spaced (at a *distance apart of approximately the floor-to-ceiling height*). Returns should be spaced so as to not interfere with air supply. Assume return air grilles at one per 400 to 600 SF.

GRILLE

DIFFUSER

NOTES

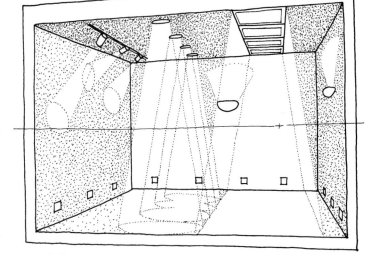

16 LIGHTING AND ELECTRICAL

NOTES

__ 1. <u>General</u>
   __ *a.* Lighting terms and concepts using the analogy of a sprinkler pipe

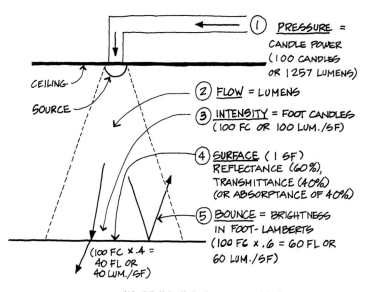

   __ (1) Visible light is measured in lumens.
   __ (2) One lumen of light flux spread over one square foot of area illuminates the area to one *foot-candle.*
   __ (3) The ratio of lumens/watts is called *efficacy,* a measure of *energy efficiency.*
   __ (4) The incident angle of a light beam always equals the reflectance angle on a surface.
  __ *b.* Considerations in seeing
   __ (1) <u>*Contrast*</u> between the object or area being viewed and its surroundings will help vision. Too little will wash out the object. Too much will create glare. Recommended maximum ratios:

__ Task to adjacent area	3 to 1
__ Task to remote dark surface	3 to 1
__ Task to remote light surface	1 to 1
__ Window to adjacent wall	20 to 1
__ Task to general visual field	40 to 1
__ Focal point: up to	100 to 1

   ___ (2) *Brightness* (How much light?). For recommended lighting levels, see d, below, or p. 414.

   ___ (3) *Size* of object or material being viewed. As the viewing task becomes smaller, the brightness needs to increase and vice versa.

   ___ (4) *Time.* As the view time is decreased, the brightness and contrast needs to increase and vice versa.

   ___ (5) *Glare.* Not only can too much contrast create glare, but light sources at the wrong angle to the eye can create glare. Typically, the nonglare angles are from 30° to 60° from the vertical.

"VEILING REFLECTIONS"

   ___ (6) *Color.* See p. 195.

   ___ (7) *Interest.*

___ c. Types of overall light sources

   ___ (1) *Task lighting* is the brightest level needed for the immediate task, such as a desk lamp. Select from table on p. 414.

   ___ (2) *General lighting* is the less bright level of surroundings for both general seeing and to reduce contrast between the task and surroundings. It is also for less intense tasks, such as general illumination of a lobby. This type of lighting can be natural and/or artificial.

   ___ (3) As a *general rule,* general lighting should be about *one-third* that of task lighting down to *20 fc.* Noncritical lighting (halls, etc.) can be reduced to *one-third* of general lighting down to *10 fc.*

      For more details, see p. 414.

___ d. Typical amounts of light

   ___ (1) Residential

      ___ *Casual* activities: 20 fc

      ___ *Moderate* activities (grooming, reading, and preparing food):   up to 50 fc

___ *Extended* activities
(hobby work, household
accounts, prolonged
reading):   up to 150 fc

___ *Difficult* activites (sewing): up to 200 fc
___ (2) Commercial
    ___ *Circulation:*   up to 30 fc
    ___ *Merchandising:*   up to 100 fc
    ___ *Feature* displays: up to 500 fc
    ___ *Specific* activities
    (i.e., drafting):   200 fc to 2000 fc
___ (3) For more detailed recommendations, see p.
414.

___ *e.* For recommended room reflectances, see p. 199.
___ *f.* *Calculation* of a point source of light on an object
can be estimated by:

$$\text{Foot-candles} = \frac{\text{Source}}{\text{distance}^2} \times \text{Cosine of incident angle}$$

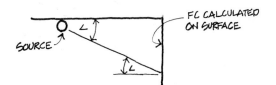

SOURCE CAN
BE IN CANDLES,
LUMENS, OR
FOOT-LAMBERTS

SOURCE

FC CALCULATED
ON SURFACE

Light hitting a surface at an angle will illuminate the
surface less than light hitting perpendicular to the
surface. The cosine of the incident angle is used to
make the correction. Doubling the distance from
source to surface cuts the illumination of the surface
to one-fourth of its previous intensity. Also, see
page 426 for other calculations.

DESIGN LIGHTING LEVELS

	TYPE OF ACTIVITY	TYPE OF LIGHTING	FOOTCANDLES X	Y	Z	TYPICAL SPACES
A	PUBLIC SPACES W/DARK SURROUNDINGS	GENERAL AREA LIGHTING THROUGHOUT SPACES	2	3	5	THEATER, STORAGE
B	SIMPLE ORIENTATION FOR SHORT TEMPORARY VISITS	→	5	7.5	10	DINING, CORRIDORS, CLOSETS, STORAGE
C	WORKING SPACES WHERE VISUAL TASKS ARE ONLY OCCASIONALLY PERFORMED		10	15	20	WAITING, EXHIBITION, LOBBIES, LOCKERS, RESIDENTIAL DINING, STAIRS, TOILETS, ELEVATORS, LOADING DOCKS
D	PERFORMANCE OF VISUAL TASKS OF HIGH CONTRAST OR LARGE SIZE	ILLUMINATION ON TASK	20	30	50	GENERAL OFFICE, EXAM ROOMS, MANUFACTURING, READING ROOMS, DRESSING, DISPLAY
E	PERFORMANCE OF VISUAL TASKS OF MEDIUM CONTRAST OR SMALL SIZE		50	75	100	DRAFTING, LABS, KITCHENS, EXAM ROOM, SEWING, DESKS, FILES, WORK BENCH, READING, MANUFACTURING, CLASSROOMS
F	PERFORMANCE OF VISUAL TASKS OF LOW CONTRAST OR VERY SMALL AREA	→	100	150	200	ARTWORK AND DRAFTING, DEMONSTRATION, INSPECTION, SURGERY, LABS, FITTING, RECORDS, CRITICAL AT WORK BENCH, DIFFICULT SEWING, MANUFACTURE ASSEMBLY
G	PERFORMANCE OF VISUAL TASKS OF LOW CONTRAST AND VERY SMALL SIZE OVER A PROLONGED PERIOD.	ILLUMINATION ON TASK BY COMBINATION OF GENERAL AND LOCAL LIGHTING	200	300	500	CRITICAL SURGERY, VERY DIFFICULT MANUFACTURING ASSEMBLY, CLOSE INSPECTION
H	PERFORMANCE OF VERY PROLONGED & EXACTING VISUAL TASK		500	750	1000	
I	PERFORMANCE OF VERY SPECIAL TASKS OF EXTREMELY LOW CONTRAST AND SMALL SIZE	→	1000	1500	2000	

% REFL.

AGE	SPEED &/OR ACCURACY
X <40	>70 NOT IMPORT.
Y 40-55	30-70 IMPORT.
Z >50	<30 CRITICAL

(41)

NOTES

NOTES

___ 2. <u>Electric (Artificial) Lighting</u>
For energy conservation, see p. 179. See p. 348 for table lamps and floor lamps.

___ *a.* <u>*Lamp types*</u>

(40 TO 150 W)

___ (1) <u>*Incandescent*</u> lamps produce a warm light, and are inexpensive and easy to use, but they have limited lumination per watt (*20 to 40*) and a short life. *Normal voltage* lamps produce a point source of light. Most common shapes are A, R, and PAR. *Low voltage* lamps produce a very small point of intense brightness that can be focused into a precise beam of light (for merchandise or art). These are usually PAR shapes or designed to fit into a parabolic reflector. Sizes are designated in ⅛ inch of the widest part of lamp. Tungsten-halogen (quartz) and low-voltage are special types of incandescent lights.

(30 TO 300 W)

(50 TO 250 W)

___ (2) <u>*Gaseous discharge*</u> lamps produce light by passing electricity through a gas. These lamps require a ballast to get the lamp started and then to control the current.

___ (*a*) <u>*Fluorescent lamps*</u> produce a wide, linear, diffuse light source that is well-suited to spreading light downward to the working surfaces of desks or displays in a commercial environment with normal ceiling heights (*8′ to 12′*). Lamps are typically 17, 25, or 32 watts. The deluxe lamps have good color-rendering characteristics and can be chosen to favor the *cool* (*blue*) or the *warm* (*red*) end of the spectrum. *Dimmers for fluorescents are expensive.* Fluorescent lamps produce more light per watt of energy (*70–85 lumens/watt*) than incandescent; thus operating costs are low. The purchase price and length of life of fluorescent lamps are greater than for incandescent and less than for HID. Four-foot lengths utilize 40 watts and are most common. *Designations are F followed by wattage, shape, size, color, and a form factor.*

___ (b) <u>*High-intensity discharge*</u> (*HID*) lamps can be focused into a fairly good beam of light. These lamps, matched with appropriate fixtures are well-suited to beaming light down to the working place from a high ceiling (*12' to 20'*). *Dimming HID lamps is difficult. The lamps are expensive but produce a lot of light and last a long time.* If there is a power interruption, HID lamps will go out and cannot come on again for about *10 minutes* while they cool down. Therefore, *in an installation of HID lamps, a few incandescent or fluorescent lamps are needed to provide backup lighting.*

    ___ <u>*Mercury vapor*</u> (the *bluish* street lamps). Deluxe version is warmer; *35 to 65* lumens/watt. They are not much used anymore.

    ___ <u>*Metal halide*</u> are often *ice blue cool* industrial-looking lamps. Deluxe color rendering bulbs are 50 to 400 watts, and almost as good as deluxe fluorescent for a warmer effect. Efficiency is *80 lumens/watt.*

    ___ <u>*High-pressure sodium*</u> produces a *warm golden yellow* light often used for highways. Bulbs are 35 to 400 watts. Deluxe color rendering is almost as cool as deluxe fluorescent for a cooler effect. Efficiency is *100 lumens/ watt.*

    ___ <u>*Low-pressure sodium*</u> produces a *yellow* color which makes all colors appear in shades of gray. Bulbs are typically 35 to 180 watts. Used for parking lots and roadways. Efficiency is *150 lumens/watt.*

___ (*c*) <u>*Cold cathode*</u> (neon) has a color dependent on the gas and the color of the tube. *Can be most any color.* Does not give off enough light for detailed visual tasks, but does give off enough light for *attracting attention,* indoors or out.

___ *b.* <u>*Lighting systems and fixture types*</u>

Note: **Costs include lamps, fixture, and installation labor, but not general wiring. As a rule of thumb, fixtures are 20 to 30%, and distribution (not included in following costs) is 30 to 70%.**

___ (1) <u>*General room lighting*</u>
A large proportion of commercial space requires even illumination on the workplace. This can be done a number of ways.
___ (*a*) <u>*Direct lighting*</u> is the most common form of general room lighting.

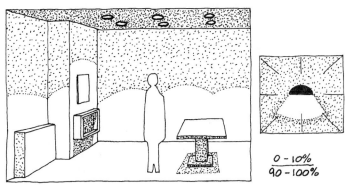

$$\frac{0-10\%}{90-100\%}$$

DIRECT

All recessed lighting is an example of a direct lighting system, but a pendant fixture could be direct if it emits virtually no light above the horizontal. Unless extensive wall washing, or high light levels (as with fluorescent for general office lighting) are used, the overall impression of a direct lighting system should be one of low general brightness with the possibility of higher intensity accents.

A guide to determine maximum spacing is the *spacing-to-mounting-height ratio*. The mounting height is the height from the working place (*usually 2.5' above floor*) to the level of the height fixtures. Note that the ratio does not apply to the end of oblong fixtures due to the nature of their light distribution.

$$\text{Spacing} = \left(\frac{S}{MH}\right) \times (\text{Mounting Ht.})$$

EXAMPLE:

WHAT IS AN AVERAGE FLUORESCENT FIXTURE SPACING IF THE CEILING IS 9' AND THE S/MH RATIO IS TO BE 1.5?

SPACING = (1.5)(9' − 2.5') = 9.75'
        SAY: 10'

Types of direct lighting are:

___ *Wide-beam diffuse lighting* is often fluorescent lights for normal ceiling heights (8' to 12'). The fixtures will produce a repetitive two-dimensional pattern that becomes the most prominent feature of the ceiling plane. Typical S/MH = *1.5*.

Typical recessed fluorescent fixture:

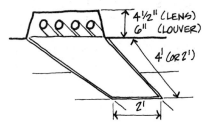

Costs:

$2' \times 4'$ = \$85 to \$135/ea (85% M and 15% L), variation of $-10\%, +20\%$.

$2' \times 2'$ = -10%

$1' \times 4'$ = $+10\%$

___ *Medium-beam downlighting* is produced with a fixture located in or on the ceiling that creates a beam of light directed downward. In the circulation and lobby areas of a building, *incandescent lamps* are often used. For large areas, *HID lamps* are often selected. In both cases the light is in the form of a *conical beam,* and *scallops* of light will be produced on wall surfaces. S/MH is usually about *0.7 to 1.3.*

Typical fixture:

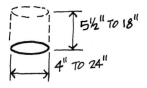

Costs:

(per fixture) (Variation of -10 to $+35\%$).

	Res.	Comm.
Low-voltage:	**\$145**	**\$300 (85% M and 15% L)**
Incandescent:	**\$65**	**\$300 (90% M and 10% L)**
Fluorescent:	**\$125**	**\$275 (85% M and 15% L)**
HID:	**\$145**	**\$450 (80% M and 20% L)**

___ *Narrow-beam downlights* are often used in the same situation as above, but produce more of a spotlight effect at low mounting heights. This form of lighting is used to achieve even illumination where the ceiling height is relatively high. S/MH is usually *0.3 to 0.9.* Typical fixture is same as above.

Cost: Same as medium-beam downlighting above.

___ (*b*) *Semidirect lighting*

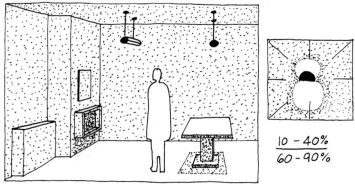

SEMI DIRECT

10 – 40%
60 – 90%

All systems other than direct ones necessarily imply that the lighting fixtures are in the space, whether pendant-mounted, surface-mounted, or portable. A semidirect system will provide good illumination on horizontal surfaces, with moderate general brightness.

Typical fixtures:

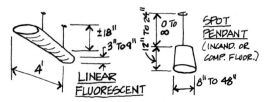

Costs: Fluorescent: $325 to $750 (90% M and 10% L)
Pendant: $150 to $450 (90% M and 10% L)

___ (c) *General diffuse lighting*

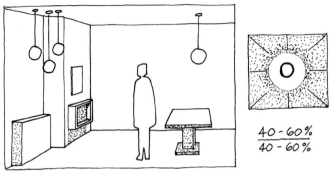

GENERAL
DIFFUSE

A general diffuse system most typically consists of suspended fixtures, with predominantly translucent surfaces on all sides. Can be incandescent, fluorescent, or HID.

Typical fixture: see sketch above

Costs: $75 to $550 (90% M and 10% L)

___ (d) *Direct-indirect lighting*

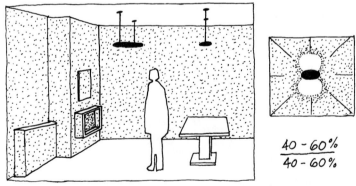

DIRECT-INDIRECT

Direct-indirect lighting will tend to equally emphasize the upper and lower horizontal planes in a space (i.e., the ceiling and floor).

Typical fixture: same as semidirect

Costs: Same as Semidirect.

___ (*e*) *Semi-indirect lighting*

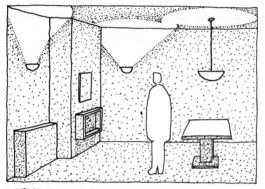

SEMI - INDIRECT

A semi-indirect system will place the emphasis on the ceiling, with some downward or outward-directed light.

Typical fixture:

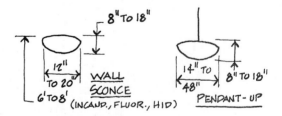

Costs: Wall sconce: $175 to $750 (90% M and 10% L)
Pendant: $350 to $2200 (85% M and 15% L)

___ (*f*) *Indirect lighting*

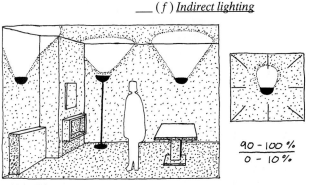

$$\frac{90 - 100\,\%}{0 - 10\,\%}$$

INDIRECT

A fully indirect system will bounce all the light off the ceiling, resulting in a low-contrast environment with little shadow.

Typical fixture: Same as direct-indirect.

Costs: Same as Direct-Indirect.

Note: ADA requires that, along accessible routes, *wall-mounted* fixtures protrude no more than *4″* when mounted lower than *6′8″* AFF.

___ (*g*) *Accent or specialty lighting*

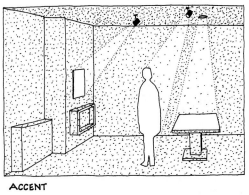

ACCENT

___ (*h*) Also see *furniture lamps* on page 348

Used for special effects or spot lighting, such as lighting art objects or products on display.

Typical fixtures:

TRACK   RECESSED ACCENT

Costs: Track: $85 to $450 (90% M and 10%L)
Recessed accent: $145 to $1000 (80% M and 20% L)

____ *c.* *Simplified calculations*
    ____ (1) For estimating light from one source (such as a painting on a wall lit by a ceiling-mounted spot) use the *Cosine Method* shown on p. 413.
    ____ (2) For general room lighting use the *Zonal Cavity Method*.

ZONAL CAVITY CALCULATIONS METHOD FOR GENERAL LIGHTING

ROOM CAVITY $= \dfrac{(5)(H)(LENGTH + WIDTH)}{LENGTH \times WIDTH}$
RATIO (RCR)

H = HEIGHT FROM THE WORK PLAN (2.5 FT. ABOVE FLOOR) TO BOTTOM OF LIGHT FIXTURES.

LENGTH & WIDTH = ROOM DIMENSIONS

NUMBER OF $= \dfrac{(FOOTCANDLES) \times (AREA OF ROOM)}{(LUMENS PER FIXTURE) \times (CU) \times (MAINT. FACTOR)}$
FIXTURES

FOOTCANDLES = THE DESIRED ILLUMINATION ON THE WORK PLANE. SEE PART 1.

LUMENS PER FIXTURE = (LUMENS PER LAMP) × (NUMBER OF LAMPS IN THE FIXTURE).

CU = COEFFICIENT OF UTILIZATION
THE COEFFICIENT OF UTILIZATION EXPRESSES THE EFFICIENCY OF THE LIGHT FIXTURE ROOM COMBINATION. IT IS DEPENDENT ON FIXTURE EFFICIENCY, DISTRIBUTION OF LIGHT FROM THE FIXTURE, ROOM SHAPE, AND ROOM SURFACE REFLECTANCES. LIGHT FIXTURE MANUFACTURERS PRINT TABLES LISTING THE CU AS A FUNCTION OF ROOM CAVITY RATIO AND ROOM SURFACE REFLECTANCES FOR EACH INDIVIDUAL LIGHT FIXTURE. SEE NEXT PAGE.

MAINTENANCE FACTOR = VARIES FROM 0.85 TO 0.65. THE MAINT. FACTOR ADJUSTS THE CALCULATION FOR THE FACT THAT LAMPS PRODUCE LESS LIGHT AS THEY GET OLDER AND FIXTURES GET DIRTY AND REFLECT LESS LIGHT OUT OF THE FIXTURE.

TYPICAL COEFFICIENTS OF UTILIZATION

INCANDESCENT PATTERN DOWNLIGHT		
ROOM TYPE	HIGH REFL. FIN.	LOW REFL. FIN.
TYP. SMALLER RMS. (MOD. LOW CL'G.)	0.70 TO 0.80	0.60 TO 0.70
TYP. LARGER RMS.		
RELATIVELY HIGH CL'G.	0.85 TO 0.90	0.80 TO 0.85
RELATIVELY LOW CL'G.	0.90 TO 0.95	0.85 TO 0.90

FLUORESCENT, 2×4, (PRISMATIC LENS)		
ROOM TYPE	HIGH REFL. FIN.	LOW REFL. FIN.
TYP. SMALLER RMS. (MOD. LOW CL'G.)	0.35 TO 0.45	0.30 TO 0.40
TYP. LARGER RMS.		
RELATIVELY HIGH CL'G.	0.50 TO 0.60	0.45 TO 0.50
RELATIVELY LOW CL'G.	0.60 TO 0.70	0.55 TO 0.60

FLUORESCENT, 2×4, (PARABOLIC LOUVER)		
ROOM TYPE	HIGH REFL. FIN.	LOW REFL. FIN.
TYP. SMALLER RMS. (MOD. LOW CL'G'S.)	0.30 TO 0.45	0.25 TO 0.35
TYP. LARGER RMS.		
RELATIVELY HIGH CL'G.	0.55 TO 0.65	0.45 TO 0.55
RELATIVELY LOW CL'G.	0.65 TO 0.75	0.55 TO 0.65

FLUORESCENT PATTERN OF INDIRECT LIGHTING		
ROOM TYPE	HIGH REFL. FIN.	LOW REFL. FIN.
TYP. SMALLER RMS. (MOD. LOW CL'G'S.)	0.35 TO 0.50	0.15 TO 0.20
TYP. LARGER RMS.		
RELATIVELY HIGH CL'G.	0.40 TO 0.65	0.20 TO 0.30
RELATIVELY LOW CL'G.	0.50 TO 0.75	0.30 TO 0.40

H.I.D. PATTERN OF INDIRECT LIGHTING		
ROOM TYPE	HIGH REFL. FIN.	LOW REFL. FIN.
TYP. SMALLER RMS. (MOD. LOW CL'G'S)	0.28 TO 0.38	0.05 TO 0.15
TYP. LARGER RMS.		
RELATIVELY HIGH CL'G.	0.40 TO 0.55	0.10 TO 0.20
RELATIVELY LOW CL.	0.50 TO 0.65	0.10 TO 0.25

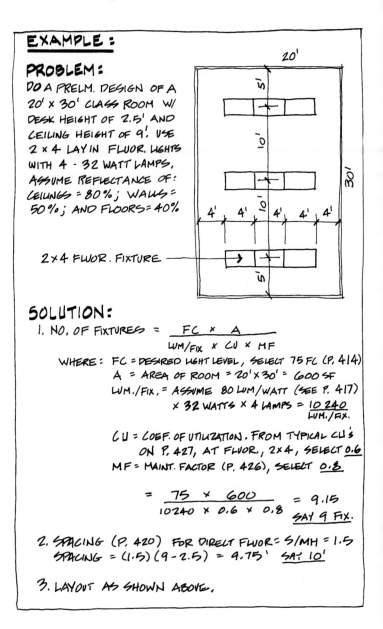

EXAMPLE:

PROBLEM:

DO A PRELM. DESIGN OF A 20' × 30' CLASS ROOM W/ DESK HEIGHT OF 2.5' AND CEILING HEIGHT OF 9'. USE 2 × 4 LAY IN FLUOR. LIGHTS WITH 4 - 32 WATT LAMPS. ASSUME REFLECTANCE OF: CEILINGS = 80%; WALLS = 50%; AND FLOORS = 40%

2×4 FLUOR. FIXTURE ——

SOLUTION:

1. NO. OF FIXTURES = $\dfrac{FC \times A}{LUM/FIX \times CU \times MF}$

   WHERE: FC = DESIRED LIGHT LEVEL, SELECT 75 FC (P. 414)
   A = AREA OF ROOM = 20' × 30' = 600 SF
   LUM./FIX. = ASSUME 80 LUM/WATT (SEE P. 417)
   × 32 WATTS × 4 LAMPS = <u>10 240</u> LUM./FIX.

   CU = COEF. OF UTILIZATION. FROM TYPICAL CU'S
   ON P. 427, AT FLUOR., 2×4, SELECT <u>0.6</u>
   MF = MAINT. FACTOR (P. 426), SELECT <u>0.8</u>

   = $\dfrac{75 \times 600}{10240 \times 0.6 \times 0.8}$ = 9.15 SAY 9 FIX.

2. SPACING (P. 420) FOR DIRECT FLUOR = S/MH = 1.5
   SPACING = (1.5)(9 - 2.5) = 9.75' <u>SAY 10'</u>

3. LAYOUT AS SHOWN ABOVE.

NOTES

NOTES

__ B. POWER AND TELEPHONE (1) (10) (20)

The interior designer will often be involved in power requirements when doing a tenant improvement or remodel. This will
probably involve working with an architect or engineer. This
section is included to give the interior designer a rough background in electrical power. For Energy Conservation, see
p. 179.

___ 1. Electrical Power

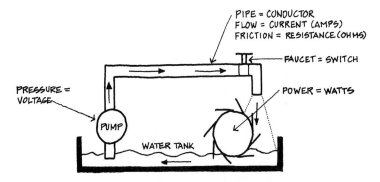

___ *a.* Water analogy (an electrical circuit)
1 volt = Force needed to drive a current of 1 amp
through a resistance of 1 ohm.
1 watt = Rate at which electrical energy is consumed
in a circuit with a force of 1 volt in a current
of 1 amp.

___ *b.* Basic formulas
___ (1) Power formula: Watts = volts × amps
Used to convert wattage ratings of devices to amps.
Wires and circuits are rated by amps.
___ (2) Ohm's law:

$$\text{Amps} = \frac{\text{volts}}{\text{ohms}}$$

Devices may draw different amperage even though
connected to the same voltage.

___ *c.* *Building power systems* consist of a *transformer* to
reduce voltage from the utility power grid, a *main
switchboard* (sometimes called *service entrance section* or *switchgear*) with main disconnect and distribution through circuit breakers or fused switches;

431

and *subpanels and branch circuits* to distribute power throughout building.

___ *d.* Detailed descriptions based on building size:

   ___ (1) *Residential and small commercial buildings* typically use *120/240 volt, single-phase* power.

      ___ (*a*) *Transformers* are pole-mounted (oil cooled, *18″ dia.* × *3′ H*) or for underground system, dry type pad mounted on ground. Both outside building.

      ___ (*b*) *Main switchboard* usually located at power entry to building and typically sized at *20″ W* × *5″D* × *30″H.*

      ___ (*c*) *Branch circuits* should not extend more than *100′* from panel. Panel boards are approx. *20″ W* × *5″D* × *30″* to *60″H.* The maximum number of breakers per panel is *42.*

      ___ (*d*) *Clearance* in front of panels and switchboards is usually *3′ to 6′.*

   ___ (2) *Medium-sized commercial buildings* typically use *120/208 volt, 3-phase* power to operate large motors used for HVAC, etc., as well as to provide 120 V for lights and outlets.

      ___ (*a*) *Transformer* is typically liquid-cooled, pad-mounted outside building and should have *4′* clearance around and be within *30′* of a drive. The size can be approximated by area served:

Area	No. res. units	Pad size
18,000 SF	50	*4′ × 4′*
60,000 SF	160	*4.5′ × 4.5′*
180,000 SF		*8′ × 8′*

      ___ (*b*) *Main switchboard* for lower voltage is approx. *6′W* × *2′D* × *7′H* (for 2000 amps or less or up to 70,000 SF bld'g.). Provide *3′ to 6′* space in front for access. Higher voltage require access from both sides. *3000 amps* is usually the largest switch-board possible.

___ (*c*) *Branch panels:* For *general* lighting and outlets is same as for residential and small commercial except there are more panels and at least *1 per floor.* The panel boards are generally related to the functional groupings of the building.

For *motor* panels, see large buildings.

___ (3) *Large commercial buildings* often use *277/480 volt, 3-phase* power. They typically purchase power at higher voltage and step down within the building system.

___ (*a*) *Transformer* is typically owned by the building and located in a vault inside or outside (underground). Vault should be located adjacent to exterior wall, ventilated, fire-rated, and have two exits. Smaller dry transformers located throughout the building will step the 480 V down to 120 V. See below for size.

___ (*b*) *Main switchboard* is approx. *10 to 15′ W × 5′ D × 7′ H* with *4′ to 6′* maintenance space on all sides. Typical sizes of transformer vaults and switchgear rooms:

Commercial building	Residential building	Transformer vault	Switchgear room
100,000 SF	200,000 SF	$20' \times 20' \times 11'$	$30' \times 20' \times 11'$
150,000 SF	300,000 SF	($30' \times 30' \times 11'$ combination)	
300,000 SF	600,000 SF	$20' \times 40' \times 11'$	$30' \times 40' \times 11'$
1,000,000 SF	2,000,000 SF	$20' \times 80' \times 11'$	$30' \times 80' \times 11'$

Over *3000 amp,* go to multiple services. XFMR vaults need to be separated from rest of the building by at least *2-hour* walls.

___ (*c*) *Branch panels*
___ Panels for lighting and outlets will be same as for medium-

sized buildings except that they are often located in closets with telephone equipment. The area needed is approx. *0.005 ×* the building area served.

___ Motor controller panel boards for HVAC equipment, elevators, and other large equipment are often in (or next to) mechanical room, against a wall. A basic panel module is approx. *1'W × 1.5'D × 7'H.* One module can accommodate 2 to 4 motor control units stacked on top of one another. Smaller motors in isolated locations require individual motor control units approx. *1'W × 6"D × 1.5'H.*

___ (*d*) *Other:* In many buildings an emergency generator is required. Best location is outside near switchgear room. If inside, plan on a room 12'W × 18' to 22'L. If emergency power is other than for life safety, size requirements can go up greatly. In any case, the generator needs combustion air and possibly cooling.

___ *e.*   *Miscellaneous electrical items*
   ___ (1) *Circuit symbols* on electrical plans

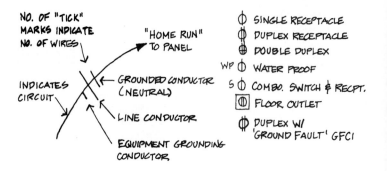

___ (2) _Residential_

    ___ (_a_) Service drops (overhead lines) must be:

        ___ _10'_ above ground or sidewalk

        ___ _15'_ above driveways

        ___ _18'_ above streets

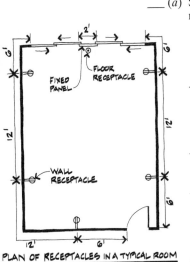

PLAN OF RECEPTACLES IN A TYPICAL ROOM

    ___ (_b_) A min. of _1 wall switch_ controlling lighting outlets is required in all rooms (but convenience outlets may apply in main rooms).

    ___ (_c_) All rooms require a convenience outlet every 12' along walls, 2' or longer.

    ___ (_d_) Provide sufficient 15- and 20-amp circuits for min. of _3 watts of power/SF. One_ circuit for every _500 to 600 SF._

    ___ (_e_) A min. of _2 #12_ wire (copper), _20-amp_ small-appliance circuits required pantry, dining, family, extended to kitchen.

    ___ (_f_) A min. of _1 #12_ wire, 20-amp circuit required for _laundry_ receptacle.

    ___ (_g_) A min. of _1_ receptacle per _bathroom_ with ground-fault circuit interrupter protection (GFCI, required within 6' of water outlet and at exteriors).

    ___ (_h_) A min. of _1_ outlet (GFCI) required in _basement, garage, and patios._

    ___ (_i_) Provide _smoke detector._ See p. 146.

    ___ (_j_) Mounting heights:

        ___ Switches, counter receptacles, bath outlets: _4'_ AFF

        ___ Laundry: _3'6"_ AFF

        ___ Wall convenience outlets: _12"_ AFF

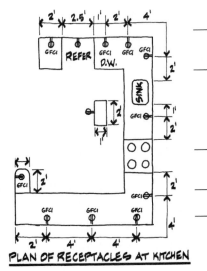

PLAN OF RECEPTACLES AT KITCHEN

___ (3) For outlets and controls required to be *HC accessible,* per ADA, place between *18″ and 4′* AFF.

___ (4) Always check room switches against *door swings.*

___ (5) Check flush-mounted wall panels against *wall depth.*

___ (6) Building must always be *grounded* by connecting all metal piping to electrical system, and by connecting electrical system into the ground by either a buried rod or plate outside the building or by a wire in the footing (UFER).

___ (7) Consider *lightning protection* by a system of rods or masts on roof connected to a separate ground and into the building elect. ground system.

___ 2. <u>Building Telephone and Signal Systems</u>

___ *a.* Small buildings often have a telephone mounting board (TMB) of ¾″ plywood with size up to *4′ × 4′.*

___ *b.* Medium-size buildings often need a telephone closet of *4′ to 6′.*

___ *c.* Large buildings typically have a *400-SF* telephone terminal room. Secondary distribution points typical throughout building (one per area or floor) usually combined with electrical distribution closets (*approx. 0.005 ×* area served).

___ *d.* ADA requires that where public phones are provided, at least *1* must be HC-accessible (1 per floor, 1 per bank of phones). See ADA for special requirements.

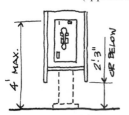

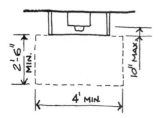

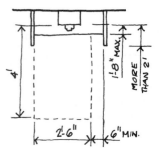

NOTES

NOTES

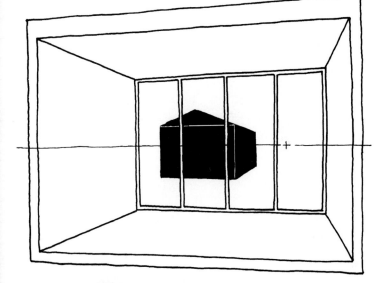

 **APPENDIX**

<u>NOTES</u>

INTERIOR COSTS AND INTERIOR DESIGN FEES BY BUILDING TYPE

Also, see p. 3.

Unfortunately, the interiors industry has not developed much data on nationwide average installation costs and design fees, at least as compared to general construction and architectural fee surveys. Perhaps future data will improve and be available for future editions.

This appendix is the best that can be done with the limited amount of data available.

The following tables are laid out as follows:

___ A. General

FF&E installed costs are in $/SF. These costs *may* include some general construction costs (ceilings, walls, etc.) beyond "furniture, fixtures, and equipment." For restaurants, of the FF&E costs, the E (kitchen equipment) is probably excluded.

Interior design fees are a percentage of the above FF&E costs. Fee data is from *1998 Fees and Pricing in Design Firms,* 13th Edition, PSMJ Resources, Inc.

___ B. This section is a summary of data available from a survey of the top 200 firms (top gross fees) in the United States. This data is *not* a national average. The data presented is for total work of the firms, not just the building type in question, and therefore is of limited value. The high and low numbers are the highest and lowest of the 20 firms surveyed. Data is from *Interior Design* magazine, January and July 1998, "100 Design Giants," Cahners Publications.

Note: All numbers in Appendix A have been rounded off.

OFFICE

A. OFFICE, LARGE (+ 50000 SF OR HIGHRISE)

		LOW	MED.	HIGH
FF & E INSTALLED COSTS	$/SF	15	35	50
INTERIOR DESIGN FEES	%	3	4	5

OFFICE, MID-RISE

		LOW	MED.	HIGH
FF & E INSTALLED COSTS	$/SF	1	1	1
INTERIOR DESIGN FEES	%	3	3	4

OFFICE, SMALL (UNDER 50000 SF, LOW RISE)

		LOW	MED.	HIGH
FF & E INSTALLED COSTS	$/SF	10	20	30
INTERIOR DESIGN FEES	%	3	4	6

B. AVERAGE OF 20 FIRMS WITH HIGHEST FEES IN OFFICE (OF TOP 200 FIRMS IN NATION FROM INTERIOR DESIGN MAGAZINE SURVEY):

		LOW	MED.	HIGH
AVE. FF & E	$/SF	18.50	42	75
AVE. FEES	%	3	6	11
AVE. FEES	$/SF	1.05	2.40	11.00

NOTE: DATA IS AVERAGE OF TOTAL WORK OF FIRMS. THERE WAS, ON AVERAGE 45% DIFFERENCE BETWEEN TOTAL FEES AND OFFICE DESIGN FEES.

FINANCIAL

		LOW	MED	HIGH
A. GENERAL				
BANKS				
FF & E INSTALLED COSTS	$/SF	10	15	20
INTERIOR DESIGN FEES	%			

B. AVERAGE OF 20 FIRMS WITH HIGHEST FEES IN FINANCIAL (OF TOP 200 FIRMS IN NATION FROM INTERIOR DESIGN MAGAZINE SURVEY):

AVE. FF & E	$/SF	25	48	68.50
AVE. FEES	%	2	5.5	11
AVE. FEES	$/SF	1.40	2.60	6.85

NOTE: DATA IS AVERAGE OF TOTAL WORK OF FIRMS. THERE WAS, ON AVERAGE, 26% DIFFERENCE BETWEEN TOTAL FEES AND FINANCIAL DESIGN FEES.

HOSPITALITY

		LOW	MED.	HIGH
A. RESTAURANTS				
FF & E INSTALLED COSTS	$/SF	30	50	100
INTERIOR DESIGN FEES	%	4	5	5
HOTELS (HIGH RISE)				
FF & E INSTALLED COSTS	$/SF	-	20	-
INTERIOR DESIGN FEES	%	5	6	7
HOTELS (LOW RISE & MOTELS)				
FF & E INSTALLED COSTS	$/SF	-	20	-
INTERIOR DESIGN FEES	%	4	5	6

B. AVERAGE OF 20 FIRMS WITH HIGHEST FEES IN HOSPITALITY (OF TOP 200 FIRMS IN NATION FROM INTERIOR DESIGN MAGAZINE SURVEY):

		LOW	MED.	HIGH
AVE. FF&E	$/SF	25	56	168
AVE. FEES	%	2	7	
AVE. FEES	$/SF			165

NOTE: DATA IS AVERAGE OF TOTAL WORL OF FIRMS. THERE WAS, ON AVERAGE 8% DIFFERENCE BETWEEN TOTAL FEES AND HOSPITALITY DESIGN FEES.

RETAIL

A. FEES (AS % OF INSTALLED COSTS)

	LOW	MED.	HIGH
SHOPPING MALLS	3	4	5
STRIP SHOPPING CENTERS	3	4	5
RETAIL SHOPS	3	5	7

B. AVERAGE OF 20 FIRMS WITH HIGHEST FEES IN RETAIL (OF TOP 200 FIRMS IN NATION FROM INTERIOR DESIGN MAGAZINE SURVEY) $

		LOW	MED.	HIGH
AVE. FF&E	$/SF	5	58	136
AVE. FEES	%	3	6.5	15
AVE. FEES	$/SF	0.50	3.30	5.00

MEDICAL

		LOW	MED	HIGH
A. HOSPITALS, NEW				
FF & E INSTALLED COSTS	$/SF	35		55
INTERIOR DESIGN FEES	%	4	4	5
HOSPITALS, REMODEL				
FF & E INSTALLED COSTS	$/SF	3	4	7
INTERIOR DESIGN FEES				
CLINICS				
FF & E INSTALLED COSTS	$/SF	3	6	6
INTERIOR DESIGN FEES	%			
MEDICAL OFFICE				
FF & E INSTALLED COSTS	$/SF	10	15	25
INTERIOR DESIGN FEES	%	4	5	7
NURSING HOMES				
FF & E INSTALLED COSTS	$/SF	3	5	7
INTERIOR DESIGN FEES	%			

B. AVERAGE OF 20 FIRMS WITH HIGHEST FEES IN MEDICAL (OF TOP 200 FIRMS IN NATION FROM INTERIOR DESIGN MAGAZINE SURVEY):

		LOW	MED	HIGH
AVE. FF & E	$/SF	13.00	67.50	280
AVE. FEES	%	1.5	6	16
AVE. FEES	$/SF	1.50	2.60	6.00

EDUCATION

A. GENERAL

	LOW	MED.	HIGH
1. CLASSROOMS (INTERIOR DESIGN FEES	4%	5%	6%
2. F.F. & E. INSTALLED COSTS ($/SF)			
COLLEGE CLASSROOMS & ADM.	6		17
COLLEGE STUDENT UNION	6		18
COLLEGE LAB	10		75
ELEMENTARY SCHOOL	5		10
JR. HIGH	5		10
SR. HIGH	5		10
VOCATIONAL	5		10

B. AVERAGE OF 20 FIRMS WITH HIGHEST FEES IN EDUCATION (OF TOP 200 FIRMS IN NATION FROM INTERIOR DESIGN MAGAZINE SURVEY):

AVE. FF & E	$/SF	8.75	48	85
AVE. FEES	%	3	7½	10
AVE. FEES	$/SF	1.00	3.75	8.80

447

GOVERNMENT

A. GENERAL

1. INTERIOR DESIGN FEES (% OF INSTALLED COSTS)

	LOW	MED.	HIGH
POSTAL	3	4	4
FEDERAL OFFICE	4	5	7
CORRECTION	3	4	5
STATE & LOCAL GOVERNMENT	6	7	8

2. INSTALLED FF & E COSTS ($/SF)

	LOW	MED.	HIGH
COURT HOUSE		30	

B. AVERAGE OF 20 FIRMS WITH HIGHEST FEES IN GOVERNMENT WORK (OF TOP 200 FIRMS IN NATION FROM INTERIOR DESIGN MAGAZINE SURVEY):

		LOW	MED.	HIGH
AVE. FF & E	$/SF	12	50	155
AVE. FEES	%	3	6	10
AVE FEES	$/SF	1.20	2.75	6.40

NOTE: DATA IS AVERAGE OF TOTAL WORK OF FIRMS. THERE WAS, ON AVERAGE, 26% DIFFERENCE BETWEEN TOTAL FEES AND GOVERNMENT DESIGN FEES.

RESIDENTIAL

	LOW	MED	HIGH
A. GENERAL			
APTS/CONDO (LARGE, 100,000 SF+, HIGH RISE)			
FF&E INSTALLED COSTS $/SF	10	15	20
INTERIOR DESIGN FEES %	3	5	6
APTS, CONDOS (SMALL, 10,000 SF−, LOW RISE)			
FF&E INSTALLED COSTS $/SF	10	15	20
INTERIOR DESIGN FEES %	4	5	5
SINGLE FAMILY			
FF&E INSTALLED COSTS $/SF	5	15	50
INTERIOR DESIGN FEES %	5	7	10
DORMS, HOUSING			
FF&E INSTALLED COSTS $/SF	4	20	
INTERIOR DESIGN FEES %	5	5	5

B. AVERAGE OF 20 FIRMS WITH HIGHEST FEES IN RESIDENTIAL (OF TOP 200 FIRMS IN NATION FROM INTERIOR DESIGN MAGAZINE SURVEY):

AVE. FF&E	$/SF	2.30	90.50	240
AVE. FEES	%	3	6.5	10
AVE. FEES	$/SF	1.00	8.00	19.00

NOTE = DATA IS AVERAGE OF TOTAL WORK OF FIRMS, THERE WAS, ON AVERAGE 14% DIFFERENCE BETWEEN TOTAL FEES AND OFFICE DESIGN FEES.

NOTES

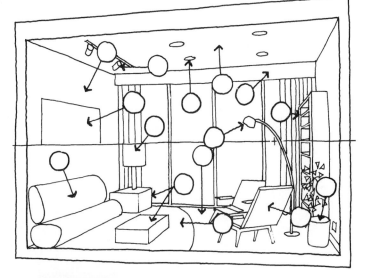

 REFERENCES /
INDEX

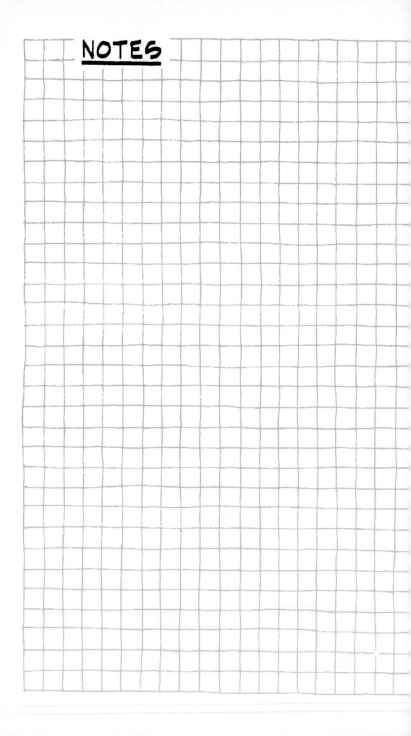

NOTES

___ REFERENCES

This book was put together from a myriad of sources including the help of consultants listed on p. 457. References shown at the front of a section indicate general background information. A reference shown at a specific item indicates a copy from the reference. The major book references are listed as follows, and many are recommended for architects' libraries:

(1) Allen, Edward, and Joseph Iano. *The Architect's Studio Companion, Technical Guidelines for Preliminary Design.* New York: John Wiley & Sons, Inc., 1989.

(2) Ambrose, James. *Simplified Design for Building Sound Control.* New York: John Wiley & Sons, Inc., 1995.

(3) American Institute of Architects. *Architectural Graphic Standards,* 6th ed., New York: John Wiley & Sons, Inc., 1970.

(4) American Institute of Architects. *Architectural Graphic Standards,* 9th ed., New York: John Wiley & Sons, Inc., 1994.

(5) American Institute of Architects. *The Architect's Handbook of Professional Practice.* David Haviland, editor, 1988.

(6) Austin, Richard. *Designing the Interior Landscape.* New York: Van Nostrand Reinhold, 1985.

(7) Ballast, David Kent. *Architect's Handbook of Formulas, Tables, and Mathematical Calculations.* New Jersey: Prentice-Hall, 1988.

(8) Ballast, David Kent. *Architect's Handbook of Construction Detailing.* New Jersey: Prentice-Hall, 1990.

(9) Better Homes and Gardens, *Decorating Book.* 1975. .

(10) Bovill, Carl. *Architectural Design, Integration of Structural and Environmental Systems.* New York: Van Nostrand Reinhold Co., 1991.

(11) Building News. *Facilities Manager's 1997 Cost Book.* William D. Mahoney, editor-in-chief. 1997.

(12) Ching, Francis. *Building Construction Illustrated.* New York: Van Nostrand Reinhold Co., 1975.

(13) Ching, Francis. *Drawing—A Creative Process.* New York: Van Nostrand Reinhold Co., 1990.

(14) Ching, Francis. *Interior Design Illustrated.* New York: Van Nostrand Reinhold Co., 1987.

(15) Construction Specifications Institute. *Master-Format, Master List of Section Titles and Numbers.* 1983.

— (16) Craftsman Book Co. *1997 National Construction Estimator.* Edited by Martin D. Kiley and William M. Moselle. 1997.

— (17) Craftsman Book Co. *1997 Building Cost Manual.* Edited by Martin D. Kiley and Michael L. Kiley. 1997.

— (18) De Chiara, Panero, and Zelnik. *Time Saver Standards for Interior Design and Space Planning.* New York: McGraw-Hill, 1991.

— (19) De Chiara and Callender. *Time Saver Standards for Building Types.* 3rd ed. New York: McGraw-Hill, 1990.

— (20) Federal Register. *Americans with Disabilities Act* (ADA). 1991.

— (21) Foote, Rosslynn F. *Running an Office for Fun and Profit: Business Techniques for Small Design Firms.* Pennsylvania: Dowden, Hutchinson & Ross, 1978.

— (22) Flynn, Kremers, Segil, and Steffy. *Architectural Interior Systems.* 3rd Edition.

— (23) Friedmann, Arnold. *Commonsense Design.* New York: Scribners, 1976.

— (24) *Human Dimensions.* New York: Interiors Magazine.

— (25) International Conference of Building Officials. *Uniform Building Code.* Tables 3-A, 3-B, 5-A, 5-B, 6-A, 9-A, 10-A, 15-A, 16-A, 16-B, 16-C, 23-11-B-1, A-29-A, and graphic 24-1, reproduced from the 1997 edition of the *Uniform Building Code*™, copyright © 1997, with permission of the publisher, the International Conference of Building Officials.

— (26) International Association of Plumbing and Mechanical Officials. *Uniform Plumbing Code.* Table 4-1 is reprinted from the *Uniform Plumbing Code* with permission of the International Association of Plumbing and Mechanical Officials copyright © 1997.

— (27) International Conference of Building Officials. *Dwelling Construction Under the Uniform Building Code.* 1997.

— (28) Knackstedt, Mary. *The Interior Design Business Handbook.* New York: Van Nostrand Reinhold, 1992.

— (29) Lockard, William K. *Drawing as a Means to Architecture.* New York: Van Nostrand Reinhold, 1968.

— (30) Lockard, William K. *Design Drawing.* Wadsworth Publications, 1982.

— (31) McGraw-Hill Book Co. *Sweet's Catalog File.* 1993.

— (32) McGraw-Hill Book Co. *Time Saver Standards.* 7th ed. John H. Callender, editor-in-chief. 1997.

— (33) Means, R. S. Co. Inc. *Means Building Construction Cost Data.* 1997.

— (34) Means, R. S. Co. Inc. *Means Assemblies Cost Data.* 1997.

— (35) Means, R. S. Co. Inc. *Means Interior Cost Data,* 1998.

— (36) Munsell, A. H. *A Color Notation.* Munsell Color Co., Inc. 1946.

— (37) Murphy, D. G. *The Business of Interior Design.* Burbank, CA: Straford House Publishing, 1975.

— (38) Peña, William, with Parshall and Kelley. *Problem Seeking.* Washington, DC: A.I.A. Press, 1987.

— (39) Piotrowski. *Professional Practice for Interior Designers.* New York: Van Nostrand Reinhold, 1989.

— (40) Reznikoff, S. C. *Interior Graphic and Design Standards.* New York: Whitney Library of Design, 1986.

— (41) Reznikoff, S. C. *Specifications for Commercial Interiors.* New York: Whitney Library of Design, 1979.

— (42) Saylor Publications, Inc. *1997 Current Construction Costs.* 1997.

— (43) Schiler, Marc. *Simplified Design of Building Lighting.* New York: John Wiley & Sons, 1992.

— (44) Sleeper, Harold. *Building Planning and Design Standards.* New York: John Wiley & Sons Inc., 1955.

— (45) Stasiowski, Frank A. *Staying Small Successfully.* New York: John Wiley & Sons, 1991.

— (46) U.S. Navy. *Basic Construction Techniques for Houses and Small Buildings.* New York: Dover Publications, 1972.

— (47) Watson, Donald, and Kenneth Labs. *Climatic Design.* New York: McGraw-Hill Book Co., 1983.

— (48) Watson, Crosbie, and Callender. *Time Saver Standards for Architectural Design Data.* 7th ed. New York: McGraw-Hill, 1997.

— (49) Wing, Charlie. *The Visual Handbook of Building and Remodeling.* Pennsylvania: Rodale Press, 1990.

— (50) Wood, R. S. and Co. *The Pocket Size Carpenter's Helper.* 1985.

Acknowledgments

Thanks to the following people for their professional expertise in helping with this book:

Special thanks to: Pat Anthony.

Also, thanks to: Steve Andros, Marcia and Ken Caldwell, Doug Collier, Ed Denham, Rick Goolsby, Glenn Heyes, Doug Hood, Norm Littler, Bill Lundsford, Randy Pace, Lorilei Peters, Dina Rosas, Sandra Warner, and L. D. Womack.

NOTES

Index

A

G

H

NOTES

ABOUT THE AUTHOR

John Patten ("Pat") Guthrie, AIA, is the Principal of John Pat Guthrie Architects, Inc., of Scottsdale, Arizona. A licensed architect in 13 states, he heads a broad-based practice that includes commercial, residential, industrial, medical, and religious facilities and that also specializes in passive solar energy design. Mr. Guthrie is author of *Cross-Check: Integrating Building Systems and Working Drawings,* published by McGraw-Hill, as well as *Desert Architecture: Climate Responsive Design as a Means to Energy Conservation in Homes and Buildings.*

NOTES

NOTES

NOTES

NOTES

NOTES